The *Peg...*

Nicholas Kenyon ha... since 1996. He was a music critic for *The New Yorker*, *The Times* and the *Observer*, and became Controller, BBC Radio 3 in 1992, responsible for the award-winning Radio 3 seasons 'Fairest Isle' and 'Sounding the Century'. He is now Controller, BBC Proms, Live Events and Television Classical Music. He wrote the history of the BBC Symphony Orchestra and edited the influential volume *Authenticity and Early Music*. In 2001 he wrote a new edition of his biography of Simon Rattle. He has edited four volumes of BBC Proms Guides to the repertory, and is a member of the boards of English National Opera and the Guildhall School of Music and Drama. He was appointed a CBE in 2001.

The Pegasus Pocket Guide to
Mozart

NICHOLAS KENYON

PEGASUS BOOKS
NEW YORK

THE PEGASUS POCKET GUIDE TO MOZART

Pegasus Books LLC
45 Wall Street, Suite 1021
New York, NY 10005

Library of Congress Cataloging-in-Publication Data is available.
ISBN: 1-933648-23-6

10 9 8 7 8 6 5 4 3 2 1

Printed in the United States of America
Distributed by Consortium

In memory of

Outstanding, inspiring, generous Mozart scholars

Contents

Introduction

As we all know, Mozart pushed things a little too far.
  Carl Friedrich Zelter, 1798

Can you put everything you need to know about Mozart in your pocket? Perhaps no composer in the history of Western music has been more written about, dissected, mythologised and fantasised over. A Google search just a year before the 250th anniversary of his birth offers some 7,930,000 current items about Mozart. Of the making of theories about Mozart's life, death, relationships, personal habits, not to mention his music, there is no end. The number of books published about Mozart ranks with those about Shakespeare, Jesus Christ and (his nearest rival among composers) Wagner. He was the subject of an acclaimed play, *Amadeus*, which has gone round the world since it was first seen in London in 1979, and became an even more popular (though completely transformed) film in the 1980s, which re-embedded myths about the man at the heart of our understanding of his music. It was doubtless partly because of *Amadeus* that Mozart, rather than any other classical composer, was in *Time* magazine's top ten cultural figures of the millennium. Today, my mobile phone's predictive text spells Mozart for me, but not Beethoven or Haydn. His music chimes in every Muzak-infested lift or restaurant or shopping centre, and in these days of eternal waiting for the call centre to answer, Mozart's must be the music you hear most often when you are on hold. Even if you claim to know nothing about classical music, you have heard of Mozart, and heard Mozart.

But just when you are about to write Mozart off as over-exploited and over-exposed, there is the sudden impact of the music, utterly direct, communicative yet emotionally elusive, simple yet infinitely complex, which has been moving listeners for over two centuries in myriads of different ways, offering different qualities to new generations. Sometimes it seems possible to read an infinite variety of meaning into Mozart's music, so open is it to interpretation and opinion, so varied in the performance styles and techniques that can be used to realise it for a contemporary audience. Equally, Mozart has now become a commercial brand: to market the supposed benefits of music on spatial-temporal reasoning in children and adults, 'The Mozart Effect' became a trademark. In this and in so many other ways, 'Mozart' has become something completely different from Mozart: it is a creation of our times, made in our own image.

We will never fully disentangle the man and the music from the myth, nor should we; for it is in the mythic power of Mozart's story that much that is so important about him survives, and it is in those stories told about him that we have articulated what we want to believe of composers, of geniuses, of those who die young, of those who create something that lasts. That is why the stories are so significant, whether or not they are entirely true.

In Mozart's case, the myths began to be created the moment he died. Mozart's wife Constanze reflected that: on the day of his death in 1791, she is reported to have been distraught, to have curled up beside his dead body in his bed, but is also supposed to have penned in her husband's album the words: 'Mozart – never to be forgotten by me or by the whole of Europe – now thou too art at peace – eternal peace!! . . . O! could I soon be joined with thee for ever.' She dated this 5 December 1791, the day of his death – but it is more likely that, rather than being her immediate reaction, those sentiments were actually those that, much later, in her new role of protector of his reputation, she felt she *ought* to have articulated at that crucial moment. Yet that makes almost more poignant the desperate vacuum that Mozart's early death left behind, and the inability of those around him to cope with his astonishing legacy – of which the endless sagas surrounding the incomplete Requiem are only the most famous example.

Of Mozart's life, there is almost too much evidence – hundreds of letters, diaries, catalogues, newspaper reports and so much else, although many of these are not about the things that really matter. How much can we believe of the welter of communication in Mozart's astoundingly vivid and turbulent letters, one of the most remarkable personal testimonies to have survived from any great artistic figure? In the biographical literature they have so often been taken as the unvarnished truth, and yet increasingly we come to realise that they are hedged around with special pleading, deliberate carelessness and dissimulation – qualities which do, of course, tell us much about the composer, but are more elusive than taking him at face value. The intoxicating aspect of the surviving Mozart evidence, including the posthumous stories and legends, is that it is all so vivid. The testimonies pulsate with life, and we feel, even at more than two centuries' distance and cultural worlds away, that we can make an immediate connection with them. That is one reason for Mozart's continuing relevance to us, yet the imagined closeness is a dangerous thing, for too often we want to believe that he had our own way of thinking, feeling and behaving.

(It is amazing how resilient both the positive and negative images of Mozart prove to be. Early in 2005, the Berlin State Library unveiled what it claimed, to some disbelief, was a lost portrait of Mozart by Johann Georg Edlinger, bought in 1934 and forgotten since. As it doesn't look much like what we know of him, it was said to show 'a graying and podgy Mozart, with heavy bags under his eyes', caused by 'his flamboyant living in his home town of Salzburg [*sic* – he actually lived at this time in Vienna] which revolved around rich foods, heavy drinking and womanising, all of which may have contributed to his premature death . . .' This report provoked an immediate reply in the *Sunday Telegraph* from a furious correspondent: 'Mozart was a good husband . . . He lived with his family all of whom were good practising Catholics. He had girlfriends and was a flirt but there is no evidence he was unfaithful to his wife.')

If you want to read what is absolutely, certainly true about Mozart, this book may be a disappointment, because the story of what has happened to him since his death has irretrievably coloured that simple tale. But at the moment that marks a quarter of a millennium since Mozart was born, the most we can do, given the infinite variety of possibilities in his music, is to provide some context – to help us hear Mozart's music freshly, and make of it what we will. Each listener will have a different reaction, just as every performer reinterprets him: here are some guides around that amazing output; from them, create your own Mozart.

The enormous amount of scholarly work on Mozart's life and music that has taken place in recent years has not yet led to a fully formed picture that can replace the pioneering work of nineteenth- and twentieth-century biographers. So many pieces of the jigsaw seem to have been thrown up in the air that it would be impossible to write a coherent, organic, musical and personal story of Mozart right now. There have been stimulating and questioning biographies, by Wolfgang Hildesheimer, Volkmar Braunbehrens and Maynard Solomon; there is a wealth of new information about his music in the work of the New Mozart Edition and its critical commentaries ('written with the utmost care, read with the minimum of attention', as one scholar wryly noted); there is a rich new sense of context from analysts and historians who are studying Mozart alongside his contemporaries and in his cultural sphere.

The insights of those who have studied Mozart's handwriting (Wolfgang Plath), copyists (Cliff Eisen for Salzburg, Dexter Edge for Vienna), editions (Gertrude Haberkamp), paper usage (Alan Tyson), sketches (Ulrich Konrad) and attitude to composition (Neal Zaslaw, Christoph Wolff and others) have turned some traditional understanding upside down. The way that Mozart wrote for particular singers and ensembles, for particular circumstances in different courts and theatres, is becoming increasingly acknowledged as a crucial influence on his style. The standard Köchel catalogue of Mozart's music (see below) is currently being rewritten.

Within all this continuing activity, the aim of this new Pocket Guide has to be very modest. It draws on a wide range of up-to-date published sources to provide as broad a guide as possible: there are countless books of Mozart biography, and there are many books which discuss his music; I hope this one manages to do some of both. We are all aware of music by Mozart that we know and love but want to find out more about, or that we do not know and would find worth exploring. Mozart's music is now available to us more easily than ever before, so this book surveys as much of his output as possible. It does not pretend to be a complete guide, or an academic treatise, though I hope it makes some newer scholarly thinking accessible.

By no means every fragment or small piece that Mozart ever wrote is included here. This book concentrates on those works which are likely to be performed, and encountered in the concert hall, on CD or on the radio. For a complete overview of his output, the magisterial work-list by Cliff Eisen and Stanley Sadie (whose death in 2005 was such a loss to Mozart scholarship) in the second edition of *The New Grove Dictionary of Music and Musicians* is the most accessible source, in print and on-line; the work-list in the forthcoming *Cambridge Encyclopaedia of Mozart*, edited by Cliff Eisen and Simon Keefe, updates that list, and I am grateful to the editors for allowing me to use it.

The material here takes advantage of programme notes and essays I have previously written; I am grateful to those who originally commissioned them and gave me the opportunity to study Mozart's music. Because of the dual structure of the book, with sections arranged around the life and the works, there is some deliberate repetition of material. The accounts of the music itself are inevitably personal; even more personal are the recommendations of recordings, as Mozart is one of the most recorded of all composers. Those listed here, including the huge achievement of the Philips Complete Mozart Edition, now available in bargain format, are a few favourites from among the many performances that might have been suggested. I am very grateful to Wiebke Thormahlen for her stimulating thoughts and suggestions, and to her, Cliff Eisen, Jane Glover and Neal Zaslaw for reading parts of the book and saving me from signal errors. Amy Carruthers and my wife Ghislaine read the proofs, but the mistakes that remain are entirely mine, and I would be very pleased to have them pointed out for any future editions.

A note on numbering

One of the most affecting documents to have survived from Mozart's life is his own thematic catalogue, where he lists all the works he finished from early in 1784; this intensely moving volume is in the British Library in London; the touching story of how it was bought by an antiquarian bookseller as the Nazis closed in on Austria, and then sold on to the collector Stefan Zweig at a loss, has been told by Albi Rosenthal. The notebook is headed 'Catalogue of my work from the month February 1784 to – 1––': the finishing date is left open, but the blank figures clearly indicate that he intended to live and compose into the nineteenth century. Mozart completed it up to November 1791, and then it contains page after page of eloquently empty staves. That brings us face to face with the reality of Mozart's early death, and with the fact that as a composer he expected to go on working. There was no sense at all in which his death can be said to be inevitable, or in which his work was done.

This catalogue covers only a small part of Mozart's composing career and is not altogether complete or reliable. There are other sources: Leopold Mozart's early catalogue of his son's music, which starts with the earliest publications, showing that it was these printed volumes rather than the now-prized earliest manuscripts that his father counted as the real achievement. Then there is the Breitkopf manuscript catalogue of around 1800, destroyed in the Second World War though copies made for Jahn and Köchel survive, which included the opening bars of some pieces that have now disappeared, and the various publishers' catalogues issued during his lifetime and after his death. The composer himself dated many of his autographs, and where these survive this is by far the most reliable evidence we have of when he was bringing a work to completion for performance (though not, as modern scholarship has emphasised, of when work on it was begun).

The detailed chronology of Mozart's music is a tortuous subject which has occupied scholars for many years and is far from resolved. The foundation of the work of cataloguing Mozart's works in the nineteenth century was admirably carried out by Ludwig von Köchel and first published in 1862; the Mozartian Alfred Einstein made a third edition of the Köchel catalogue in 1947 which relied on his stylistic instincts and is now unreliable, while a sixth edition of 1964 has also been widely used though it has many problems of its own. So Köchel's work has been subject to frequent revision in the course of the years as scholarship has advanced, and one of the problems this has created is the different alternative and appendix numberings of Mozart's works as they were fitted into Köchel's original chronological sequence. Hopefully a benchmark for our present understanding of Mozart's work will be set in *The New Köchel*, to be published under the editorship of the leading American Mozart scholar Neal Zaslaw. This will revert to the original numbering wherever possible. Before that, there will be a new 'Little Edition' of Köchel in 2006, edited by Cliff Eisen and Ulrich Konrad.

In this practical guide I have adopted the numbers and titles most frequently and currently used for performances and recordings, retaining the first edition of Köchel; for works not in the first edition, the sixth edition's number is used. (Thus there is a caveat that no Köchel number can be taken as implying our present understanding of exactly when a work of Mozart's was written. Early Köchel numbers are still mainly early works, and late Köchel numbers are mainly late works, but more than that it would be unwise to assume.) There is a particular issue with works that may be by Mozart but for which no authentic sources survive; I have either omitted these, where they are rarely performed, or signalled them with a question mark where they are likely to be heard under Mozart's name. In referring to works I have used the convention that works are in the major key unless they are otherwise described: 'Symphony No. 41 in C' is in C major, whereas Symphony No. 40 is described as being 'in G minor'.

The trouble with Mozart's music is that it can fill not just a pocket, but a life. Because there are so many pieces and because you may want some recommendations for beginning to listen, I have rashly given the works discussed a very personal star rating:

****the essential Mozart: you cannot be without these unquestioned masterpieces
***wonderful pieces, among the finest of their kind
**a really good work of its genre
*well worth exploring

NK
27 January 2005
249th anniversary of Mozart's birth

The Mozart 'Top 10'

The popular image of Mozart is created by a very small number of oft-repeated pieces:

Ave verum corpus K618
Clarinet Concerto in A K622
Eine kleine Nachtmusik K525
Exsultate jubilate K165
Overture: *The Marriage of Figaro* K492
Piano Sonata in C K330
Piano Concerto No. 21 in C K467
Requiem K626
'Rondo alla turca' from Piano Sonata in A K331
Symphony No. 40 in G minor K550

. . . as well as some popular operatic excerpts and arias from *Die Zauberflöte, Don Giovanni* and the other great operas. But it is an oddly limited list in terms of the expressive range and technical variety of Mozart's music.

My 4-star Mozart

New listeners start here: these are the pieces of Mozart I have come to value most highly over the years.

Adagio for piano in B minor K540
Clarinet Concerto in A K622
Così fan tutte K588
Die Zauberflöte K620
Divertimento in E flat for string trio K563
Don Giovanni K527
Fantasia in F minor for mechanical organ K608
Idomeneo, re di Creta K366
Le nozze di Figaro K492
Mass in C minor K427
'Nehmt meinen Dank', aria K383
Piano and Wind Quintet in E flat K452
Piano Concerto No. 19 in F K459
Piano Concerto No. 20 in D minor K466
Piano Concerto No. 21 in C K467
Piano Concerto No. 24 in C minor K491
Piano Concerto No. 25 in C K503
Piano Concerto No. 27 in B flat K595
Piano Quartet in G minor K478
Piano Sonata No. 8 in A minor K310
Requiem in D minor K626
Rondo for piano in A minor K511
Serenade in B flat K361
Serenade in C minor K388
Sinfonia concertante in E flat for violin and viola K364
Sonata for piano duet in F K497
String Quartet in C, 'Dissonance' K465
String Quintet No. 2 in C K515
String Quintet No. 3 in G minor K516
Symphony No. 38 in D, 'Prague' K504

Symphony No. 39 in E flat K543
Symphony No. 40 in G minor K550
Symphony No. 41 in C, 'Jupiter' K551
'Vorrei spiegarvi', aria K418

Things people said about Mozart

JOHANN ADOLF HASSE 1771
This boy will confine us all to oblivion!

EMPEROR JOSEPH II (ATTRIB.) 1782
Too many notes, my dear Mozart.

ERNST LUDWIG GERBER 1790
This great master, through his early acquaintance with
harmony, had become so profoundly intimate with it that
the unpractised ear has difficulty in following his works.
Even practised ones must hear his pieces several times . . .

Journal des Luxus und der Moden 1793
Mozart's talent appears to be an original one, which nevertheless tends towards affectation, towards bizarre, surprising
and paradoxical passages, both melodic and harmonic, and
avoids natural flow so as not to become ordinary . . . His
melody is overburdened with too many harmonic changes,
accompaniments, and difficult striking intervals which are
often hard for the singer to intone and remember . . . a
genius who worked according to a plan in which one cannot
sanction the harsh modulations, improper imitations, and
intricate accompaniments.

GIUSEPPE SARTI *c.*1800 (PUB. 1832)
The composer, whom I do not know and do not want to
know, is a clavier player with a depraved ear; he follows that
false system which divides the octave into semitones . . .
'de la musique pour faire boucher les oreilles' [music to
make you block your ears].

KARL DITTERS VON DITTERSDORF 1801
I have never known any other composer to possess such a
wealth of ideas. I wish he were not so profligate with them.
He does not give the listener time to catch his breath, for no

sooner is one inclined to reflect upon a beautiful idea than another appears, more prominently, which drives away the first and this continues on and on, so that in the end one is unable to retain any of these beauties in the memory.

FRANZ SCHUBERT 1816
[On hearing the *Figaro* overture] That is the most beautiful overture in the whole world . . . but I had almost forgotten *Die Zauberflöte*.

A light, bright fine day this will remain throughout my whole life. As from afar the magic notes of Mozart's music still gently haunt me . . . O Mozart, immortal Mozart, how many, oh how endlessly many such comforting perceptions of a brighter and better life hast thou brought to our souls!

JOHN KEATS 1818
She kept me awake one night, as a tune of Mozart's might do.

HANS GEORG NÄGELI 1826
Great was his genius, but just as great was the failing of his genius, in that he created effects through contrast . . . it was destructive, primarily for Mozart himself, because as perpetual contrast is elevated to the primary means of effect, one disregards the beautiful proportion of the parts of a work of art.

HECTOR BERLIOZ
One of the most flagrant crimes recorded in the history of art against passion, feeling, good taste and good sense . . . I found it hard to forgive Mozart for this enormity ['Non mi dir' from *Don Giovanni*] . . . The marvellous beauty of his quartets and quintets, and of some of his sonatas, first converted me to this celestial genius, whom thenceforth I worshipped.

JOHANN WOLFGANG VON GOETHE 1829
A phenomenon like Mozart remains an inexplicable thing . . . a latent, procreative force which is continuously effective from generation to generation, and is not likely soon to be exhausted.

MUZIO CLEMENTI

Mozart has reached the boundary gate of music, and has leapt over it, leaving behind the old masters, the moderns, and posterity itself.

LUDWIG VAN BEETHOVEN

I could not compose operas like *Don Giovanni* and *Figaro*, they are repugnant to me. I could not have chosen such subjects; they are too frivolous for me . . .

I have always counted myself among the greatest admirers of Mozart and shall remain so until my last breath.

FRIEDRICH NIETZSCHE

Mozart, a delicate and lovable soul, but quite eighteenth-century, even when he is serious.

STENDHAL

Mozart is like a mistress who is always serious and often sad, but whose very sadness is a fascination, discovering ever deeper springs of love.

ROBERT SCHUMANN

Ah Mozart, Prince of Spirits in that other world founded by the most beautiful of human faiths . . . Does it not seem as if Mozart's works become fresher and fresher the more often we hear them?

ANDRÉ GIDE

Of all musicians Mozart is the one from whom our epoch has taken us farthest away; he speaks only in a whisper, and the public has ceased to hear anything but shouts.

ROSSINI 1860

I take Beethoven twice a week, Haydn four times, Mozart every day . . . Mozart is always adorable. He was lucky enough to go to Italy when he was very young at a time, too, when they still knew how to sing.

TCHAIKOVSKY 1878

It is thanks to Mozart that I have devoted my life to music

. . . Mozart is the highest, the culminating point that beauty has attained in the sphere of music. No one has made me weep, has made me tremble with rapture, from the consciousness of my nearness to that something which we call the ideal, as he has done.

WILLIAM MAKEPEACE THACKERAY 1879
A new world of love and beauty broke upon her when she was introduced to those divine compositions . . . how could she be indifferent when she heard Mozart? The tender parts of *Don Juan* awakened in her raptures so exquisite that she would ask herself when she went to say her prayers at night whether it was not wicked to feel so much delight as that with which 'Vedrai carino' and 'Batti batti' filled her gentle little bosom?

When she comes into the world, it is like a beautiful air of Mozart breaking upon you.

CHARLES GOUNOD 1882
Oh Divine Mozart! . . . For prodigal heaven has given thee everything, grace and strength, abundance and moderation, luminous spontaneity and ardent tenderness in the perfect equilibrium which constitutes the irresistible power to charm, and has made thee the unexcelled musician – more than the first – the only Mozart!

SIR HUBERT PARRY 1890
Mozart was not naturally a man of deep feeling or intellectuality, and the result is that his variation building is neither impressive nor genuinely interesting.

RICHARD WAGNER PUB. 1892–8
The perpetually recurring and garrulous half-closes make the impression as if I were hearing the clatter of a prince's plates and dishes set to music . . .

The most prodigious genius raised him high above all masters of arts and every country.

JOHANNES BRAHMS (WRITING TO DVOŘÁK) 1896
If we cannot write with the beauty of Mozart, let us at least try to write with his purity.

CAMILLE SAINT-SAËNS 1899
Give Mozart a fairy tale and he creates without effort an immortal masterpiece.

HANS VON BÜLOW
Mozart is a young man with a great future before him

SIR EDWARD ELGAR 1905
Turning from a modern score to this small attenuated orchestra [for the G minor Symphony], we may wonder how it is possible that a great art-work could be evolved from such sorry materials . . . We have to marvel that with such a selection of instruments, a variety and contrast can be found sufficient to hold the attention for thirty minutes.

FERRUCCIO BUSONI 1906 (PUB. 1921)
This is how I think of Mozart: he is up to the present the most perfect manifestation of musical talent.

His short life and fecundity enhance his perfection to the point of the phenomenal.

The untroubled beauty of his work irritates.
His sense of form is almost superhuman. Like a masterpiece of sculpture, his art, viewed from any side, is a perfect picture . . .

With the riddle he provides the solution.

GEORGE BERNARD SHAW 1921
Mozart was the greatest of all musicians. He taught me how to say profound things and at the same time remain flippant and lively.

HERMANN HESSE 1927
. . . And I heard from the empty spaces within the theatre the sounds of music, a beautiful and awful music, that music from *Don Giovanni* that heralds the approach of the guest of stone. With an awful and an iron clang it rang through the

ghostly house, coming from the other world, from the immortals. 'Mozart,' I thought, and with the word conjured up the most beloved and the most exalted picture that my inner life contained . . . [*Steppenwolf*]

CECIL GRAY 1928
[The piano concertos are] wayward and nonchalant in form, full of charming ideas which he hardly takes the trouble to work out.

ARNOLD SCHOENBERG
From Mozart I learned
  1 Inequality of phrase-length
  2 Co-ordination of heterogeneous characters to form a thematic unity
  3 Deviation from even-number construction in the theme and its component parts
  4 The art of forming subsidiary ideas
  5 The art of introduction and transition.

WANDA LANDOWSKA
The works of Mozart may be easy to read, but they are very difficult to interpret. The least speck of dust spoils them. They are clear, transparent, and joyful as a spring, and not like those muddy pools which seem deep only because the bottom cannot be reached.

RICHARD STRAUSS (ATTRIB. BY NORMAN DEL MAR)
I cannot write about Mozart, I can only worship him.

FREDERICK DELIUS
If a man tells me he likes Mozart, I know in advance that he is a bad musician.

VIRGINIA WOOLF 1917
Then onto *Figaro* at the Old Vic. It's perfectly lovely, break-ing from one beauty into another, and so Romantic as well as witty – the perfection of music, and the vindication of opera.

EDWARD MACDOWELL

Mozart's sonatas are compositions entirely unworthy of the author of *The Magic Flute*, or of any composer with pretensions to anything beside mediocrity. They are written in a style of flashy harpsichord virtuosity such as Liszt never descended to . . .

AARON COPLAND

Mozart tapped the source from which all music flows, expressing himself with a spontaneity and refinement and breathtaking rightness.

BENJAMIN BRITTEN

All his life, Mozart had the wit to be influenced by great composers, but then he assimilated these influences and made them part of his character.

GEORGE ANTHEIL

The 'fun' in a Mozart symphony is not entirely unlike that of a baseball game. In baseball, all plays are strictly within the rules . . . Mozart's mastery was so superb, so utterly top-notch, that Mozart fans experienced exactly the same sensation which a modern baseball audience might feel today should its home town team be blindfolded and still win hands down against a super-excellent non-blindfolded visiting team.

GLENN GOULD

Mozart was a bad composer who died too late rather than too early.

MARIA CALLAS

Most of Mozart's music is dull

ARTHUR MILLER

Mozart is happiness before it has gotten defined.

LEONARD BERNSTEIN

Mozart is *all* music; there is nothing you can ask from music that he cannot supply . . . bathed in a glitter that could have come only from the eighteenth century, from that age of light, lightness and enlightenment. It is a perfect product of the age of reason – witty, objective, graceful, delicious. And yet over it all hovers the greater spirit that is Mozart's – the spirit of compassion, of universal love, even of suffering – a spirit that knows no age, that belongs to all ages. [*Infinite Variety of Music*]

VICTOR BORGE
In my dreams of heaven, I always see the great Masters gathered in a huge hall in which they all reside. Only Mozart has his own suite.

See also *Mozart in Retrospect* by Alec Hyatt King, *Mozartiana* by Joseph Solman, *Viva Mozart* by George D. Snell.

Mozart 2006

For many years now, over half a million people a year have fought their way through the narrow streets of Salzburg to visit Mozart's birthplace on the third floor of a medieval town house in the Getreidegasse. It is the place to go, even if you are really here only for the shopping or the *Sound of Music* tour. If you go up the narrow stairs, past the factitious 'Mozart kitchen', into the room which houses facsimiles of autograph scores and early printed editions, you can see a few impressive relics such as Mozart's child-sized violin and his adult viola, as well as a supposed lock of his hair (which is generously granted the status of a '?' in the guide). Here in the hushed voices of tour guides the stories of 'little Wolfgang's' youthful prowess in playing and composition are embroidered; here are absurd guesses about which corner of the room he was supposedly born in; here is the clavichord on which a little faded label signed by his wife in the nineteenth century explains that he is supposed to have composed *Die Zauberflöte* and the other works of his last year on it – 'such a quiet instrument, so as not to disturb his dear Constanze who was so ill'. (He is also said to have composed the piece in the much-restored and rebuilt wooden summer house which was moved from Vienna to Salzburg and stands in the garden of the nearby Mozarteum, but no matter.) Here are the trinkets: his tobacco case, his snuff-box, a wallet, buttons from one of his jackets, and a mother-of-pearl case. But there are far fewer genuine musical items than there used to be, doubtless because of security and preservation concerns: in particular, not a single real Mozart manuscript – they're now stowed away in a safe across the river.

There are a couple of powerful artworks which speak across the years: the Lorenzoni portrait of Mozart aged seven in his gleaming formal dress, hung next to those of his sister, mother and father, and the wonderful unfinished portrait of the composer at the piano by Joseph Lange, which more than any other depiction allows us to approach the darker side of Mozart's intense personality. (Unfortunately this is placed near fairly gruesome reproductions and laser prints of other Mozart portraits.) The piano that Mozart played, made by Anton Walter, albeit much restored, which allows us a glimpse of how his music might have sounded, has been transferred across the river to the safer display arrangements of a new Mozart museum, though there is a copy here and fine recordings have been made on the original by András Schiff and others. Increasingly what remains in the birthplace – in shiny new, brightly lit wooden cases – are copies, photo-copies, prints and facsimiles, as if it doesn't matter that no one can tell the difference from the real thing.

The Mozart industry is one metaphor for the tumult and contradictions that surround the composer on the 250th anniversary of his birth: the noise of jarring claims and counterclaims, the vigorous grinding of biographical axes, the combination of genuine admiration and simplistic exploitation, and above all the confusion of demonstrable fact, tentative hypothesis, meaningful myth and ludicrous fiction that goes to make up the history of a genius. For Mozart is now big business, as the city of Salzburg – which reckons to receive over half its multi-million-pound tourist income directly from the Mozart industry – is the first to acknowledge.

This is ironic, since for a long time Salzburg erased Mozart from its history, and it was not until 1880, nearly a century after his death, that a Birthplace Museum was first created: a statue had been erected in 1842. The Mozarteum bought the property in 1917, and the exhibitions have developed and expanded there (to include scenic designs of Mozart's operas, more recently accompanied by brief video extracts, and a re-creation of a typical middle-class apartment) in the years since 1956. Then the Mozart industry took a bigger leap of faith in his staying power. When you buy your Mozart mug and Mozart postcards, the Mozart liqueurs or Mozart candles from the birthplace shop, you are helping pay for investment in the rebuilding of a remarkable 'new' Mozart house. The Mozart Wohnhaus, where the family lived from 1773, was across the river from the birthplace, in the Makartplatz. It was the Salzburg dancing master's house before Leopold Mozart bought it, and balls were held there. The Mozarteum had begun to turn it into a museum at the end of the 1930s, but then it was badly bombed during the war in October 1944; only a couple of rooms survived, and a nasty office block was built over the site, selling Mercedes cars. The Mozart Foundation went into debt to raise the 26.5 million schillings (a snip at £1.3 million) needed to buy the block. It raised another few million pounds and dollars (or more likely yen) to knock it down in 1994 and – thanks to the precision of the Nazis in recording every detail of the Mozart dwelling – reconstructed a version of the whole building. So now there is a bright new Mozart relic in Salzburg, housing an audio-visual museum and an ultra-secure storage space for the manuscripts and letters and much else, aiming to attract visitors across the river from the old town. All the features of present-day tourism – the audio guide, trendily designed display cases (by the same artist who created the covers of the Philips Mozart CD edition) and the souvenir shop equipped with everything except Mozart's own scores – are present. Some original features are missing, including the musicians' balcony in the great room where dances would have been held in Mozart's day. It may be over the top, but in much more culturally aware Vienna, the site of the apartment where Mozart died in 1791 is still marked by little more than a potted plant in the corner of a department store. And it is also a peculiar sort of reparation from the city that, once he left under clouded circumstances, more or less erased Mozart from its history for generations.

Now Salzburg is investing heavily in Mozart. The second theatre of the Festspielhaus – unbeloved by performers and audiences alike – has been demolished, and a new theatre significantly called 'Haus für Mozart' is due to open in 2006, if several million more euros can be raised. Just opposite, private donations have built a swish new entrance to the restored University Hall, where Mozart first appeared when he was seven. There is even an avant-garde sculpture by the river devoted to Mozart: a hugely tall, thin metal chair, with the instruction 'Sit on the Chair / Close your eyes / Contemplate'. Salzburg is taking Mozart back to its heart, as if he had never been rejected.

This is a risk, for Mozart has by no means always been the world's most popular composer. Right now it just seems that way; and everything Mozart touches turns to gold, or at least into a Mozart chocolate. Even at a time of seismic change in the classical music world, we seemingly cannot get enough of Mozart. The 'Mostly Mozart' Festival has filled halls for years at Lincoln Center in New York and, more recently, so has its spin-off at the Barbican Centre in London. At a time of declining CD sales, Mozart is still successful on disc, and there are websites from which you can download his out-of-copyright music in all sorts of performances, including inhuman synthesised versions supplied as MIDI files. A massive quasi-scientific industry has been built in America on the (somewhat dubious) association of Mozart and classical music generally with special mental skills, marketed under the trademarked brand name 'The Mozart Effect'.

Yet at the beginning of the twentieth century in Britain, to pick just one moment in the fluctuating history of Mozart's reputation, there were only isolated figures like George Bernard Shaw, E. J. Dent and Donald Tovey who argued for Mozart's supreme greatness. Alec Hyatt King well described Tovey as 'a beacon in the fog which then shrouded English Mozart scholarship'.

The academic consensus was sniffy; Parry famously dismissed one great set of variations as 'mere notespinning'. Sir William Hadow said the great operas contained 'no coherent story nor even any serious attempt at dramatic illusion'; when the Royal Musical Association eventually devoted a whole lecture to Mozart in 1906 (though, as the speaker noted, he had 'once shared attention with Beethoven in a lecture discussing the treatment of the Rondo form') it was called, with nicely judged severity, 'Mozart's Early Efforts at Opera'.

In the 1930s even Ernest Newman, no mean Mozartian, was still describing Mozart's symphonic form as 'really rather rudimentary' compared with that of Sibelius, and a relatively small number of the symphonies were performed. Thomas Beecham was an early advocate of the operas, but it is easy to forget, at a time when the popular six operas are now the staple of the repertory in opera houses, how recently they have become re-established. The earlier operas are now revived with increasing frequency, and the Salzburg Festival is boldly performing every Mozart opera in the anniversary year of 2006.

The insights of German scholars, especially those of Alfred Heuss and Hermann Abert, who in the early twentieth century were exploring the darker side of Mozart's character and music with considerable analytical insight, were rarely acknowledged. (Heuss wrote an important article on 'The Demonic Element in Mozart's Work' in 1905.) True, the standard British reference work, Cobbett's *Encyclopedia of Chamber Music*, published in 1929, did commission an entry on Mozart from Abert; but the editor found it so disturbing that although he published it, he added a note disowning it! 'Dr Abert reads into his music qualities of tragic intensity, sullenness, even demonaic fury, and this will, I think, excite the astonishment of some of our readers . . . a Mozart record is a veritable nest of singing birds . . .' (a sentiment which would appeal to the mass-marketers of Mozart CDs today).

In one sense this reductionist approach to Mozart's music should not cause surprise; in an age which saw music as ever improving, as it became larger and more complex, Mozart was bound to appear a mere precursor to Romanticism. He would be the composer who prepared the way for Beethoven, who prepared the way for Brahms, who prepared the way for Wagner. To Wagner, Mozart was the master of endless melody who composed 'thoughtlessly', without reflection.

Just as Schubert and Gounod and Tchaikovsky adored Mozart, Wagner worshipped him for his preternatural innocence. The legend of the eternal child, which, as we shall see, originated in a bizarre way, became extended to the music in the nineteenth-century vision: though connoisseurs and composers like Brahms appreciated Mozart's depths, too often he was seen as the creator of naive but inspired miniatures that prepared the way for 'real' music.

But the German writers saw beyond this limited vision. They harked back to the 'demonic power' that had been discerned in Mozart's music very soon after his death by Goethe ('a procreative force', he said of Mozart) and E. T. A. Hoffmann. Hoffmann had analysed Mozart's music deeply, and had rewritten *Don Giovanni* as a visionary Romantic moral tale. This was the tradition that Heuss and Abert sought to revive for the generation of Mahler and Schoenberg. But Abert's powerful biography of Mozart (a revision of Otto Jahn's pioneering work) was never translated into English – except for William Glock's publication of the fascinating chapter on *Don Giovanni*. So Abert's view did not make an impact in this country, and the notion of a grave, demonically inspired and even neurotic Mozart never caught on here.

That view was radically diluted, too, by the distinctively bourgeois and popular (and readily available in English) version of Mozart the Romantic offered in Alfred Einstein's warm-hearted biography of 1944. This portrayed an essentially warm and smiling figure, one with human failings but able to rise above them – a reassuring portrait, even a touch cosy amid the tribulations of war. Much of Einstein's response to the music is admirable and detailed, but his scholarly hypotheses about the chronology of Mozart's music, which he formulated in his third edition of the Köchel catalogue, have since been largely discredited.

The deeply sentimental view of Mozart so prevalent in the popular literature across two centuries had its roots much further back, however, in the very first decades after his death.

In what now seems a remarkably effortless struggle to establish his respectable credentials as a timeless genius, Mozart's biography, eminently suitable for Romanticisation, was transformed. To meet the needs of the age that followed him, the workmanlike composer became the inspired artist; the servant-artisan became the free-spirited creator, and a tiny part of the music was preserved in the repertory to serve the biographical fiction that Mozart was always a child. Where did this come from?

In a seminal but apocryphal statement from his deathbed recorded by his early biographer Niemetschek, Mozart was made to declare: 'Now I must leave my Art just as I had freed myself from the slavery of fashion, had broken the bonds of speculators, and won the privilege of following my own feelings and composing freely and independently whatever my heart prompted!' This summed up everything the Romantics wanted a composer to be, and which Mozart was not. He had just spent much of his last year composing two operas that were commissioned and specifically tailored to very different performing circumstances, as well as sets of dances for immediate use, written as part of his job in Vienna. We cannot be sure if 'composing freely' is a concept Mozart would have understood or desired: all the evidence is that he yearned to be needed and appreciated – to be asked to write music because people wanted it, to show off the skills of his singers and players as well as possible, to make the most of whatever practical performing circumstances he was faced with. Yes, he wanted his audiences to enjoy his music, and to show by their attention that they were enjoying it. Yes, he wanted his music to be better, cleverer, more passionate, and more memorable than everyone else's, and probably believed it to be so, but there is not a shred of support for the idea that he ever consciously wrote for some far-distant future.

The image of the bourgeois, respectable Mozart was an astoundingly rapid creation of the late 1790s. And this icon had its roots, ironically for those who believe that Mozart became an exploitable proposition only in our age, in commercial necessity. Constanze Mozart, the widow he left with-out financial resources, had only one source of income, and that was her husband's music and reputation: she could sing his arias, she could sell his scores. Encouraged by her future second husband, the Danish diplomat Georg Nissen, who wrote most of her letters for her, she negotiated with pub-lishers to make the most of these precious assets. Breitkopf und Härtel, one of the leading music publishers of the day, planned to publish an 'Oeuvres Complettes' of Mozart's music and a biography of the great composer. But myths about Mozart were already becoming well established, thanks to the collection of biographical information about him from those with axes to grind. It may now seem irrelevant where these ideas originated, but given that some of them appear in every popular Mozart biography, knowing where they come from is critical to our understanding of his story.

There were two fundamentally different biographical trad-itions in the years immediately after Mozart's death. One orig-inated with his wife Constanze in Vienna, the other with his sister Nannerl in Salzburg; Constanze and Nannerl had drift-ed far apart in the years since Wolfgang's marriage and Leopold's death. Nannerl had not visited Vienna since her childhood, and never after Mozart moved to the city; she knew little of Mozart's existence there. On the other hand Constanze knew little of Mozart's gilded childhood in Salzburg. 'Biography is a contest for possession,' Maynard Solomon has written, and how well that is demonstrated here.

Constanze's views are reflected in the supportive, pro-Mozart biography written by their Prague friend Franz Xaver Niemetschek, published anonymously in 1797 and repub-lished under his name in 1798, which relates many stories about Mozart's good nature and loving marriage based on the Vienna and Prague years. Here are the origins of Joseph II's remark, 'Too many notes, my dear Mozart!' and Mozart's reply: 'Exactly as many as are necessary, your Majesty!' (The exchange is glossed with the generous thought that the monarch was 'at heart delighted with this new and deeply expressive music'.) Here are many of the Requiem legends, including Mozart's immortal line 'Did I not say that I was writing this Requiem for myself?' and his fear that he was being poisoned; here too Mozart's special successes in Prague and Bohemia are highlighted. The emphasis of Niemetschek's book is that Mozart's glorious genius was not fully recompensed with the appointments and financial success that should have been his. This helped Constanze to account for her poverty on his death: it is not hard to see here a purely self-justificatory element in Constanze's story, supporting the (perfectly true) notion that she was left with a financial burden after Mozart's death, which her performances and the sale of his manuscripts then went to alleviate. Niemetschek's eulogy pushed Mozart inexorably into the world of the isolated nineteenth-century Romantic artist who struggled for his existence; but much recent work has stressed how comparatively successful Mozart actually was for much of his Vienna period.

The Nannerl line is rather darker and more complex. Mozart's first obituarist was the scholar and lawyer Friedrich Schlichtegroll, who compiled books of obituaries from 1790 and wrote Mozart's in the second part of his *Nekrolog auf das Jahr 1791*, published in Gotha in 1793. To prepare it he wrote to the Salzburg court official Albert von Mölk for information. The von Mölks had been family friends of the Mozarts, and indeed Nannerl had been romantically involved with one of his sons, so von Mölk was able to pass the enquiry on to Nannerl, who was still in Salzburg. She responded with lengthy memories of his early years and tours, doubtless using her meticulous diaries and Leopold's letters as a source. Nannerl's memories of her brother are fresh and positive: 'He was never forced to compose nor to play, on the contrary he always needed to be restrained, he would otherwise have remained sitting over his clavier or his compositions day and night.' Nannerl also wrote to the family friend Johann Schachtner asking for some stories of Mozart's earliest days, which he cheerfully supplied and are uncritically repeated in many biographies. But Nannerl then said: 'for the events of his later life, you must make enquiries in Vienna, as I can find nothing from which I could write anything thorough'; this extended as far as claiming not to know 'as also who his wife was, how many children they had of their union, how many of them are still alive, etc.'. She was firmly drawing a line and saying that she did not wish to be taken as an authority on this period of Mozart's life. However, without her knowledge (according to the latest exhaustive research into this episode by Bruce Cooper Clarke), Nannerl's comments were supplemented by von Mölk in forwarding the letter on.

Von Mölk added a devastating little postscript undoubtedly reflecting the Salzburg feeling of the time. The first part describes and praises Nannerl herself (which makes it clear that the extra material was not written by her) and then says: 'Apart from his music he was almost always a child, and thus he remained, and this is the main feature of his character on the dark side; he always needed a father's or a mother's or some other guardian's care; he could not manage his financial affairs . . . [he] married a girl quite unsuited to him, and against the will of his father, and thus the great domestic chaos at his death.' In spite of the fact that the last part of this (after the dots) was scribbled out, this view of Mozart began to take root, doubtless fuelled by existing gossip and rumour.

Schlichtegroll, who pulled together the materials for his obituary from a variety of sources, did not actually print von Mölk's last comment, and was positive about Mozart's marriage to Constanze; but he did let stand the comment that Mozart was incapable of looking after his own affairs, because that had actually been supported by Nannerl. He wrote, 'In Vienna he married Constanze Weber and found in her a good mother of two children conceived with her, and a worthy wife, who sought to restrain him from his many excesses.' But that was enough to rouse Constanze to fury; she later claimed that she bought and destroyed all six hundred copies of the 1794 Graz reprint of this obituary, now independently published as a single volume under the title *Mozarts Leben*.

(Though her claim has never been contested, it is inherently bizarre, especially as some copies survive.) Her objections can be glimpsed in a surviving copy of Schlichtegroll in which a few lines have been scribbled out by an interested party (italics here show the erased sections): 'He never learned to discipline himself, he had no inclination for domestic orderliness, for appropriate use of money, *for moderation and judicious choice in gratification*' (in this case it is surely surprising that the beginning of the sentence was left to stand). 'As considerable as his income was, on account of his *preponderant sensuality and* disorder, he bequeathed to his survivors nothing more than the fame of his name.'

The point that Mozart was not good with money was acceptable because it helped Constanze's claim of impoverishment, but it seems to be the only criticism of him that she was prepared to accept. There is a narrow line here between one excess and another: even Nannerl admitted in her comment, when pressed for his faults, that she could 'only charge him with a single one . . . he had too soft a heart and did not know how to handle money'. This, she said, was why Leopold constantly supervised him, why his mother went to Paris with him, and why he got into financial difficulties later. However, there was a big difference between admitting this and suggesting that he was excessive in his gratifications, sensuality, lacking in moderation, and unable to control himself! Nannerl never endorsed those views, which led in a quite different direction: to rumours of dissolute living and womanising, which it is easy to see that both she and Constanze wanted to eradicate from any view of the great composer.

The most respectable musical journalist of the day, Johann Friedrich Rochlitz, knew better than these vile rumours, for at the age of eighteen he had briefly met Mozart in Leipzig in 1789 and set out to become the self-appointed guardian of his spirit. In 1798, in Breitkopf und Härtel's house journal, the *Allgemeine muskalische Zeitung*, he set out to publish a series of stories about Mozart with the specific aim that 'the despicable, malevolent and repugnant anecdotes that are still being told about Mozart' would be contradicted. He was not aiming to write a biography as such, but to collect incidents which supported his righteous view of Mozart. Whether or not Rochlitz acted with the support of Constanze (who did not supply the detail of the anecdotes, for many of them appear to have been completely invented by Rochlitz), it is easy to see here a direct connection with the forthcoming sale of Mozart's music from the same publisher. Rochlitz, without embarking on a full-scale biography, was attempting to build the cultural image of the great composer which would enable his works to be accepted by a new age. He succeeded.

Rochlitz's anecdotes are remarkable documents of their time, cast in the form of mini-novelettes that became increasingly popular in Germany and which spawned a whole Mozart fiction industry in the century that followed. Often drawn from Niemetschek's biography and grandly elaborated, they were as based on rumour as the vile stories they aimed to supplant. But because they are not actually verifiable or true, it does not mean they are not important. Here is Mozart, the carelessly generous man, who has no money only because he has overpaid the tradesmen. Here is Mozart, turning down a lucrative offer of a job in Berlin because of his devotion to Joseph II, once again suggesting why Mozart remained poor. Here is Mozart, ruthlessly exploited by publishers and performers, but always overlooking their malice towards him because of his forgiving heart. The picture of a dissolute Mozart who is out of control, or even a poorly-organised Mozart who cannot cope, is replaced by that of an unworldly, innocent Mozart, existing above all trivial and mundane matters of the world: it is an alluring image.

The fact that the anecdotes were essentially fictional had little effect on their staying power, because they portrayed the Mozart that the nineteenth century wanted. And some of them undoubtedly have more than a grain of truth: they simply dramatise that truth in the form of a story. Rochlitz has a famous anecdote of Mozart poring over the parts of a motet by Johann Sebastian Bach which he had heard in Leipzig, exclaiming, 'Here's something from which one can learn!' This may or may not have happened quite like that (though at least in that case Rochlitz was actually present, and Mozart's autograph copy of the motet survives), but it points up an important moment in Mozart's intense involvement and identification with the music of the baroque, which is highly significant for Mozart's creative process. Other anecdotes refer to characteristics of Mozart's generosity which may have their origins in truthful memory; it would be wise not to dismiss them out of hand.

Maynard Solomon has suggested that 'eventually, Mozart's widow and sister were reconciled to the biographies of Mozart which the other had shaped.' I wonder: the relationship between the two during the years they both lived in Salzburg after Mozart's death is shadowy. Though the English couple Vincent and Mary Novello painted a generous picture when they visited Salzburg, the two women were very distant, making contact mainly through Constanze's son Wolfgang. When Constanze went so far as to bury her second husband Nissen in the Mozart family vault, and placed his name prominently on the headstone, Nannerl bitterly changed her will and moved her intended grave. In considering the biography that Breitkopf was planning, Constanze recommended only that 'Niemetschek's work and the *good part* of [Schlichtegroll] would permit one to make a whole.' Nannerl's testimony was that when she finally read Niemetschek's account of Mozart's struggles in Vienna it 'again so totally animated my sisterly feelings towards my ardently beloved brother that I was often dissolved in tears'. That is a touching moment: a biographical picture of Mozart designed to form an image of him as a neglected genius affected even his own sister, because it told her about a part of his life from which she had been totally excluded.

So into one fluid and ever-shifting historical picture came together the memories of those who had a stake in Mozart's life, the myths they wanted to preserve as his heritage, and their aspirations for who they wanted 'Mozart' to be in the future. The person who should have taken all this material and welded it into an authoritative Mozart biography was Constanze's second husband, Georg Nissen. He accumulated vast amounts of material from many sources, including the letters, published biographies and obituaries, and the Rochlitz anecdotes, but he seemed defeated by the task: he was completely unable to sort them into any logical order. Constanze described to her son a picture any writer will recognise, of her husband 'sitting day and night, buried in piles of his books and newspapers, within which he can barely be seen'. He worked tirelessly, but was unable to complete the work before he died. But Constanze desperately needed the book to be published and sold, so in a process which remarkably resembles her attitude to the Requiem after Mozart's death, it was hurriedly edited, or perhaps just bundled and thrown together, by Johann Feuerstein, a medical man with few qualifications for biography. The result is generally agreed to be a total mess. ('It is difficult to credit the apparently unlimited extent of Nissen's incompetence,' writes Solomon. But for the twenty-first century it might be an interesting exercise to unpack his book and establish where all the many bits of it came from.) One of the most creative uses of Nissen's material and other early sources to assemble an early Mozart biography in English is a fine book, *The Life of Mozart* by Edward Holmes, published in 1845, as beautifully written and organised as Nissen's was not, which has been reprinted in Everyman's Library.

By the mid-nineteenth century Mozart's life had irretrievably taken on the character of a novel. The irony is that although the 'scientific' Mozart writers, the early positivist scholars, laboured long and hard to ascertain 'facts' about Mozart, and thus rejected Rochlitz's fabrications, they were ineluctably touched by his sentimentalising intent. The great Mozart biography of the 1860s by the classicist Otto Jahn, which is often biographically reliable and musically perceptive, outlawed Rochlitz as 'completely untrue', and dismissed Nissen as 'enough to drive one to absolute despair . . . a con-

fused and ill-proportioned mass'. He endorsed Edward
Holmes's book as 'without a doubt the most reliable and serv-
iceable biography that could be achieved by the skilful use of
the material generally accessible'. But Jahn's wholly
admirable and objective view of Mozart is still essentially
devoted to the creation of an appropriate image, bathed in a
penumbra of warmth which praised the achievements of its
German hero: 'While our gaze is lifted in reverence and
admiration to the great musician, it may rest with equal sympathy and love upon the pure-hearted man.'

In the twentieth century, scholars who sought verifiable
truth classed Rochlitz with fiction: the anecdotes in their full
original form have only very recently appeared in English
with an excellent commentary by Maynard Solomon (in
Mozart Studies, edited by Cliff Eisen); they were excluded by
Otto Erich Deutsch from his magisterially compendious
Mozart: A Documentary Biography, which does, however,
include some semi-fictional material, and accounts that,
though fascinating, are not reliable. The most gripping story
of Mozart's last days is the emotional letter of 1825 – which
reads just like a novelette – by Constanze's sister Sophie Haibl.
This (doubtless entirely sincere) letter was written thirty-four
years after the events it describes, and draws on already published sources such as Niemetschek's biography to elaborate
her personal testimony. Even the immensely likeable account
of Mozart's childhood music-making which Nannerl requested from the court trumpeter Johann Andreas Schachtner ('He
would often ask me ten times a day if I loved him') was written
in 1792, over thirty years after the events it describes. Both
these documents were specifically tailored to provide information for biographies of the dead genius. They are testimony to an idea about Mozart, a conviction in their writers –
amply borne out by events, of course – that he was greater
than ordinary mortals. But as biographical fact, we have to
recognise that they may be no more reliable than the Gospels.

In line with the demythologising trend that marked the
latter part of the twentieth century, modern research has

produced some deflating facts about Mozart as a prodigy. Not until Wolfgang Plath got to work on the handwriting in the autograph scores did we realise quite how much of the very early works were actually written down (or just corrected? or edited? or half-composed?) by his father Leopold. Much is made of Mozart's admission to the famous Accademia Filarmonica in Bologna when he was fourteen, but the documents that survive show that his entrance composition was heavily corrected before acceptance. Leopold Mozart, so intent on demonstrating his son's genius, quickly turned him into a presentable composer, but the American scholar Christoph Wolff has questioned whether Mozart was as good a composer at sixteen as was Mendelssohn. Essentially, Mozart taught himself from other people's music, with brilliant resourcefulness and amazing speed. Leopold's presentation of his early work was principally motivated by his desire to further Wolfgang's career, and any 'help' he gave would have been both logically and generously motivated. But what then happened was that Mozart radically over-fulfilled his father's expectations, and went his own way, musically and personally, leading to huge tensions in their relationship.

Research has also revealed new facts about Mozart's working methods. Alan Tyson's important hypothesis, from study of the music paper Mozart used, is that he sometimes started works and then broke off for anything up to a couple of years before completing them, presumably under the pressure of a deadline or a commission. Many fragments of great promise remained unfinished, probably simply because of lack of opportunity for performance. One cannot rule out creative block, but given the fecundity of Mozart's ideas that seems inherently unlikely. A more likely scenario is rapid rejection of the second-rate: Mozart must have daily been his own fiercest critic, for there was literally no one else around him who really understood his music. So he would start pieces, toy with ideas, and then decide that they would not work and move on. These sketches, the try-outs that Mozart made in the course of composition, are fascinating, and some are of the highest quality; much work remains to be done with them. There are not nearly as many as from Beethoven, even supposing that many have been thrown away, but quite enough to counter the notion that Mozart always wrote down fully finished pieces straight out of his head. The fact that he carefully kept so many fragments, Neal Zaslaw suggests, means that they were ready to be worked on for some future performance. In the sketches, we can see him working through the tricky contrapuntal combinations of some moments, sketching ideas and sequences and trying out melodic shapes. We know that he did perform works which he had thought out but never written down, especially when performing as a pianist; but equally the sketches show that crucial moments had to be prepared and worked at. That was surely the 'long and laborious labour' that Mozart referred to in the dedication of six quartets to Haydn, a composer with whom he could talk on equal and genuinely admiring terms.

Demythologising has also been brought to bear in great detail on Mozart's finances, to demonstrate that he probably earned far more than we thought in Vienna, and was not as impoverished as was claimed. This research is a two-edged sword: if he earned so much more, where did the money go? Certainly the life of a freelance composer and teacher that he created for himself in Vienna was an expensive one to sustain, and there were few precedents. He had to be present at social events, dress accordingly, and maintain a certain standard of living. Teaching was unreliable, though it has been pointed out that his arrangements with pupils showed a strong business sense, in that he contracted for series of lessons so that he earned his income 'irrespective of the lady's weekly whims'. Have his famous begging letters to Michel Puchberg survived only because Puchberg decided to keep them? Might there have been many others? And what of the extraordinary new evidence which emerged only in the 1990s that at the time of his death Mozart was actually being sued by his patron Prince Lichnowsky for money owing him?

That evidence comes from Vienna court papers, but is nowhere mentioned in Mozart's own letters or the resources of his estate after his death. The Lichnowsky lawsuit emerged mysteriously, and may well have been abandoned when he died, but it suggests there may well have been other financial dealings and problems of which we know nothing.

In the years since the hyperactive Mozart bicentenary of 1991, Mozart scholarship has continued, out of the limelight, to revise our perceptions of significant parts of his output. Mozart's interaction with the culture of the cities within which he worked and by which he was commissioned has received close attention; this extends not only to instrumental forces but to local ideas, individual singers, the state of operatic development and so on. This is a much more fruitful way forward than the simple interaction of biography with composition that had been the usual way of describing Mozart's motivation (which gives rise to so many problems: if he wrote intense minor-mode works as a reaction to his mother's death, why did he finish off *A Musical Joke* after his father died?). And while we have found it possible to move past some of the ideas about Mozart that the nineteenth century imposed on him, we are still too often bound by nineteenth-century concepts of genius, their ideas of the nobility of instrumental music – the vision of what the symphony became after Mozart's death, for example – and the relation between 'the composer' and 'the work', which is something that Mozart would scarcely have recognised. What was 'a work' to Mozart? It was surely something very fluid and flexible, often changing from performing circumstance to performing circumstance, changing from autograph to copyist to printed edition.

There is a particular problem here, because for much of the twentieth century it was precisely the period of the late eighteenth century, when Mozart worked, that provided the ideal model of what an artist was. This was the moment when the artist was gradually becoming a free agent, a force for social criticism and political change; hence there has been an easy assumption that Mozart was part of this process, that he set Beaumarchais's *Figaro* because he wanted to be a revolutionary, writing his three last symphonies not for performance but because he wanted to change the world. Mozart worked within the conventions of his time, stretching them to their limits, but our view of how far he broke those bounds altogether will depend on how far we want to identify him with the generations that followed, and how far with those from which he emerged.

What has happened in the musical world's understanding of Mozart's music during the last half century can be summed up in a phrase: Mozart suddenly became serious. W. H. Auden noticed in 1956:

> We know the Mozart of our fathers' time
> Was gay, rococo, sweet, but not sublime
> A Viennese Italian; that is changed
> Since music-critics learned to feel *estranged*:
> Now it's the Germans he is classed amongst
> A *Geist* whose music was composed from *Angst*
> At International festivals enjoys
> An equal status with the Twelve-Tone Boys . . .

(and since 1956, one might add, rather greater status than the dodecaphonists). Kenneth Clark in his TV series *Civilization*, which formulated the accepted enlightened views on so many cultural issues, described how he used to see Mozart depicted in 'horrible plaster casts which made him look the perfect eighteenth-century dummy. I bought one of those busts when I was at school, but when I heard the G minor Quintet I realised that it could not have been written by the smooth white character on my mantelpiece and threw the bust in the wastepaper basket.' Yet the plaster-cast view of Mozart survives in record-company marketing departments around the world, and other mythical stories bubble away beneath the surface and then burst forth. That was what happened in the 1980s with Peter Shaffer's outstanding play *Amadeus*, and then the film, rewritten by Shaffer but shaped by director

Milos Forman. Serious Mozartians may wish to dismiss both the play and the film as irrelevant, but they are central to the understanding of the composer by a new generation, and it is interesting to see an increasing acceptance of their relevance to Mozart reception in the new *Cambridge Companion to Mozart*.

Paradoxically, it was exactly the seriousness with which we now view Mozart's music that made the violent contrasts of *Amadeus* possible: Shaffer's much-criticised reduction of Mozart's personality became the dramatic device through which he pointed up the chasm between the (over-emphasised) scatological nature of his chit-chat and his sublime music, whose importance and power Shaffer never for a minute diminishes. Shaffer's Salieri declares: 'Tonight at an inn some-where in this city stands a giggling child who can put on paper, without actually setting down his billiard cue, casual notes which turn my most considered ones into lifeless scratches.' Salieri's acceptable mediocrity is set against Mozart's unac-ceptable genius: it is a clever dramatic conceit, albeit one drawn directly from Pushkin's 1830 drama on the same sub-ject. It enables Shaffer to draw on all manner of Mozart stories and legends to prove his point. In the play, Mozart's music was superbly used, half-heard and distorted (through the agency of another composer, Harrison Birtwistle), to recreate its impact on Salieri; in the film the music was fatally changed into an extravaganza (with such appalling solecisms as editing together two movements of the Serenade in B flat K361). And the touching fiction at the heart of *Amadeus* is that Salieri is the person who really did appreciate Mozart's music and, as a second-rate composer, saw its first-rate qualities. In real life Mozart was probably much lonelier: with whom could he actually discuss the subtleties of what he was creating, after he had left his father behind? Surely only Joseph Haydn, a first-rate composer in his own right, really penetrated the full scope of Mozart's genius.

In our age, when the idea of musical progress has col-lapsed, and an ever-wider chronological and geographical range of music is relished by listeners, Mozart has come into his own. For how long? One might have thought that the height of Mozart's fame would turn out to have been the period between the two bicentenaries of 1956 and 1991, when so much attention was given to his work. But as we approach the 250th anniversary period, from 2006 to 2041, there is no sign that Mozart has lost his relevance among classical composers. He still matches with uncanny precision the temper of our troubled times: our emotional uncertainty, our ability to perceive serenity fleetingly, but never to attain it. One of the best summaries for us of Mozart's paradoxes remains Donald Mitchell's prophetic essay of 1956: 'What amazes, and sometimes confuses, is Mozart's mercurial synthesising . . . his essential ambiguity . . . Mozart sounds those deep recesses of the human spirit where opposites are identical.' And by 1991, for the author who has done more than anyone to articulate the story of Mozart for our generation, H. C. Robbins Landon, the composer had become something almost apocalyptic: 'as good an excuse for mankind's survival as we shall ever encounter, and perhaps, after all, a still small hope for our ultimate survival'. The central focus of the ever-shifting image of Mozart continues to elude us. But the music continues to speak with unrivalled force across more than two centuries, and that, we might guess, would satisfy a man who knew the supreme worth of what he was creating.

Verse on Mozart

O where is justice when the sacred gift,
Immortal genius, comes not in reward
For toil, devotion, prayer, self-sacrifice –
But shines instead inside a madcap's skull,
An idle hooligan's? O Mozart, Mozart . . .
I cannot bend the course of destiny –
For I am chosen, I must stop him now,
Or he will be the downfall of us all,
Us ministers and acolytes of music,
Not only me of humble fame . . . What good
If Mozart should live on to reach new heights?
Will music be better? Not at all . . .

PUSHKIN, *Mozart and Salieri*, 1830
(TRANS. ANTONY WOOD, ANGEL BOOKS, 1987)

Almost before the lisping tongue can form
The words, the waves of love and harmony
Combine to whisper, Mozart, in thine ear!
He listens to the enchanting interplay
Of sounds, seeks to match note with note, and halts,
Fascinated, to mark the swelling tones
That form the perfect triad!
Kissing a hundred times his father's cheek
'Do you love me?' he asks on every hand
and should the father, jesting, answer 'no',
the tears of chagrin glisten in his eyes.
Still, at the long day's end, the tired child
Insists on music as he goes to bed.

LUDWIG RITTER VON KÖCHEL, FROM *Twelve Canzonen*
(TRANS. MARTIN COOPER)

Better – than Music! For I – who heard it –
I was used – to the Birds – before –

This was different – 'Twas translation –
Of all tunes I knew – and more –

'Twasn't contained – like other stanza –
No one could play it – the second time –
But the Composer – perfect Mozart –
Perish with him – that Keyless Rhyme!
  EMILY DICKINSON, *c.*1862

The beauty of perfection makes me weep
With helpless ecstasy. O rare Mozart!
Prince of the sweet untroubled countenance . . .
  ALFRED DOUGLAS, 'TRIO'
  (ON 'AH, TACI INGIUSTO CORE' FROM *Don Giovanni*), 1897

Nay come not thus; white lilies in the spring
Sad olive-gardens, or a murmuring dove,
Teach me more clearly of thy life and love
Than terrors of red flame and thundering;
Fruit-laden vines dear memories of thee bring;
A bird of evening flying to its nest
Tells me of One who had no place of rest;
I think it is of thee the sparrows sing . . .
  OSCAR WILDE, 'SONNET' (AFTER HEARING THE 'DIES IRAE'
  FROM THE REQUIEM), 1877

Show me again the time
When in thee Junetide's prime
We flew by meads and mountains northerly! –
Yea, to such freshness, fairness, fullness, fineness, freeness,
Love lures life on.

Show me again the day
When from the sandy bay
We looked together upon the pestered sea!
Yea, to such surging, swaying, sighing, swelling, shrinking
Love lures life on . . .
  THOMAS HARDY, 'LINES TO A MOVEMENT IN MOZART'S E FLAT
  SYMPHONY', 1898

. . . all that joyous is, and young, and free
That tastes of morning and the laughing surf;
The dawn, the dew, the newly turned-up turf,
The sudden smile, the unexpressive prayer,
The artless art, the untaught dignity;
You speak them in the passage of an air.

    MAURICE BARING, 'MOZART'

To the supreme pig the archbishop of Salzburg
Lasting filth and perdition
Since your exalted pustulence is too stingy
To give me a decent salary . . .

    EZRA POUND, CANTO XXVI

. . . That lucid souvenir of the past,
The divertimento,
That airy dream of the future,
The unclouded concerto . . .
The snow is falling.
Strike the piercing chord.

Be thou the voice,
Not you. Be thou, be thou
The voice of angry fear,
Thee voice of this besieging pain.

Be thou that wintry sound
As of the great wind howling,
By which sorrow is released,
Dismissed, absolved
In a starry placating.

We may return to Mozart.
He was young, and we, we are old.
The snow is falling
And the streets and full of cries.
Be seated, thou.

    WALLACE STEVENS, 'MOZART', 1935

The extraordinary extension of the tune
is like being asked where you want to go
To Italy
Italy of the climate,
Not the Italians
but with the Lion of St Mark's in every square
And the dash and jangle of the 'Turkish music' in the air . . .
SACHEVERELL SITWELL, 'ON THE JANISSARIES' CHORUS
FROM *Il Seraglio*'

We who know little (which is just as well)
About the future can at least foretell,
Whether they live in air-borne nylon cubes,
Practise group-marriage or are fed through tubes,
That crowds two centuries from now will press
(Absurd their hair, ridiculous their dress)
And pay in currencies however weird
To hear Sarastro booming through his beard,
Sharp connoisseurs approve if it is clean
The F in alt of the nocturnal Queen . . .

How seemly, then, to celebrate the birth
Of one who did no harm to our poor earth,
Created masterpieces by the dozen,
Indulged in toilet-humour with his cousin,
And had a pauper's funeral in the rain,
The like of whom we shall not see again . . .
W. H. AUDEN, 'METALOGUE TO *The Magic Flute*', 1956
SEE ALSO P. 39

MOZART: THE LIFE

A chronology

The perils of writing anything reliable about Mozart's life are huge. The copious material from his lifetime, especially the Mozart family's voluminous letters, are a remarkable source but need to be treated with some care. In her book *The Mozart Family*, Ruth Halliwell has wisely characterised the 'widely held view that the material is sufficiently well known for quick, confident and uncomplicated judgements to be made about the characters of the people concerned in it, and the relationships within the family. This view, I believe, is seriously misguided . . .' Although many letters survive, many are also missing, lost, destroyed or never kept, and there are some that are preserved not in autograph but only in edited versions in Nissen's biography. Emily Anderson's classic translation, an extraordinary achievement for its time (updated by Stanley Sadie and Fiona Smart for the third edition of 1985, which is used here), is now being supplemented by other translations which catch more of the flavour of Mozart's often eccentric writing, especially Robert Spaethling's *Mozart's Letters, Mozart's Life*.

Many contemporary references and authentic documents were collected by Otto Erich Deutsch in *Mozart: A Documentary Biography*, which has been supplemented by Cliff Eisen's *New Mozart Documents*. The account below is deliberately bald, but it is hopefully not too embroidered.

1756

In January 1756 Mozart was born, the seventh child of Leopold and Anna Maria Mozart, who had married in 1747. Their first, second, third, fifth and sixth children had all died. Their fourth child, Maria Anna, known as 'Nannerl', had been born in July 1751. On 26 January, Leopold was writing to his publisher in Augsburg that he was busy 'partly because of the operas at court, partly because of my pupils, and partly because of other matters that hinder me'. One of the latter was the impending birth of Johannes Chrysosto[mos] Wolfgangus Theophilus, who was born at 8 p.m. on 27 January. Leopold wrote that 'my dear wife was happily delivered of a boy; but the placenta had to be removed, so she was therefore astonishingly weak. Now however (God be praised) both mother and child are well.' In the same year Leopold had issued by his publisher, Johan Jakob Lotter, a progeny of which at that moment he was probably even more proud: his *Violin School*, a well-reviewed and influential method for teaching the violin. From 13 November, Leopold was officially a violin teacher at the Kapellhaus in Salzburg.

- Britain declares war on France
- William Pitt the Elder becomes Secretary of State
- Black Hole of Calcutta: British soldiers die in massacre
- Britain driven from the Great Lakes by France
- Outbreak of Seven Years' War
- Russia joins Alliance of Versailles with France and Austria against Prussia

1757

In January 1757 Mozart turned one. His father is described as 'Hofkomponist' by Marpurg in his account of Salzburg musical life, but this seems to have had no official recognition. The information in Marpurg came from Leopold himself: it reports that the establishment consists of ninety-nine musicians plus three organ-blowers, for church and secular occasions, that most of the musicians are Italians (though some were German and Austrian), and that the fifteen choir-boys had to be trained in Italian. Leopold's report speaks warmly of Johann Ernst Eberlin, the organists Anton Cajetan Adlgasser and Franz Ignaz Lipp (who was also a tenor), but not of vice-Kapellmeister Giuseppe Lolli. Of Eberlin, Leopold Mozart reported to Marpurg that 'he writes with such quickness that many people would take for a fairy-tale the manner in which this profound composer brings this or that composition to the music-stand' – which goes to show that it was not only the young Wolfgang about whom such tales were told.

- Seven Years' War: the Empire declares war on Prussia
- France and Empire sign second treaty of Versailles
- British army beaten at Hastenbeck and surrender at Kloster Seven
- Frederick II wins battles at Rossbach and Leuthen

1758

In January 1758 Mozart turned two. Leopold was now the second violinist of the Salzburg court, and the fame of his violin treatise was spreading. Around this time, Nannerl much later recalled, Wolfgang 'spent much time at the clavier, picking out thirds, which he was always striking, and his pleasure showed that it sounded good'.

- Russians victorious in East Prussia
- British subsidise Prussian army
- French defeated at Crefeld
- Austria defeats Prussia at Hochkirch

1759

In January 1759 Mozart turned three. Nannerl received on her eighth name-day a music book, 'Pour le clavecin', from her father, which was soon to be turned to other uses as her brother's musical skills became apparent. Originally a forty-eight-page bound volume of blank music paper, this fascinating volume was gradually filled by pieces written out by Leopold and at least two other local musicians. In later years individual pages were removed or given away. In Nannerl's own account 'the son was three years old when the father began to instruct his seven-year-old daughter in the clavier,' at which she showed great promise.

- Prussians defeated by French, Russians and Austrians
- Prussian surrender at Maxen
- British take Quebec
- Death of Handel
- Expulsion of Jesuits from Portugal
- British Museum opens

1760

In January 1760 Mozart turned four. During the year, according to Leopold's notes, he learnt to play eight minuets in Nannerl's music book, as well as an Allegro and another Minuet. Leopold himself published keyboard sonatas in Nuremberg this year. The court trumpeter Johann Andreas Schachtner later told a compelling story about the four-year-old Mozart. He said he was writing a keyboard concerto:

> The first part is nearly finished. Papa: Show me. Wolfg: it's not ready yet. His father took it from him and showed me a smudge of notes, most of which were written over ink-blots which he had rubbed out . . . at first we laughed, but his father then began to observe the most important matter. And then tears, tears of joy and wonder fell from his eyes. Look, Herr Schachtner, he said, see how correctly and properly it is all written, only it can't be used. For it is so very difficult that no one could play it. Wolfgangerl said: That's why it's a concerto, you must practise it until you get it right.

No matter how much this story had been polished in the thirty-two years before it was written down, it contains some important kernels of truth about the individual vision of the young Mozart.

- Death of George II; reign of his grandson George III begins
- Tax on colonies to finance Britain's war with France
- Prussian army suffer continuing defeats
- British capture Montreal
- Russians occupy and burn Berlin

1761

In January 1761 Mozart turned five. 'This piece was learnt by Wolfgangerl on 24 January 1761, 3 days before his 5th birthday, between 9 and 9.30 in the evening,' Leopold noted under a Scherzo by Wagenseil in Nannerl's music book. 'This Minuet and Trio was learnt by Wolfgangerl within half an hour on 26 January 1761, a day before his fifth birthday, at about half past 9 at night.' On 4 February he learnt a march. On 6 February he learnt a Scherzo by Wagenseil. Between February and March he wrote his two earliest-recorded compositions, noted by Leopold as written 'in the first three months after his 5th birthday', K1a and 1b. Nannerl later noted, 'He made such progress that at the age of five he was already composing little pieces, which he played to his father who wrote them down.' Leopold did this in Nannerl's own book (one wonders how she felt about this); clearly from the earliest moment Leopold preserved his son's achievements with what Cliff Eisen describes as 'painstaking orderliness'. Wolfgang is also recorded on 1 September as taking part as a dancer in the end-of-term performance at the university of the play *Sigismundus Hungariae Rex*, in the presence of the Archbishop. In December he wrote two more pieces, an Allegro K1c and a Minuet K1d, and around then the most famous of these early pieces, the Minuet in G and Minuet in C K1, preserved on a leaf taken from Nannerl's music book now in the Salzburg Museo Carlino Augusteum.

- France opens peace negotiations with England
- William Pitt resigns
- Austrian troops blockade Frederick II

1762

In January 1762 Mozart turned six. During the year the family made their first exploratory tour, travelling to Munich, where they met the Elector Maximilian Joseph III. In the Trinity Inn, Linz, on 1 October, Mozart gave what some claim was his first public performance. In Vienna they were received by the Empress Maria Theresa and the Emperor Francis I; Wagenseil was also present and was summoned to turn pages for Mozart. (Wolfgang's reported request is absolutely to the point: 'Where is Herr Wagenseil? . . . *He understands*.') Among the many memories of these tours, this contemporary diary item by Count Zinzendorf rings true: 'Then at Thuns, where the little child from Salzburg and his sister played the harpsichord. The poor little fellow plays marvellously, he is a Child of Spirit, lively, charming . . . Mlle de Gudenus, who plays the harpsichord well, gave him a kiss, and he wiped his face.' Leopold's letters to his friend Lorenz Hagenauer in Salzburg describe the visits in detail; Mozart fell ill with scarlet fever on 21 October and had to stay in bed.

During January, Wolfgang wrote the Minuet in F K2, on 4 March he wrote the Allegro in B flat K3, on 11 May the Minuet in F K4, and in July the Minuet in F K5. All these were originally written (in Leopold's hand) in Nannerl's music books, but the pages were removed over time.

It was of this period that Schachtner told the story of Mozart asking to join in a performance by playing the second violin part, even though he had had no tuition on the violin. When refused, 'Wolfgang began to weep bitterly and stamped off with his little violin. I asked them to let him play with me . . . I soon noticed I was quite superfluous, I quietly put my violin down and looked at your papa.' The purpose of these stories was not only to recall the accomplishment of the young Mozart, but also the 'tears of joy' they provoked in his father. However, Daniel Heartz points out that the idea that the young boy could not play the violin at all at this stage is challenged by Leopold's letter of 16 October, which describes Wolfgang charming the customs official in Vienna by playing a minuet on his little violin.

- Britain declares war on Spain and Naples
- Alliance between Russia and Prussia
- Tsar Peter III is killed and succeeded by his wife Catherine II

- Peace between Sweden and Prussia in Treaty of Hamburg
- Prussia defeats Austria at Burkersdorf and Freiburg
- Peace plans between France, Spain and Britain
- Truce between Prussia and the Empire

1763

In January 1763 Mozart turned seven. His father was appointed deputy Kapellmeister, after the death of the Kapellmeister Eberlin; though he might have hoped to succeed Eberlin, the post went to Lolli. Word of the young Mozart's exploits was beginning to spread and the *Augsburg Ischer Intelligenz-Zettel* wrote on 19 May, quoting a letter that had been sent from a Vienna resident:

> We fall into utter amazement on seeing a boy aged 6 at the clavier and hear him, not by any means toy with sonatas trios and concertos, but play in a manly way, and improvise moreover for hours on end out of his own head, now cantabile, now in chords, producing the best of ideas according to the taste of the day and even accompany at sight symphonies, arias and recitatives at the great concerts. Tell me, does this not exceed all imagination?

On 28 February Mozart played the harpsichord and violin at the Archbishop's birthday concert 'to everyone's astonishment'.

On 9 June the first of the Mozarts' great tours began. In Munich, Wolfgang performed for the Bavarian Elector again; then they visited Ulm, Ludwigsburg and Bruchsal. And in Schwetzingen the children performed for Elector-Palatine Karl Theodor. At Frankfurt four concerts were given and the fourteen-year-old Goethe was in the audience. They stopped in Coblenz, Bonn and Cologne, and performed at Aix-la Chapelle for Princess Amalia of Prussia. A concert was given in Brussels for the Governor-General of the Austrian Netherlands (whose successor would later be fêted in Vienna with *Der Schauspieldirektor*). Then the Mozarts went to Paris, arriving on 18 November and moving on to Versailles at the end of December.

- End of Seven Years' War
- Peace of Paris between Britain, France and Spain
- India and New World ceded by France to Britain
- Peace of Hubertusburg: Silesia kept by Prussia
- King of Poland Augustus III dies

1764

In January 1764 Mozart turned eight. His first sonatas for keyboard with violin accompaniment were published, Op. 1 in February (K6–7) and Op. 2 in April (K8–9), the first works in Leopold's catalogue of his son's music. Leopold wrote proudly: 'My little girl, although only 12 years old, is one of the most skilful players in Europe, and, in a word, my boy knows in his eighth year more than one would expect from a man of 40.' At other times it seems that Leopold was not entirely accurate about his children's ages, just as he had not been completely truthful with his employers about the facts of his life.

Their first Paris concert was on 9 March and the second on 9 April. While in Paris, Leopold recommended their servant and hairdresser Sebastian Winter, the Figaro of his day, to the Princess of Furstenberg. On 10 April they left Paris for London, travelling via Calais and Dover, during which journey they were seasick. On 23 April they arrived and stayed at the White Bear Inn in Piccadilly. Then they found lodgings with John Cousins in Cecil Court off St Martin's Lane (now the street of the music shop Travis and Emery). On Friday 27th they were received by King George III and Queen Charlotte at Buckingham House, the predecessor of the present Palace. During May two concerts were given at Hickford's Music Room in Brewer Street, Soho, on the 17th and 22nd. There was a concert at Ranelagh House which presented Mozart in the middle of other entertainments: this would have given him the chance to hear for the first time music by Handel from *Acis and Galatea* and *Alexander's Feast*, two works Mozart subsequently rescored for performance in Vienna.

In July, Leopold became ill, and the family moved in August to Chelsea, lodging with the Randall family at Five Fields Row, now 180 Ebury Street (which was renamed Mozart Terrace in a ceremony in 1991). In September, Leopold wrote 'there is a sort of national disease here which is called a "cold" . . . for people who are not very strong the best advice is to leave England.' While in Chelsea, Wolfgang spent some time filling a notebook with musical sketches, 'di Wolfgango Mozart a Londra'; it probably dates from late 1764 and early 1765, and is undoubtedly authentic (the book did not resurface before the end of the nineteenth century and the music was first published in 1909). This is probably the first music that Wolfgang wrote that does not show signs of the intervention of Leopold, and demonstrates his unfettered if sometimes chaotic invention beginning to emerge.

According to Nannerl, much later, Wolfgang also wrote his 'first' symphony at this time, 'with all the instruments of the orchestra especially trumpets and kettledrums. I had to transcribe it as I sat at his side. While he composed and I copied he said to me "Remind me to give the horn something worthwhile to do . . .".' It's a nice picture, but that scoring does not match the Symphony No. 1 K16, which is the only one to have survived from 1764. Perhaps the memory became mixed with the writing of a later symphony, or the work is lost.

- John Wilkes is expelled from Commons for libel, causing London riots
- American colonies taxed in Sugar Act
- New King of Poland
- Jesuits suppressed in France

1765

In January 1765 Mozart turned nine. His six sonatas for

keyboard with violin and cello Op. 3, K10–15 were published and dedicated to Queen Charlotte with a most effusive dedication supposedly written by Wolfgang himself. The Mozarts gave a concert at the Haymarket on 21 February. 'All the Overtures will be from the Composition of those [*sic*] astonishing Composers, only eight years old.' Possibly the symphonies K19 and K19a (the latter turned up only in 1981 in Munich) were heard. But the event was not well attended. In April the children were made available at home each weekday from twelve to three, except Tuesday and Friday: anyone who had bought the sonatas, or a ticket to their concert, could hear them play and 'likewise try his [Mozart's] surprising musical capacity by giving him anything to play at sight, or any music without bass, which he will write upon the spot, without recurring to his harpsichord'. On 13 May there was another concert at Hickford's, also 'with all the overtures of this little boy's own composition'.

In the summer Mozart was examined by the scientist Daines Barrington, and this remains the most reliable account of the abilities of the young prodigy. In July the Mozarts visited the British Museum and presented the manuscript of the motet to English words 'God is our refuge' K20, which Leopold helped Wolfgang to write out. On 24 July the Mozarts left London and spent the night in Canterbury. Then they went from Dover to Dunkirk, and on to Lille in August, Antwerp in September, and then The Hague. Nannerl became ill in September with intestinal typhoid and received the last sacraments on 21 October, but she recovered. Wolfgang caught the illness less severely in mid-November and was in danger for two months. In December he wrote another symphony, K22.

- Stamp Act passed to tax American colonies, Congress in New York challenges the Act
- Emperor Francis I dies
- Joseph II becomes Holy Roman Emperor, but only as co-regent with Maria Theresa in Bohemia and Hungary

- Dauphin of France dies, and Louis succeeds (heir to the French throne, later to be Louis XVI)

1766

In January 1766 Mozart turned ten. He had very nearly died of typhoid. But instead of relaxing the pace or returning home, Leopold pressed on with an ambitious programme of concerts, including some more of Mozart's music on 22 January and 29 January, and then on 26 February in Amsterdam. In March Wolfgang wrote the amusing quodlibet *Gallimathias Musicum* K32, which seems to have formed part of the celebrations of the installation of William Prince of Orange – the first of many occasions when Mozart attached his music to regal celebrations of one sort or another. On 8 May the family arrived in Brussels and then via Valenciennes they went to Paris, and on to Versailles, returning to Paris on 28 May. 12 June saw the completion of a Kyrie, perhaps for local church use. On 9 July the family left Paris for Dijon and on the 26th arrived in Lyons, where a single concert was held at the Place des Cordeliers. On 20 August the family travelled to Geneva, and then went to Lausanne, where two concerts were given on 15 and 18 September. They left for Berne and then travelled to Zurich, giving two concerts at the Collegium Musicum on 7 and 9 October. On 13 September they went from Zurich to Winterthur and Schaffhausen and thence to Donaueschingen. On 9 November they were back in Munich, and played again before Elector Maximilian III. Wolfgang was again ill from 12 to 21 November. Finally on 29 November they returned to Salzburg, and the diary of a local friend recorded that he had met them and seen all the many presents they had received on their journey. A 'symphony', perhaps a church sonata, was performed at the cathedral on the day of their return.

- Stamp Act repealed, but Declaratory Act reaffirms Britain's ability to tax colonies
- William Pitt Prime Minister

• Secular education introduced in Spain

1767

In January 1767 Mozart turned eleven. This was a decisive year for Mozart as a musician. It is clear that Leopold now realised the potential of his son as a composer, not just as a keyboard player, and set out both to train him and to acquire him commissions. In February a 'Licenza' by Wolfgang, a tribute aria, for the end of an opera, probably K70, was performed. In March he contributed to the composition of *Die Schuldigkeit der ersten Gebots* K35 (Part One; the music for the other parts was by Michael Haydn and Adlgasser), and in April he composed the *Grabmusik* K42, for Good Friday. This is the piece of which the story is told (as with similar early pieces written in Vienna and Milan) that Wolfgang was locked up in a room to write it: perhaps the suspicion that Leopold was helping his son to an unwarranted extent needed to be disproved. In May he wrote his first operatic essay, later called *Apollo and Hyacinthus*, to be performed between the acts of the university play. In June and July he arranged the pasticcio concertos K37 and 39–41; then in September Leopold took his son to Vienna with the hope of gaining commissions there. They saw Hasse's opera *Partenope*, which they admired. But in October smallpox was raging in the city, so they left for Brno and then Olmutz, where Mozart contracted smallpox and was ill for two weeks. They returned to Brno from Olmutz, where they stayed with the brother of the Archbishop of Salzburg and gave a concert on 30 December. One diary report says 'they were accompanied on various instruments by inhabitants of Brno . . . but he [Mozart] could not endure the trumpets, because they were incapable of playing completely in tune with one another.' The leader of the city waits later said, however, that Mozart 'was very pleased with the orchestra here and would not have believed that my colleagues could accompany so well at the first rehearsal'!

- Public meeting in Boston protests against new taxes and bans imported goods
- Burmese invade Siam
- Prusso-Russian alliance revised to support possible war with Turkey
- Jesuits expelled from Spain by Charles III

1768

In January 1768 Mozart turned twelve. Leopold described him famously in a letter as 'a miracle which God caused to be born in Salzburg'. They left Brno, went back to Vienna and were finally received by Maria Theresa on 19 January between 2.30 p.m. and 4.30 p.m., with her son Joseph II. Leopold's court salary was withheld in March for his extended absence from Salzburg. They performed for Prince Galitzin, Russian Ambassador at Vienna, on 24 March. Mozart wrote *La finta semplice* K51, following a hint from Joseph, but no performance resulted. Leopold wrote a long petition to the Emperor dated 21 September to complain about the failure to perform the piece, which can scarcely have increased his standing. Meanwhile Wolfgang was already onto the next work: a little opera, *Bastien und Bastienne* K50, to be performed at Dr Mesmer's house. Then there was the opportunity to write new church music, the *Waisenhausmesse* K139 (and a lost offertory and a trumpet concerto 'for a boy' mentioned by Leopold), for the dedication of the chapel of an orphanage in Vienna which the Empress attended. Reports say it was conducted 'with the greatest accuracy . . . to general applause and admiration; and apart from this Mozart also sang in the motets'. Other music from this time includes the Symphony K48, the Missa Brevis K49 and the song 'An die Freude' K53.

- John Wilkes elected to Parliament
- Secretary of State for Colonies appointed
- Massachusetts Assembly dissolved for refusing to house troops and collect tax
- Turkey declares war on Russia

1769

In January 1769 Mozart turned thirteen. At the beginning of the year the family travelled from Linz to Salzburg, returning on 5 January. Mozart was writing symphonies and cassations during this period for use in outdoor entertainments in Salzburg, as well as another Mass, K65, which was sung on 5 February. Leopold petitioned the Archbishop for the pay which had been withheld during his trip. He also made an immediate attempt to arrange a Salzburg performance of *La finta semplice*, and a libretto was printed, but other records of the performance do not survive.

Probably from this year, and seemingly authentic, there is a first surviving undated letter from Mozart to an unidentified girl, teasing her about her knowledge of Latin and asking for 'a reply by one of Hagenauer's maids'. (A story relates that when this letter was shown to Constanze Mozart for authentication later in life, she threw it contemptuously to the ground.) In the autumn Mozart wrote another setting of the Mass, K66, this time to celebrate the first Mass of his friend Cajetan Hagenauer (son of Leopold's correspondent), performed at St Peter's. In October Mozart was promoted to be co-leader of the Salzburg court orchestra. In December he and his father left again, this time for a tour of Italy, and arrived in Verona.

- John Wilkes elected Alderman of London and expelled from Parliament
- Bourbons demand the end of the Jesuits
- Britain decides to retain tea duty
- Virginia Assembly is dissolved for protesting against trials in London
- Prusso-Russian alliance renewed, Russia occupies Bucharest

1770

In January 1770 Mozart turned fourteen. His voice broke. He wrote the first of his dated letters to have been preserved, asking Nannerl to kiss their mother millions of times. With his father he toured Italy with great success, listening to and absorbing the music of Italian opera. He reportedly wrote down Allegri's *Miserere* from memory. (Or was it simply the castrato's decorations that he memorised? It is actually a fairly simple choral chant that is repeated several times.) He was elected to the renowned Accademia Filarmonica of Bologna, and acquired a commission for which he had longed: to write a grand Italian *opera seria*. *Mitridate* was first performed on 26 December and received twenty-two performances to considerable acclaim. Mozart also composed symphonies and arias. It was the beginning of a newly mature period of his youth, when boyish promise grew into real achievement. And he would have started to become aware of the wider world.

In 1770 there were new artistic notions stirring elsewhere: the births of Ludwig van Beethoven, William Wordsworth and Friedrich Hölderlin in that year marked the origins of the ideas of Romanticism they would help create. Goldsmith was writing; Gainsborough was painting. The favourites of the musical world were Gluck in Vienna, J. C. Bach in London, Piccinni and Sammartini in Italy. In England in 1770 it seemed likely that war might break out with Spain over Spain's attack on the Falkland Islands, which Britain had occupied four years earlier. Exploration continued around the world: Captain Cook landed at Botany Bay, and James Bruce reached the source of the Blue Nile. It was a time of discovery with revolutionary implications.

- Lord North British Prime Minister
- The Boston Massacre
- Some taxes on colonies repealed, but that on tea remains
- Dauphin marries Joseph II's sister, Marie Antoinette
- Russian fleet defeats Turkish navy
- French foreign minister prevents war between Spain and Britain over Falkland Islands

1771

In January 1771 Mozart turned fifteen. He was still touring Italy with his father, but his thoughts sometimes turned towards home. He was becoming extensively interested in the opposite sex, and his letters to his sister towards the end of the tour (usually postscripts added to the end of Leopold's letters) send good wishes to various anonymous girls whom Nannerl is expected to identify. To another friend, one Johannes, he says that he must soon come back to Venice and submit to the *attacco*, that is, have his bottom spanked when he is lying on the ground, so that he may become a true Venetian. 'They tried to do it to me – the seven women all together – and yet they could not pull me down.' Wolfgang also read: the *Arabian Nights* in Italian, and more ambitiously *Télèmarque*, the novel written by Rousseau's predecessor, Fénélon, are two of the books he claimed to have enjoyed at this time, though the evidence that he read much more widely than this is not clear. The Mozarts had travelled to Venice from Milan, thence to Verona, and back to Salzburg via a freezing-cold Innsbruck. *La betulia liberata*, commissioned in Padua, was written on return to Salzburg. But they returned to Milan later in the year for the rehearsals and performances of *Ascanio in Alba*, arriving back in Salzburg at the end of the year.

Mozart's musical skills were now beyond question. In a note to his mother this year he complained that 'there is a performance of Hasse's opera today, but as papa is not going out, I cannot be there.' Then he adds chirpily: 'Fortunately I know nearly all the arias by heart and so I can see and hear it at home in my head.' Music in his head: that is one clue to the flowering of Mozart's talent around this time. His facility was phenomenal, perhaps dangerously so; but because of lack of opportunity much of his talent appeared latent, just waiting for the right commission to realise its potential.

- Composition of Haydn's 'Sun' Quartets
- Publication of Klopstock's *Odes*

- Falkland Islands ceded by Spain to Britain
- Russia completes conquest of Crimea
- Austria and Turkey unite against Russia

1772

In 1772 Mozart turned sixteen. He was ever more confident of his skills, ever more anxious to realise his talents fully, and in no doubt of the approval which he deserved. His letters are effervescent and exuberant: one he writes to his sister had every other line written upside down. There were few shadows; Mozart was alert to international events, at least when his mother back in Salzburg needed to be reassured of his safety in Italy – 'There is no truth in the report of an Italian war or of the fortifying the castle of Milan.' He could scarcely have been as concerned about the dividing up of a third of Poland between its neighbours Austria, Prussia and Russia; this brutal arrangement was ratified in the Treaty of St Petersburg in August but brought condemnation on the Empress Maria Theresa, who had objected to the annexation but allowed Austria to profit from it.

It was a time of change in Salzburg. Following the death of Schrattenbach, in March, after a long wrangle and very unexpectedly, Hieronymous Colloredo was elected Prince-Archbishop, and the consequences for the Mozarts and their travels were to be considerable. Though he was a product of the Enlightenment and something of a musician himself, determined to restore the finances of the court which had been lavishly spent by his predecessor, Colloredo was an old-fashioned master who treated his servants as property rather than as people; he expected unquestioning service, and the gradual emancipation of the musician from servant to independent artist which the Mozart family represented was not something he was likely to encourage.

For the enthronement of the archbishop, Mozart wrote *Il sogno di Scipione*, a work which has been the most rarely revived of any of his full-length pieces. It seems that the work was originally planned to mark the fiftieth anniversary of Schrattenbach's ordination in January 1772, but when that was cancelled following his death, the work was revised and replanned to welcome the new Archbishop. In August the new Archbishop confirmed Wolfgang's appointment as Konzertmeister with a salary of 150 gulden. Such an appointment must have been a welcome acknowledgement of his talent, but it was to tie Mozart's strings to his home base far too closely for comfort: life was to become increasingly restrictive under the new archbishop. However, in October Leopold and Wolfgang set off again for Milan, where the new opera *Lucio Silla* was rehearsed and performed for the first time on 26 December. Although the tenor had to be replaced by a church singer and the performance started late, it was a success.

- Cook's second journey around the world
- Publication of Lessing's *Emilia Galotti*
- First partition of Poland
- Boston threatens secession from Britain
- Royal Marriage Act for all descendants of George II
- Gustavus III re-establishes monarchy in Sweden

1773

In January 1773 Mozart turned seventeen. It was the year the Pope suppressed the Jesuits, a move that had direct repercussions around the Mozart family and was a subject of lively debate in their circle. Wolfgang was about to become disheartened by his drudgery at Salzburg, and he tried once more and failed once more to penetrate the closed artistic circles of Vienna. Was there a suspicion that he had hit his peak in making the transition from prodigy to maturity? One of Charles Burney's correspondents suggested that 'if I may judge of the music which I hear of his composition in the orchestra, he is one further instance of early fruit being more extraordinary than excellent.' That opinion, which Burney must have later regretted giving currency in his 1773 volume *The present state of music in Germany* . . . , is the first of several from those who found Mozart's novelties too spicy to stomach.

In January 1773 Mozart wrote a demonstrative motet, *Exsultate jubilate*, for the castrato Venanzio Rauzzini who had triumphed in the opera *Lucio Silla*. It has since become one of his most popular works, demonstrating the complete sureness of touch which he appears to have acquired quite suddenly in different genres. Milan still feted Mozart, but there was no job to be had. Leopold tried to put off their return to Salzburg. He had a good excuse in the crippling rheumatism which was affecting him, but he also thought there might be a chance of an appointment in Florence for Wolfgang.

Soon after they returned to Salzburg, Leopold planned a trip to Vienna; as the new Archbishop was absent from Salzburg, they were allowed to go. But the trip was not a success, and Leopold had ignored the opinion Maria Theresa expressed to her son that the Mozarts should not be hawking their children around Europe. They made many friends and were entertained splendidly, in particular by the Dr Mesmer who later became famed for his cures by magnetism, to whom Mozart paid humorous tribute in *Così fan tutte*. The court musical director, Florian Gassmann, was increasingly ill and was to die the following January. Leopold implied that people thought that was why the Mozarts were in Vienna, to bid for his job – but as he wrote, 'fools everywhere are but fools!' Meanwhile Salieri's *La locandiera* was performed in Vienna with success, C. P. E. Bach dedicated six symphonies to the Baron van Swieten, who was soon to assume an important place in Mozart's musical development, and Haydn wrote operas for Eszterháza. But this was a very fertile year musically, with symphonies and string quartets especially prominent in Mozart's output.

- Publication of Goethe's *Götz von Berlichingen*, *Urfaust*
- Completion of Klopstock's *The Messiah*
- C. P. E. Bach Six Symphonies, Wq 182
- Haydn *L'infedeltà delusa*, Eszterháza

- Pope Clement XIV dissolves the Jesuits
- France restores Avignon to the Papacy
- Boston Tea Party on 16 December

1774

In January 1774 Mozart turned eighteen. It was a year in which the shadows began to loom in Europe: Louis XVI succeeded Louis XV in France, and the journey to the French Revolution had begun. Russia gained an important foothold on the Black Sea in the settlement of the Turkish War, in spite of having suffered previous reversals. Turkey was left weakened, a situation which suited Austria well; it claimed new territory in the following year. But within Austria, Joseph II was anxious to begin a programme of reform; it was not to be until 1780 with the death of Maria Theresa that the way would be open for him. The peasants of Austria, frustrated by the promise of reform and their continued servile dependence on their landowners, rose in revolt this year.

Once again, Mozart was obsessed with opera: *La finta giardiniera*, commissioned for the following year's carnival season in Munich, was occupying his time, and he and his father travelled there in December. But there was much other composing activity. At the end of the previous year he wrote a piano concerto which was to become the first of a sequence of wonderfully original works (K175 in D); he also wrote one of his most ingratiating concertos, for bassoon, (K191 in B flat) in which the capabilities of an instrument then used only rarely as a soloist were understood and exploited to the highest degree. Perhaps most significantly in terms of his compositional development, his symphonies broke through to unquestioned maturity. From the Symphony in G minor K183 of October 1773, he moved onto the Symphony in A K201, two fine works as strongly contrasted as those in the great final trilogy of symphonies written in 1788.

By the end of the year, Mozart is writing a satirical letter to his sister dated the '1774th day of the year 30'.

- Gluck *Iphigénie en Aulide*, Paris
- Publication of Goethe's *Die Leiden des jungen Werther*
- Birth of Caspar David Friedrich

- Louis XVI succeeds his grandfather Louis XV
- Declaration of Rights and Grievances in Philadelphia
- Boston harbour closed
- Russia and Turkey sign peace
- John Wilkes Lord Mayor of London

1775

In January 1775 Mozart turned nineteen. While the War of Independence was launched in America, the peasants' revolts in central Europe grew stronger; in both Bohemia and Russia there were major uprisings this year. But for Mozart one thing was uppermost: his new opera. He had hoped that it would be staged in Munich the previous December, and he set out there with his father at the beginning of that month. Wolfgang's sister Nannerl joined them on 4 January, missing some performances of Mozart's sacred music on New Year's Day. There were further delays with the opera, and *La finta giardiniera* was not performed until 13 January 1775: 'Thank God!' reported Mozart, 'My opera was performed yesterday, the 13th, for the first time and was such a success that it is impossible for me to describe the applause to Mamma . . .' Archbishop Colloredo came to Munich, but missed the opera and was reportedly embarrassed by its success; according to Leopold's biased report, everyone had a good opinion of it.

While still in Munich, Mozart was asked to write some church music, and also took part in a piano-playing contest with Ignaz von Beeke. A correspondent of C. F. D. Schubart reported that 'Mozart's playing had great weight, and he read at sight everything that was put before him. But no more than that. Beeke surpassed him by a long way. Winged agility, grace, melting sweetness and a quite peculiar, self-formed taste are clubs which nobody is likely to wrest from this Hercules.' The same correspondence suggested that in

Mozart's opera 'flashes of genius appear here and there, but there is not yet that still altar-fire that rises towards Heaven in clouds of incense.'

The Mozarts left Munich on 6 March. Leopold reported testily that 'we are to bring with us from Munich a young lady, who would like to stay with us for three or four months and improve her harpsichord playing. Up to the present I have refused this.' He goes on to fuss a good deal about the practical arrangements. Is it fanciful to see here one of Wolfgang's first serious attachments? In any case, the threat, or whatever it was, never materialised. April was devoted to *Il re pastore*, and this year also saw the sequence of violin concertos which were probably written for Mozart himself to play; when the new concertmaster of the Salzburg orchestra Antonio Brunetti arrived in 1776, the concertos became part of his repertory and Mozart wrote a new movement for him. As part of his Salzburg duties, Mozart also wrote serenades and marches with increasing resourcefulness and originality.

- Goethe at the Weimar court
- Premiere of Beaumarchais's *Le barbier de Seville*
- Grétry *Cephale et Procris*, Paris
- Boccherini Symphonies Op. 21
- Birth of J. M. W. Turner

- Bohemian peasants' revolt
- American War of Independence: battles of Lexington and Concord
- Famine in Paris
- George Washington appointed commander-in-chief of American forces
- British victory at Bunker Hill

1776

In 1776 Mozart turned twenty. If it was a landmark for him, it cannot have been a very happy one, for he was reaching the heights of frustration with his position in Salzburg, and longed for a position elsewhere. He was already looking towards Vienna, where in this year Joseph II took over the Burgtheater in the beginnings of his theatrical reforms. Further afield, how aware was Mozart of major developments shaking the world? It was the year of the American Declaration of Independence on 4 July, the year of Adam Smith's revolutionary economic theories and of Edward Gibbon's epoch-making historical work *The Decline and Fall of the Roman Empire*. For the emerging study of musical history, too, the year was a landmark: the first volume of Charles Burney's *History of Music* and the whole of Sir John Hawkins' rival treatment were published in London.

We know too little about Mozart's life in this year: because the family was in Salzburg during 1776, there are no letters documenting its events. Unusually, however, we can follow some of the Mozarts' social round through the diary of a friend, Joachim Ferdinand von Schiedenhofen, a Salzburg councillor who lived in the Getreidegasse, just near Mozart's birthplace, with his sister Nannerl. He was a close friend of the Mozarts, and from 1774 we find reports of his evenings out in their company. Such reports increase in frequency during 1776. On 3 January he attended the play *Thamos, King of Egypt*, with Mozart's music. On 18 February he tells of a lively masquerade that lasted until 4 a.m., 'the elder Mozart as a porter and the younger as the hairdresser's boy'; the next night he went again, and 'among the curiosities was an operetta by [Leopold] Mozart'. On 31 March, Palm Sunday, he was in more sober mood at the cathedral, and on Easter Sunday reported that a new Mass by Wolfgang was heard there. On 18 June there was music composed for the Countess Ernst Lodron. On 7 July there was music at the Antrettern family residence, where he went with the Mozarts. On 21 July, 'I went to the bridal music which young Herr Haffner had made for his sister Liserl. It was by Mozart and was performed in the summer-house at Loreto': thus originated the great 'Haffner' Serenade K250.

- J. C. Bach *Lucio Silla*, Mannheim
- Salieri *Daliso e Delmita*, Vienna
- Gibbon's *The Decline and Fall of the Roman Empire* begun
- Concerts of Academy of Ancient Music begin in London
- John Constable born
- Birth of E. T. A. Hoffmann

- American Declaration of Independence approved by Congress
- British evacuate Boston
- Cook's third journey around the world
- Torture abolished in Austria
- American troops driven from Canada
- France makes war loan to Americans
- Washington forced to retreat from New Jersey to Pennsylvania

1777

In January 1777 Mozart turned twenty-one. It was a year when his compositional achievements were increasingly matched by professional frustration, leading to his first break with Salzburg. This year and the next were to be a watershed in his life. From various accounts we can piece together the kind of life that Mozart lived during this year, making music with friends and colleagues: here a serenade, a friendly performance of a piano duet, a visit for talk or a walk in the gardens; for instance at the house of Johann Gusetti a flute concerto, violin concerto and a symphony by Mozart were played on 26 July. But it was clearly not enough: as early as March 1777 Leopold petitioned the Archbishop of Salzburg for further permission to travel. What became of this document is unknown, but it was unsuccessful, for it is not until August that we find Wolfgang himself addressing a petition to the Archbishop. He reminded his employer that he and his father had remained in Salzburg 'in readiness for the impending visit of His Majesty the Emperor', but now that this was no longer necessary, he wished again to travel. 'Our circumstances are pressing: my father has decided to send me off by myself.' But even this was refused. 'To profit from our talents is taught us by the Gospel,' writes Mozart in a phrase doubtless suggested to him by Leopold; the archbishop scribbled curtly on the document, 'Father and son herewith granted permission to seek their fortune according to the Gospel.' Wolfgang and his mother left together. Fatefully, Leopold did not accompany his son on this trip. Perhaps he decided he could not afford to leave the Archbishop's service altogether. We know he was ill at the time 'with a heavy catarrh'. In the end – and in retrospect this can be seen as one of the crucial decisions of Mozart's life – he stayed at home; and Mozart's mother, who had far less experience of the political and social problems which the Mozarts encountered on their musical travels, accompanied him. Nannerl, clearly appalled by the thought of having sole responsibility for looking after her father, collapsed on the day of their departure.

The next few months were a disaster whose every move can be traced in the voluminous correspondence. Leopold lectures, hectors, advises, reprimands, and tries quite unsuccessfully to control the course of events by letter from Salzburg. Mozart has no success with the Elector of Munich and moves to Augsburg, where he is equally unsuccessful but strikes up a very close friendship with his cousin Anna Maria which revels in the scatological language that was not uncommon within families at the time. (The relationship probably went beyond friendship, too, and it is hardly too subtle to connect this little explosion of sexuality with his first-ever period away from his father.) Then mother and son go to Mannheim, and Mozart suddenly feels completely at home. He is overcome by the musicality of the court and its orchestra, strikes up numerous friendships with the leading players in the superb orchestra, and generally has a whale of a time which with typical lack of diplomatic tact he relates to his father in some detail. Leopold is appalled. He is more interested in the post of court organist in Salzburg which is vacant on the death of Adlgasser in December.

- Gluck *Armide*, Paris
- Haydn *Il mondo della luna*, Eszterháza
- Gazzaniga *La bizzaria degli umori*, Bologna

- Washington defeats British at Princeton and Bennington
- British occupy Philadelphia
- British lose at Saratoga
- Congress adopts Articles of Confederation
- Karl Theodor becomes Elector of Bavaria

1778

In January 1778 Mozart turned twenty-two. He now fell seriously in love for the first time, with Aloysia Weber, a fine singer and daughter of the prompter at the Mannheim court theatre whose wife, Aloysia's mother, ruled the family vigorously. (Again, is it mere coincidence that Wolfgang, escaping from a family with a dominant father, falls into the lap of a family with a dominant mother?) When Leopold appeals to Mozart to think of making money, he responds with hugely unrealistic plans to take Aloysia on a singing tour of Italy and to get her work in the opera there. This is the last straw for Leopold, who fulminates against his son and tells him to leave: 'Away with you to Paris, and as speedily as you can, put yourself in the company of the great.'

Unfortunately, without Leopold's guiding hand through the social channels of the city, Paris was also fated to be unsuccessful. The father sends lists of names and contacts to follow up, but that was not Wolfgang's way. Mozart and his mother left Mannheim on 14 March 1778 and arrived in a Paris that was in political turmoil and musical turmoil as well, since the quarrel between the supporters of Gluck and Piccinni was rapidly assuming huge proportions. Thanks to his Mannheim friends, the wind players Wendling and Ramm, Mozart ingratiated himself into Parisian musical life and received some commissions. But there were intrigues against him, and the patron in whom Leopold had trusted, Baron Grimm, eventually despaired of Mozart's ways – wishing, in a deadly reflection of the problems of Mozart's personality, that Mozart had half as much talent and twice as much social grace.

Into this already unpleasant scenario the illness and death of Mozart's mother on 3 July came like an overwhelming blow. We cannot really tell how Mozart felt: what does emerge from his letters with extreme vividness is his fear of his father at this moment. He finds it impossible to communicate the news directly, and merely warns Leopold of her illness. Then he writes to a friend in Salzburg, the Abbé Bullinger, to ask him to tell his father that his mother has died. Is this the result of 'a new maturity and sensitivity' (as *The New Grove* has it)? Or is it an act of elemental cowardice? Leopold virtually blames the son for the mother's death, and frets endlessly over the many arrangements which he felt Wolfgang incapable of making.

Perhaps the most extraordinary feature of the letter which Wolfgang wrote to his father during the night when his mother died is its manic exuberance. After he makes his warnings about her health, he feels the need to distract Leopold with all manner of jolly chatter. It is from this document that we learn the circumstances surrounding the performance of the 'Paris' Symphony (see p. 163). He then writes that 'I was so happy that as soon as the symphony was over, I went off to the Palais Royal, where I had a large ice, said the Rosary as I had vowed to do – and went home – for I am and always will be happiest there' (an extremely ironic statement at that moment, in a gloomy apartment with his dead mother in the next room). Displacement activity does not come much more radical than this.

Mozart was prepared to do anything to delay returning to face his father and employer in Salzburg, and instead went to Strasbourg, where he gave three poorly attended concerts, and then on to Mannheim and Munich, where he stayed with the Weber family. This is one of the most musically unproductive periods of his entire life, as he was preoccupied with the arrangements following his mother's death and the endless bickering by correspondence with his father. Although there is music from the first part of 1778, and then the effervescent 'Paris' Symphony from later in the year, only the highly original and forceful Piano Sonata in A minor K310 and the similarly minor-mode Violin Sonata in E minor K304 stand out. He planned a drama, *Semiramis*, in Mannheim, but nothing came of it and there are no surviving sketches.

- Salieri *L'Europa riconosciuta*, Milan; *La scuola de gelosi*, Vienna
- Death of Voltaire
- Death of Rousseau

- Karl Theodor leaves Mannheim for Munich
- France and United States sign treaties
- Britain declares war on France
- British evacuate Philadelphia
- British defeated at Monmouth, New Jersey
- Prussia declares war on Austria, war of Bavarian Succession

1779

In January 1779 Mozart turned twenty-three: he returned to Salzburg from his travels a chastened man, and travelled home via Augsburg, bringing his cousin with him, perhaps to protect himself from the full force of Leopold's wrath. Life seemed to have become more problematical for him than he could ever have expected as a young, favoured, protected genius. His first love, Aloysia Weber, had deserted him, his mother had died in traumatic circumstances, and his father was less than warm towards him for his dilatoriness and lack of success in Europe:

> I am tired of your projects with which you have destroyed the excellent plans I have often had; which you can never realise because you can't or won't think over anything in cold blood and without prejudice; often it is true that you are carried away in an instant by the fire of your youth

and the flattering suggestions made to you by this or that person, and see everything as gold which is in fact only tinsel.

Meanwhile, Wolfgang dreaded a return to the servitude of Salzburg; to the Abbé Bullinger, who had been his confidant over the death of his mother, he wrote:

> Salzburg is no place for my talent. In the first place, professional musicians there are not held in much consideration; and secondly, one hears nothing, there is no theatre, no opera; and even if they really wanted one, who is there to sing? For the last five or six years the Salzburg orchestra has always been rich in what is useless and superfluous, but very poor in what is necessary, and absolutely destitute of what is indispensable; and such is the case at the present moment.

In the same letter he speculates hilariously on the possibility that since the castrato Ceccarelli is the only decent singer in the city, he would have to take the roles of both *prima uomo* and *prima donna* in a specially written opera where the two never meet. 'In this way the castrato could play the parts of both the lover and his mistress and the story would prove more interesting – for people would have to admire the virtue of the lovers which is so absolute that they purposely avoid any occasion of speaking to each other in public!'

On his return, Mozart petitioned for the post of court organist, but one can guess that his heart was not in it. He did receive the appointment, though it did him little good. The remainder of the year produced some good music, including the Symphonies No. 32 K318 and No. 33 K319, but it was an uneventful period.

- Gluck *Iphigénie en Tauride*, Paris
- Goethe *Iphigenis auf Paurios*
- Lessing *Nathan der Weise*
- Sheridan *The Critic*

- British conquer Georgia and South Carolina
- Louis XVI abolishes serfdom
- France defends Senegal against British
- Spain declares war on Britain; siege of Gibraltar
- Congress sends army to fight Indians in the Wyoming Valley
- French fleet in English Channel

1780

In January 1780 Mozart turned twenty-four. His life in Salzburg was increasingly unsatisfactory, and his mind turned more and more towards freedom, and especially towards the composition of opera. In the summer Mozart received a commission for which he had longed, to compose a grand opera for Munich: that was to produce *Idomeneo*, the first great outpouring of his operatic skills and arguably his first dramatic masterpiece.

1780 was a crucial year for Austria: it was the year in which Joseph II finally succeeded Maria Theresa and became Emperor. One of his priorities was to create a National Singspiel theatre in Vienna; he had already proclaimed a 'Nationaltheater' in the spring of 1776, and two years later had placed a German company in the Burgtheater, performing works by such composers as Ignaz Umlauf which were essentially spoken plays with interspersed music. It may well be this that spurred the composer into action to write a German-language music-drama during that year, and produced the incomplete but musically outstanding fragments of *Zaide*.

We know too little about Mozart's relationship with the other arts, but it can be safely stated that he loved the theatre. He wrote to his sister while in Vienna that he spent a great deal of time there, and while he was still in Salzburg he seems to have made friends easily among actors and managers. In December 1779, for instance, he saw a comedy by Goldoni, *Il bugiardo*, at the Salzburg Theatre, performed in German by the company of Johann Heinrich Böhm. Goldoni's plays were to have a considerable influence on the libretti of Lorenzo Da Ponte, and his distinctive mixing of serious and comic elements is something that became central to Mozart's operatic art over the next few years. Böhm's company was in Salzburg for several months, from September 1779 to the following March, and Mozart probably attended many performances. Mozart provided music for Böhm's company: one of his symphonies was used as an overture, and the fine incidental music for the play *Thamos, King of Egypt* may also have been used by Böhm's company. A further stimulus to theatrical activity was the arrival in Salzburg of Emanuel Schikaneder's company in July and August 1780: Mozart was eventually to write *Die Zauberflöte* for Schikaneder. In November of this year Mozart went to Munich for the rehearsals of *Idomeneo*, which he recounts in a long series of fascinating letters to his father, one of the most detailed accounts of the gestation of an opera production that survives.

- Piccinni *Atys*, Paris
- Salieri *La dama pastorella*, Rome
- Birth of Ingres

- Britain declares war on Holland
- Serfdom abolished in Bohemia and Hungary
- Maria Theresa dies, Joseph II succeeds in Austria, Bohemia and Hungary
- French troops arrive in America
- Gordon Riots in London
- Irish free trade with Britain

1781

In January 1781 Mozart turned twenty-five. The death of Maria Theresa on 29 November 1780 and the accession of the Emperor Joseph II to full power was a landmark for Austrian life. It was also to be a landmark for Mozart, who was reaching the central crisis of his career. After all the success of *Idomeneo* in Munich (it was performed, after many delays, on 29 January 1781), and the respect with which he was treated at the Munich court, he found himself with the unwelcome prospect of a return to his less privileged life in Salzburg. He was about to make a decisive break.

A return was delayed for a while because the Archbishop's entourage had travelled to Vienna to take part in the celebrations in Joseph II's honour. In March 1781 Mozart too was summoned to Vienna, where he was poorly treated and expected to give concerts for the Archbishop when he could have been earning a great deal more money playing for the Emperor. Perhaps because of his flighty behaviour over the past months, he was expected to lodge in the Archbishop's house with the staff and servants, and not to have separate quarters like the violinist Brunetti or the castrato Ceccarelli. His discontent with his situation came to a head.

It would be implying too much to interpret Mozart's furious rows, leading to the suspension of his employment, purely as the spirit of the incipient Romantic artist asserting himself against the will of authority. Mozart perhaps thought – and in this he was, much to his father's surprise, not entirely mistaken – that it would be possible to earn better money by operating as a freelance musician in Vienna, giving concerts, teaching, and receiving commissions. He also certainly hoped to be close to the Emperor in case opportunities should arise at court. In addition, there was another factor keeping him in Vienna that he mentioned to his father only in passing. He had moved into the Weber household, where although his first love, the eldest daughter, Aloysia, had now married, he was showing a distinct interest in her younger sister Constanze, encouraged, we may presume, by her mother.

We do not have Leopold's replies to his son's increasingly pressing letters from this period, but we may judge them to have been so violent in their reaction to Mozart's aggressive opposition towards authority that the son in one letter had to 'confess that there is not a single touch in your letter by which I recognise my father!' Partly writing in code, Wolfgang rails against his employer and Salzburg: 'to waste one's life in inactivity in such a beggarly place is really very sad – and it is such a loss.' He asks for advice, but one senses that his mind is made up and that he is about to force a conflict. In Vienna on 9 May Mozart had a fierce exchange with the Archbishop, and asked to be released from service. The colourful account given in Mozart's letter to his father – a drama which resounds across the ages as a picture of the creative artist standing up to thoughtless authority – is clearly only one side of the story: Mozart hedges around the tangled issue of why he could not leave Vienna on the day he was ordered to – this probably had more to do with the Webers (mother and daughter) than with the Archbishop.

On 9 June he saw the Archbishop's chief steward, Count Arco, and received the immortal 'kick on the arse' which sent him to his fate and, as some would have it, into the modern world of the freelance musician. But in discussion before this violent conclusion the Count was more interesting. In reply to Mozart's ambitions towards Vienna he argued:

> Believe me, you allow yourself to be far too easily dazzled in Vienna. A man's reputation there lasts a very short time. At first, it is true, you are overwhelmed with praise and make a great deal of money into the bargain – but how long does that last? After a few months the Viennese want something new.

Mozart reported these prophetic words but did not heed them. Indeed he countered them with an increasingly manic set of objections: that his honour had been insulted, that he would make money, that Vienna was 'the land of the clavier'. In any case, he was soon left to find out whether he could survive there. He set up as a freelance musician, and apart from the fact that the Webers were feeding him it is difficult to see how he survived at first. The letters to his father report that he has only one pupil, though he says he could acquire more if he lowered his terms, which he thought it unwise to do. A note of formality then creeps in: 'Unless I have something particularly important to tell you, I shall only write to you once a week, as I am very busy just now.' This was perhaps the nearest Wolfgang came to a firm declaration of independence from his father.

- Haydn String Quartets Op. 33
- Boccherini *Stabat mater*
- Paisiello *La serva padrona*, St Petersburg
- Cimarosa *Il pittore parigino*, Rome

- Austro-Russian treaty against the Turks
- Americans defeat British at Cowpens, North Carolina
- British defeat Americans at Guilford, North Carolina
- Joseph II gives religious freedom and tolerance to Austrian press
- Joseph II makes monastic order independent of Rome
- British troops under Cornwallis surrender at Yorktown

1782

In January 1782 Mozart turned twenty-six. It was a crucial year for him; certainly the most significant of all in non-musical terms. It was the year he married, and thus confirmed the independence which he had sought by settling in Vienna. In doing so, Mozart formed the only relationship which was to be remotely comparable with the one that had sustained him through his entire early creative life so far, that with his father Leopold. And in marrying Constanze Weber on 4 August 1782, in haste and without his father present, he risked irrevocably breaking that bond. That the relationship with his father survived during Mozart's married life, albeit with many conflicts and problems, is testimony to its importance. From Constanze, Mozart acquired something very different from the emotional links his father had offered: a feeling not of dependence but of independence, a sense not of perpetual challenge but of perpetual support, and centrally, not an essential coldness but an essential warmth.

Even Mozart, on whom external political events rarely impinged, could not fail to notice that in 1782 the Pope, Pius VI, made a wholly unprecedented visit to Vienna. The composer was vague as to its purpose, and it is probable that the conflicts regarding the authority of Joseph II over the church in the Habsburg dominions were not something that greatly troubled him, unless it affected the way church music had to be written. But the Emperor's high-handed assertion of control over the ecclesiastical institutions in his land was unpopular both with the Pope and with his own people. Joseph II doubtless had the best intentions at heart in suppressing what he saw as wasteful contemplative orders and redirecting the money towards the secular clergy. But the implications in terms of property and tradition were immense, and Joseph's reforms, as so often, were only half thought through. He wished to be a bold moderniser, dragging a backward Austria into the modern age; but he only partly succeeded.

1782 was also an important year in terms of Mozart's position in Vienna: Joseph II's efforts to establish a German theatrical life bore fruit with the staging of Mozart's drama *Die Entführung aus dem Serail* at the Burgtheater. It proved to be a short-lived tradition, but Mozart's enthusiastic contribution to the form shows how anxious he was to ingratiate himself with the Emperor. The significance of the famous if undocumented anecdote – that Joseph II said 'Too many notes, my dear Mozart,' and Mozart replied, 'Just as many as are necessary,' relates to the importance of Mozart's desire to be accepted by Joseph II; it sums up nicely both the problems Mozart created for himself in writing so originally, and the creative confidence with which he answered his critics. The opera's success preceded Mozart's marriage by only a fortnight: was its triumph the final stimulus that he needed to act independently and decisively?

The wrangles and upheavals of this year's events in the Mozart household and especially in the household of his bride-to-be, the Webers, have something of the flavour of an eighteenth-century soap opera. The year begins with

Mozart in a difficult situation, having incurred his father's wrath by signing a marriage contract for Constanze, 'or rather a written assurance of my honourable intentions towards the girl', in order to placate the Weber family. Their daughter Aloysia, Mozart's first love, had married in 1780, and Mrs Weber may well have had her eye on Wolfgang as a suitable match for one of the younger sisters. After Constanze's father died, the person responsible for her welfare was her guardian Johann von Thorwart. He is an important and neglected figure in the Mozart story, for he was part of the composer's great and abiding fascination with the theatre, being Imperial and Royal Court Theatrical Supervisor; he was not an artistic figure, but was certainly an important administrator.

Thorwart had received rumours (from the composer Peter von Winter among others) that, as Mozart graphically put it, 'I have no settled income, I was far too intimate with her, I should probably jilt her, the girl would then be ruined, and so forth. All this made him smell a rat . . .' Mozart's accounts of the situation to his father are certainly biased, and it is difficult to know how far to believe their particulars. We cannot tell what Leopold wrote to him in return, for (maybe because of their strong content) these letters were not kept or were later destroyed, perhaps by Constanze herself. Mozart was undoubtedly naive: in the marriage settlement of Aloysia Weber with Joseph Lange (the actor who was later to paint the best portrait of Mozart) a substantial annuity for Madame Weber was agreed, and the payment subsequently reduced Lange to penury. Still, his first-hand account of the disputed contract was that though he agreed to write it out, Constanze herself tore it up with the words 'Dear Mozart, I need no written assurance from you. I believe what you say.'

Throughout this year, and through the to-and-froing of this lurid domestic drama, Mozart attempts to assure his father that he is living an organised and profitable life. 'Every morning at six o'clock my friseur arrives and wakes me, and by seven I have finished dressing, I compose until ten, when I give a lesson to Frau von Trattner and at eleven to the Countess Rumbeck.' He even breaks off one letter in January 1782 as if by way of demonstration, as his friseur has arrived. We may doubt that Mozart's schedule – at least his composing schedule – was so meticulous, for all the evidence suggests that he wrote with great fury when a deadline approached, less so when it did not loom. *Die Entführung*, for example, had been slow to materialise, and though Act II was previewed earlier, the composition was only completed in May 1782 under the pressure of the rehearsals which were to begin. Mozart attempts to reinforce this idea of his organised life in another, less convincing, letter of this year to his sister, which changes several of the facts (here he composes until nine) and is marked by that curious mixture of coldness and hypocritical gushing which seems to characterise his contacts with his sister in the period after he meets Constanze.

Again, Mozart is clearly replying to his father's concerns when he spells out to him three possible sources of income in Vienna, including patronage from Prince Lichtenstein who wants to form a wind band, Archduke Maximilian (a very strange thought, that Mozart might have been made Kapellmeister in Cologne), and the Emperor himself. Another letter mentions that 'at table the other day the Emperor gave me the highest praise, accompanied by the words "*C'est un talent, decidé!*"' – a well-attested remark, but less famous, because rather less memorable, than 'too many notes'. Mozart's speculations here seem optimistic, to say the least, and it is interesting that what proved to be his most lucrative source of income – giving concerts as a keyboard player – is not mentioned at this point.

Apart from his teaching and composing, how did Mozart establish himself as a performer in Vienna? The arrangements under which concerts were given there have been studied in increasing detail by Dexter Edge and Mary Sue Morrow; there is an interesting letter from Mozart to his father in May 1782. He explains that:

a certain Martin organised last winter a series of amateur concerts which took place every Friday in the Mehlgrube. You know that there are a great many amateurs in Vienna, and some very good ones too, both men and women. But so far these concerts have not been properly arranged. Well, this Martin has now got permission from the Emperor under charter (with the promise too of his gracious patronage) to give twelve concerts in the Augarten and four grand serenades in the finest open places of the city. The subscription for the whole summer is two ducats. So you can imagine that we shall have plenty of subscribers, the more so as I am taking an interest in it and am associated with it. Assuming that we get only a hundred subscribers, then each of us will have a profit of three hundred gulden (even if the costs amount to two hundred gulden, which is most unlikely). The orchestra consists entirely of amateurs, with the exception of the bassoon players, trumpets and timpani.

- Premiere of Schiller's *Die Räuber* in Mannheim
- Choderlos de Laclos publishes *Les liaisons dangereuses*
- Birth of Niccolò Paganini
- Death of Johann Christian Bach
- Death of Pietro Antonio Metastasio
- Haydn *Orlando paladino*, Eszterháza; *Missa cellensis*

- Spain captures Minorca from British
- Pope Pius VI visits Vienna
- Spain completes conquest of Florida
- Gibraltar relieved
- Peace planned by Britain and United States

1783

In January 1783 Mozart turned twenty-seven. He and his wife had their first child, who died later that year. In this year, too, Joseph II was pushing on with his legal, constitutional and theatrical reforms. Following the suspension of the national Singspiel company at Easter after a string of failures (Mozart denounced one of the offerings, by Umlauf, as 'execrable'), Joseph was attempting to assemble a troupe of *opera buffa* singers who would outshine those all over Europe, attracting leading Italians to Vienna. He favoured Salieri as the agent through which this operatic revolution might happen: the librettists Casti and Da Ponte were Joseph's favourites, and the music included the lighter operas by composers such as Paisiello, Cimarosa and Sarti, the Viennese favourites in the first half of the decade. Operatically, in spite of the success of *Die Entführung*, Mozart's time had not yet come, but the singers that Joseph II drew to Vienna in 1783 were to be enormously influential in creating his comic opera style. Mozart made only one impression on the new operatic scene in Vienna during this year, writing two arias for Aloysia Lange and one for the tenor Adamberger to sing in an opera by Anfossi, *Il curioso indiscreto*: the brilliant Lange pieces were successes but caused something of a scandal, while Adamberger was advised to turn down his newly written rondo, as a result of which, Mozart tells us, his performance was a failure.

In January he was still trying to placate his father, whose wrath he had incurred the previous year by his sudden marriage. A letter makes enigmatic reference to a promise he had made (see p. 265).

But what promise did he make? It is difficult to say precisely, since Leopold's letters on the other side of this correspondence do not survive (perhaps because of the reservations they contained towards Mozart's new wife). In later years Constanze said that, rather than the promise being linked to her illness before their marriage, Wolfgang had pledged to write a mass on the arrival of their first child. In any case there is a surviving torso of a magnificent mass setting: the great C minor Mass. Why was it never completed? If Constanze's account is correct, the death of their first child (see below) might have been one personal reason to abandon the work. However, one of Joseph II's reforms was to dis-

courage the use of elaborate liturgical music in church, and in
1782 a report from Vienna suggested that 'orchestrally
accompanied music has now been entirely eliminated from
the churches, except for very important feast days'. This may
well be an exaggeration, but it could also suggest why Mozart
had no incentive to complete the mass written to mark his
marriage: it would have had few opportunities for future performance in Vienna.

In 1783 Mozart was already heavily and successfully
involved with Viennese social life. One of the central features
of that life was the dance, and the carnival period which took
place each year from January to Lent. 'You are doubtless
aware that this is carnival time and that there is as much dancing here as in Salzburg and Munich,' writes Mozart to his
father on 22 January. 'Well, I should very much like to go as
Harlequin (but not a soul must know about it) – because here
there are so many – indeed nothing but – silly asses at the
Redoutes [the Redoutensaal in Vienna where the balls were
held]'. Mozart asks his father to send him his harlequin costume, and to do so quickly because they will not be able to
attend until it arrives. He also explains that Constanze and he
gave a private ball in their own rooms in new lodgings lasting
some eleven hours. In March, having received the costume,
Mozart relates to his father that he and his friends performed
a half-hour pantomime in between the dances, for which he
also wrote the music.

1783 was also a year of great success for Mozart in the concert life of Vienna. There was a benefit concert for his former
love Aloysia Lange on 11 March; as Mozart reported, 'the
theatre was very full and I was received again by the Viennese
public so cordially that I really ought to feel delighted. I had
already left the platform, but the audience would not stop
clapping and so I had to repeat the rondo, upon which there
was a regular torrent of applause.' Then there was a very varied concert later in the same month, on the 23rd, which the
Emperor attended, with a programme which typically mixed
symphonies, concert arias, concertos and keyboard solos by

Mozart himself. Slowly but surely (to adopt a proverb which Mozart himself used to his father), Mozart was ingratiating himself into Viennese social life and was becoming an important figure.

This must partly account for the saga of Mozart's reluctance to leave the city with Constanze and pay the long-overdue and long-promised visit to his father and sister in Salzburg. He thought up all manner of reasons during the earlier part of 1783 for failing to travel, including the fear that he might be arrested by the archbishop for reneging on his contract in Salzburg. More pertinent considerations included the forthcoming birth of the Mozarts' first child. In April Mozart cheerfully states that 'as soon as my wife has sufficiently recovered from her confinement, we will be off to Salzburg at once', but following the birth there are complications, about which Mozart explains, concerning the nursing and care of the new child:

> I was quite determined that even if she were able to do so, my wife was never to nurse her child. Yet I was equally determined that my child was never to take the milk of a stranger. I wanted the child to be brought up on water, like my sister and myself. But the midwife, my mother-in-law, and most people here have begged and implored me not to allow it, if only for the reason that most children here who are brought up on water do not survive . . . that induced me to give in.

Even so, young Raimund died during his parents' absence, on 19 August.

The 'Linz' Symphony was apparently written during the space of his stay in Linz (on the way from his visit to Salzburg) between 30 October and 4 November – a date mentioned in a letter, where he says 'I am giving a concert in the theatre here, and, as I have not a single symphony with me, I am writing a new one at breakneck speed.' Perhaps the speed was unusual, but the length of composition would have to have allowed time for the work to be copied and, who knows, perhaps rehearsed as well. This would have been exceptional, as sightreading of symphonies was common by bands skilled in the style, as a review of some symphonies by Vanhal in 1781 suggests: 'It would not be advisable to perform them without having played them through first with all the instruments at least once.' (Haydn requested the same when he sent his Symphonies Nos. 95 and 96 to Vienna in 1791.) So a full-scale symphony might be conceived and actually written out in score by Mozart within two or three days if he worked into the night. How far had he worked it out in his head? We shall never know precisely. In this case the symphony had a public rehearsal at Count Thun's palace before it was performed at a theatre in Linz the following day.

We can only presume that the visit to Salzburg was not really a happy one, and that the poor relationships established between Constanze on the one hand and Leopold and Nannerl on the other continued. At any rate, Constanze writes no more letters to the Mozart household, at least none that have survived, and Mozart's tone towards his sister becomes somewhat distant, or else takes refuge in banter, as in this PS from a letter to his father in the last month of 1783:

> We both send Nannerl
> 1. a couple of boxes on the ear
> 2. a couple of slaps on the face
> 3. a couple of raps on the cheek
> 4. a couple of whacks on the jaw
> 5. a couple of smacks on the jowl
> 6. a couple of cuffs on the mug.

The unspoken rift between Constanze and Nannerl was to have the greatest consequences for the development of our picture of Mozart after his death: their views were diametrically opposed, and they influenced different biographers who wrote about Mozart (see p. 28–31).

- Haydn *Armida*, Eszterháza
- Piccinni *Didon*, Fontainebleau

- Sacchini *Renaud*, Paris
- Treaty of Versailles: Britain, France, Spain and the United States
- Joseph II enforces German language in Bohemia and suppresses the Diet
- Russia seizes Crimea and enforces sovereignty over Georgia

1784

In January 1784 Mozart turned twenty-eight. It was one of the most sheerly successful years of his life, when he was attaining his peak of public success in Vienna and producing masterpieces with astonishing speed while making many private and public appearances as a performer. It was the year when his standing with the Viennese public was at its height, too, and those who supported him were drawn from the cream of Viennese society. The foundation of his success was the piano concerto, the genre which he fostered as a vehicle for his own talents and did so much to develop.

Vienna, with a population of something under a quarter of a million, was small among Europe's capitals at the end of the eighteenth century (London was over three times as big) but very large among German-speaking cities. With Austria in the ascendant in the East, the nobility of Eastern Europe often visited Vienna. So it flourished through its status as a cultural centre, because of the influence of the court, and the nobility who, though they numbered under ten thousand among the population, wielded great power and influence. The Viennese were serious about their culture, and music 'is the only thing about which the nobility shows taste. Many houses have their own band of musicians, and all the public concerts bear witness that this aspect of art is in high repute here.' That report, written by a travelling Frenchman, was first published in this year 1784, in Cramer's *Magazin der Musik*, and was translated by H. C. Robbins Landon in his great biography of Haydn. This exceptionally interesting

document gives the lie to some of the complaints about contemporary performance in Mozart's day:

> The number of real virtuosi is small, but as far as the
> orchestral musicians are concerned, one can hardly imag-
> ine anything in the world more beautiful. I have heard 30
> or 40 instruments playing together, and they all produce
> one tone so correct, clean and precise that one might
> think one is hearing one single string instrument. The
> violins play as if with one stroke of the bow, the wind
> instruments with one breath.

We should add to this Mozart's own testimony about his 1784
concert in which the Quintet for Piano and Wind was given
its first performance, 'I would have wished you could hear it!
and how beautifully it was performed!' No dissatisfaction
there, and indeed one suspects that Mozart stressed to his
father the excellence of Viennese performers in order to
remind him that they were definitely better than those in
Salzburg.

Mozart was now in great demand. Private patrons solicited
his appearances, and it is worth recalling the astonishing list
which he provided to his father, clearly with some defensive
pride, of his appearances in March 1784. (These were concert
appearances during Lent, when the opera was closed, so he
was actually untypically busy.) These fall into a regular pattern: Mondays and Fridays at Esterházy's, Thursdays at
Galitzin's, Saturdays at Richter's, plus private and public concerts of his own: twenty-two appearances in three weeks.
Mozart explains that Georg Friedrich Richter, 'the clavier
virtuoso, is giving six Saturday concerts . . . the nobility subscribed, but remarked that they really did not care much
about going unless I played. So Richter asked me to do so. I
promised to play three times and then arranged three concerts for myself, to which they all subscribed.' (Mozart later
provides a list of the subscribers, and of these it has been estimated that about half were from the established nobility,
about forty per cent from lower nobility or those who had

bought titles, and only some eight per cent from the bour-
geoisie. Most were men, though presumably most bought
two tickets.)

Of the other patrons, Prince Dimitri Galitzin was the
Russian ambassador, a regular musical patron whose concerts
Mozart must have relished for their social contacts: the
ambassador was close to the Emperor and exerted considerable
influence. Robbins Landon has established the entertaining
information that when he died in 1793 his will contained references to 254 paintings and drawings in his possession, as
well as fourteen carriages, eleven horses and 552 bottles of
rare wine. It is also thanks to Robbins Landon that the identity of the Esterházy who was Mozart's patron has been clari-
fied as Count Johann Baptist and not, as had been previously
believed, Johann Nepomuk (who indeed lived in Vienna but
was absent from the city on important occasions during most
of this period, including Mozart's concerts of March 1784).

Perhaps Mozart began to feel the need to keep track of his
compositions more rigorously during 1784: it was early in
this the year that he began the thematic catalogue of all his
works from February onwards which still survives in the
British Library in London. On 21 September his second son,
Carl Thomas, was born, and the Mozarts moved to a more
expensive apartment in the Domgasse. Mozart joined the
Masonic lodge 'Zur Wohltätigkeit' (Beneficence) on 14
December; he was now part of the Vienna establishment.

- Beaumarchais's *La folle journée, ou Le marriage de Figaro*
- Death of Diderot
- David's painting *The Death of the Horatii*
- Grétry *Richard Coeur-de-Lion*, Paris
- Birth of Louis Spohr

- Britain reduces duties on tea and spirits
- East India Company under government control
- Joseph II suppresses Hungarian constitution and transfers
  power to Vienna
- Joseph II breaks off relations with Holland

1785

In January 1785 Mozart turned twenty-nine. His success in
Vienna continued, and he found wide fame, as the *Wiener
Zeitung* reported in December of that year: 'Our praise is
superfluous in view of the deserved fame of this master, as
well known as he is universally valued.' We have a vivid and
immediate picture of the composer's life in the first few
months of this year because his father Leopold visited him,
perhaps partly to check up on his domestic situation, partly to
remove any ill-feeling left by the visit of Wolfgang and
Constanze to Salzburg in the previous year – but most of all
to participate in his son's tremendous musical triumphs.

At the end of 1784, Mozart had taken a decisive step and
joined a Viennese lodge of the Freemasons. Freemasonry
was at the height of its popularity in the Vienna of the early
1780s, and one report from Georg Forster, who came into
contact with the Viennese lodges in 1784, said 'Freemasonry
is thriving'. It was not officially approved at this time,
though Joseph II was sympathetic to its aims, and a year later
he regularised the Masons' activities but at a cost of some
independence. Forster was particularly strong in his praise of
the lodge 'Zur wahren Eintracht' (True Concord), which
Haydn joined in 1785, though he did not attend any further
meetings:

> [It] is the one most actively working for enlightenment.
> It publishes a Freemason's journal in which everything –
> faith, the oath and ceremonies, and even fanaticism – is
> more openly discussed than at home in Saxony. The best
> poets and scholars are members of this lodge. They make
> light of the whole idea of secrecy and have transformed
> the entire thing into a society of rational, unprejudiced
> men dedicated to enlightenment.

In fact this lodge survived Joseph II's regularisation less well
than Mozart's. And Mozart's involvement with the Masons
came at the very end of their power in Vienna: after Joseph

II's death his successor Leopold II was much preoccupied
with the possibilities of Masonic plots in Prague, and in 1793
Francis II banned secret societies entirely, an edict which
later in the year was interpreted to include Masonic lodges.
Mozart did not live to see that reduction in their influence:
for him the contact with Masonry ensured him a circle of
close-knit, often wealthy friends on whose support he did not
hesitate to call in the years ahead.

Leopold Mozart arrived in Vienna on 11 February, and
stayed until 25 April. It was a good moment to view his son's
work positively, for Mozart's activity in Vienna was now at its
peak. He gave a series of six subscription concerts in the
Mehlgrube, three in February and three in March, featuring
his own playing. Leopold was extremely responsive to the
events of the household, particularly their financial implications, and his letters home to his daughter tell us much of
Mozart's life at that time:

> That your brother has very fine quarters with all the nec-
> essary furniture you may gather from the fact that his rent
> is 460 gulden. On the same evening we drove to his first
> subscription concert, at which a great many members of
> the aristocracy were present. Each person pays a sou-
> verain d'or or three ducats for these Lenten concerts.
> Your brother is giving them at the Mehlgrube and only
> pays half a souverain d'or each time for the hall. The con-
> cert was magnificent and the orchestra played splendidly.
> In addition to the symphonies a female singer of the
> Italian theatre performed two arias. Then we had a new
> and very fine concerto by Wolfgang which the copyist was
> still copying when we arrived, and the rondo which your
> brother did not even have time to play through as he had
> to supervise the copying.

It was this year that Haydn heard three of Mozart's quartets dedicated to him, and complimented Leopold Mozart on
his son's accomplishments. Haydn and Leopold Mozart also
became masons during the period of Leopold's visit, and

Wolfgang's cantata *Davidde penitente* was performed, reusing sections of the C minor Mass.

- Haydn Symphonies Nos. 83, 87, String Quartet Op. 42
- Storace *Gli sposi malcontenti*, Vienna
- Cimarosa *Il marito disperato*, Naples
- Birth of Manzoni
- Salieri *La grotta di Trofonio*, Vienna

- Joseph II tries unsuccessfully to exchange Bavaria for Austrian Netherlands
- William Pitt's parliamentary reforms defeated
- Prussia signs commercial treaty with United States
- Alliance of France and Holland
- Cardinal de Rohan arrested and Marie Antoinette blamed in Diamond Necklace Affair

1786

In January 1786 Mozart turned thirty. In that year, you could buy his variations, arias, chamber music and symphonies from the music shops in Vienna, and Mozart stood alongside 'the most celebrated masters, viz Herr Gluck, Mozart, Paisiello, Salieri and Grétry'. He was at the centre of artistic life, in all but one field, that of comic opera. Even that was to change during the year, for there was a court commission planned. At the start of the year Mozart wrote *Der Schauspieldirektor* for festivities at the palace of Schönbrunn. And then, on 1 May, *Le nozze di Figaro* finally came to birth: the opera which would eventually establish Mozart's claim to be the greatest, most subtle *opera buffa* composer of his time.

Vienna in 1786 was the subject of entertaining investigation by Johann Pezzl, a fellow Freemason of Mozart's whose articles about the city H. C. Robbins Landon has translated in part. He paints a vivid picture of conditions in Vienna without avoiding the less favourable aspects:

The constant dust in warm weather is one of Vienna's great plagues. It is the dried-out dust of chalk and gravel,

it irritates the eyes and causes all sorts of lung complaints
. . . Many carriage wheels and horses' hooves, incessantly
passing along the streets at all hours, stir it up and if there
is a little more wind than usual, the city, the suburbs and
especially the Esplanade are covered with it. If you leave
your house at eight o'clock on a Sunday evening after a
lovely warm day, it is like entering a fog.

Pezzl's observations on the state of the city range far and
wide (including a list of consumption in 1783 ranging from
40,029 head of oxen to 1,265,180 bundles of straw), but his
remarks on income are highly relevant to Mozart, since they
enable direct comparison with his known fees from concerts
and outlay on rent. Pezzl tried to set aside the extremes of 'a
countess who is free to spend a thousand gulden a day, and
the seamstress in the suburbs who earns three and a half
kreuzer for a long day's work', and to estimate what a modest
man would require for middle-of-the-road needs:

Assuming that you have no family, that you are not
employed in a public office, that you are not a gambler,
and that you do not keep a regular mistress – these are
things which cause complications and require a certain
type of wardrobe, and also involve a good deal of continuous unregulatable expenses – you can live fairly comfortably in Vienna for the following annual outlay, which will
enable you to move in respectable middleclass circles . . .
total 464 fl. I leave to your imagination and your purse
the question of how much you wish to spend on theatres
and private pleasures. You can manage quite comfortably
on 500 or 550 gulden.

Mozart, however, clearly could not. He required special
clothing for his court appearances, and we know that in this
one year he was paying almost Pezzl's entire estimated budget
for rent alone. On the other hand, he also made that much
from a single academy concert at the height of his success in
1785, which earned 559 gulden. Then there were teaching

fees and publishers' income. When Joseph II came to one concert he sent twenty-five ducats (112 florins or gulden) in advance. Mozart was paid 225 gulden for *Der Schauspieldirektor*, 450 for *Le nozze di Figaro*. When he sold three piano concertos to Donaueschingen, also in this year, he received eighty-one gulden, but these were not new works.

We will never know in detail about Mozart's expenses. But we can judge them to have been high, for Mozart played a full part in the social life of the city, as he had always done since his arrival. On 19 February, for example, he attended a masked ball in the robes of an oriental philosopher, and handed out copies of a sheet containing eight riddles and fourteen proverbs. His father received a copy, and was so impressed with them that he forwarded them to his daughter, with the note that the proverbs 'are really good and true from first to last and should really be taken to heart'.

The first half of the year was dominated by *Le nozze di Figaro*, his new opera for Vienna, which was eventually performed for the first time on 1 May. 'It will be surprising if it is a success,' wrote Leopold Mozart to his daughter, 'for I know that very powerful cabals have ranged themselves against your brother. Salieri and all his supporters will again try to move heaven and earth to down his opera. Herr and Mme Dušek told me recently that it is on account of the very great reputation which your brother's exceptional talent and ability have won for him that so many people are plotting against him.' Well, it was not quite as simple as that. *Figaro* was a controversial choice for an opera, because Beaumarchais's play, first performed in Paris in April 1784, had incurred the displeasure of Joseph II himself, perhaps especially because of Figaro's last-act outburst, in a long and powerful speech, denouncing despots and tyrants who controlled people's lives.

On 18 October Constanze gave birth to their third son, but he lived for only a month.

• Haydn Symphonies Nos. 82, 84, 86

- Salieri *Prima la musica e poi la parole*
- Martín y Soler *Una cosa rara*

- Belgian protests against Joseph II
- Pitt financial reforms in England
- Friedrich Wilhelm II of Prussia succeeds Frederick of Prussia

1787

In January 1787 Mozart turned thirty-one. Following the huge success of *Le nozze di Figaro* in Prague during December 1786, Mozart and Constanze travelled to the city and the 'Prague' Symphony was performed there. But although the year started well, it was the beginning of a difficult period, and the downturn in the economic climate, combined with a falling-off in his fashionable appeal, led to the eventual abandonment of his subscription concerts. In the spring of 1787 the Mozarts moved from the splendid apartment he had occupied on the Domgasse to a much smaller one at Hauptstrasse 224. 'He does not say why he has moved,' wrote Leopold bitterly to his daughter, 'but I can guess the reason why.' The rent was 50 gulden, just about what Pezzl estimated was necessary for a member of the modest middle class without any children.

However in one respect things improved: he was finally given a court position, that of Kammermusicus following the death of Gluck. His salary was 800 fl. ('but no other member of the chamber receives as much', he told his sister), a small sum compared to the 2000 fl. that Gluck had been receiving, but comparable to court officials of the middle rank. So Mozart had achieved what he had been longing for since arriving in Vienna at the start of the decade: official recognition from the Emperor. It must have felt somewhat half-hearted after the public acclaim he had already received.

The third event of 1787 that was crucial to Mozart's life was the death of his father on 28 May. His relationship with his father, often stormy, had been without doubt the most

profound of his life, surpassing in complexity and power his
rather warmer and simpler relationship with his wife.
Wolfgang had heard of Leopold's serious illness a month
before, and had written a remarkable letter in which he gathered together some thoughts about death. It is clearly
inspired by Masonic writings, and recycles some precepts
which Mozart would have learnt and taken to heart. But there
is more than a touch of personal ownership in his statement
that 'I have now made a habit of being prepared in all affairs
of life for the worst.' He claimed to have been brought closer
to an understanding of death by the death of his friend and
exact contemporary, Count von Hatzfeld. His letter may simply have been a reconciling attempt to heal the wounds with
his father by saying the right thing to him at the right time.

When Leopold died, Mozart scribbled a PS on a letter to
his friend Gottfried von Jacquin: 'I inform you that on
returning home today I received the sad news of my most
beloved father's death. You can imagine the state I am in.' But
that soon turned to practicality as he made arrangements
with his sister Nannerl for the splitting of their father's estate.
First he requested an inventory before the public auction of
his effects, 'so that I could select a few items for myself, but if
there is a *disposito paterna inter liberos* . . . I need to know what's
in that disposition before I can decide about anything else.'
There is evidence of a quarrel, and he wrote brusquely to her
in words which seem more immediately convincing than his
letter to his father: 'If you were still single and unprovided
for, all this would not be necessary. I would most gladly leave
everything to you, as I have thought and said a thousand
times before; but because the property is now of no use to
you, yet on the other hand of considerable value to me, I
regard it as my duty to think about my wife and child.'
Eventually the matter was settled through Nannerl's husband, and Mozart received 1,000 gulden, but he asked for it
in Viennese currency, and as a bill of exchange, which made it
worth a little more. Brother and sister drifted further apart,
and indeed after Mozart's death Nannerl claimed to know

nothing of his circumstances in Vienna and to be deeply moved by his plight when she read about it in Niemetschek's biography.

Perhaps all this took its toll on Mozart: 1787 shows a falling-off in the amount of music he produced, though this may well be accounted for by the huge labour of *Don Giovanni*, commissioned by Bondini while he was in Prague. Another significant change is the gradual move towards writing chamber music for performance in middle-class homes and for publication, rather than concertos for performance in the homes of the nobility: Mozart clearly saw an opportunity here in the freelance world of Viennese music-making. Among the musical highlights of the year are the remarkable Rondo in A minor for piano K511, the Sonata in C for piano duet K521 (sent to Jacquin on the day he learnt of his father's death), and the great String Quintets in C and G minor K515 and 516. And among the puzzles are the two little serenades, *A Musical Joke* and *Eine Kleine Nachtmusik*, an unclouded work of complete perfection which has since become one of the most popular works of classical music in the world.

The autumn of 1787 was dominated by the rehearsal and premiere of *Don Giovanni* in Prague; Mozart directed four performances from 29 October and the work was deemed an overwhelming success.

- Haydn String Quartets Op. 50, Symphonies Nos. 88 and 89
- Salieri *Tarare*, Paris
- Paisiello *Pirro*, Naples
- Dittersdorf *Die Liebe in Narrenhause*, Vienna
- Martin y Soler *L'arbore di Diana*, Vienna
- Death of Gluck

- Joseph II annexes Austrian Netherlands, provoking riots
- Alliance between Joseph II and Catherine II
- New American constitution drafted at Philadelphia and signed on 17 September
- Cardinal Etienne Brienne becomes French minister of finance

- French Parlement demands the summoning of the States-General; Parlement banished by Louis XVI and then recalled, summoning States-General for 1792
- Turkey declares war on Russia

1788

In January 1788 Mozart turned thirty-two. Back in Vienna after the successes of Prague, things did not go well for Mozart. He was now unfashionable; that much was clear. The performances in Vienna of his new opera *Don Giovanni* came in for much criticism, and no appearances by the composer as a concert soloist can be confirmed. He could not raise enough subscribers to publish his three string quintets, masterpieces though they were.

The picture may, however, be more complicated than the simple one of declining popularity which has been accepted until recently by Mozart's biographers. The artistic situation in Vienna was complicated by the closing of the Kärntnertor theatre and the disbanding of Joseph II's old German opera company. Only the Burgtheater remained available for opera, and that was circumscribed because of the economic situation. The central fact of Viennese existence from February 1788 onwards, which had a bearing on the whole artistic life of the city and affected Mozart as much as anyone, was that Austria was at war. On 9 February hostilities had been formally declared with the Ottoman Empire, though there had been war since the end of 1787: these ill-considered Turkish wars were to have a catastrophic effect on the economy of Austria in general and the reputation of Joseph II in particular.

There were continual conflicts elsewhere, making matters increasingly difficult for Joseph II. His domination of Hungary was not accepted by the nobility there, who resented his unfair taxation system; there was increasing disturbance in the Netherlands. Even in Vienna, there were publications with titles like *Why is Emperor Joseph Not Loved by His*

People? That 1787 pamphlet by Joseph Richter praised many aspects of Joseph's activities and his personal care towards his subjects, but then pointed out that many people had good cause to be resentful of his reforms, including the clergy, the aristocracy, government officials and others. Volkmar Braunbehrens summarises the situation accurately:

> This catalogue of complaints shows that although the Emperor had many achievements to his credit, he had forfeited public approval through arrogant behaviour and decisions he made without thought for their conse- quences. The reference to the many enemies of reform was a warning to Joseph that he must not alienate his sup- porters or he would be totally isolated.

That, however, was exactly what he did, plunging the country into crisis, and creating such difficulties that he had to undo his own reforms before he died. It is also highly rel- evant to the operatic situation in Vienna that although per- formances continued through the year, Joseph II decided in August to suspend the season of Italian opera because the deficit run up on the previous season had been so great. That decision was not in the end carried through, so performances of *Don Giovanni* continued. But the atmosphere must have been unpleasant: when Joseph came back to Vienna on 5 December, he was at the lowest point of his popularity, and when on 15 December he attended the opera (he had already expressed an opinion, without seeing it, that it was 'too diffi- cult for the singers'), he was apparently given such a cold reception that he left long before the end.

So it may well be that the falling-off in popularity we per- ceive for Mozart in this year was really a reflection of a gen- eral recession: more work needs to be done on the prevailing climate of the time. At any rate, Mozart remained popular with the connoisseurs in Vienna: just the day after war was declared, we read of him playing at a private concert given by the Ambassador of Venice, in which singers from the opera took part, along with 'a certain Muller, a shoemaker's daughter'. Count Zinzendorf, the indefatigable diarist, recorded: 'I was afflicted with spleen.'

One of Mozart's continual supporters through this period was Gottfried van Swieten, the son of Maria Theresa's doctor and a highly cultivated man who was prefect of the court library (a position he inherited from his father) and who in 1782 had become president of the Commission on Education and Censorship. He was no mean composer himself, and through time he spent in Germany, where he made the acquaintance of Carl Philip Emanuel Bach, he had acquired an extensive knowledge of baroque music and baroque composers, admiring especially J. S. Bach and Handel. Whether van Swieten stepped into the breach as an employer of Mozart primarily as an act of charity it is difficult to say, but from the beginning of 1788 onwards we find him playing an increasing role in providing Mozart's income; for van Swieten in February, Mozart directed (and rearranged one aria of) C. P. E. Bach's *Resurrection Oratorio*, and in November he arranged and performed Handel's *Acis and Galatea*.

- Goethe *Egmont*
- Haydn String Quartets Opp. 54 and 55, Symphonies Nos. 90 and 91
- Salieri *Axur, re d'Ormus*, Vienna
- Birth of Arthur Schopenhauer
- Death of C. P. E. Bach

- Austria declares war on Turkey
- Alliance between England and Holland
- Sweden declares war on Russia; Swedish fleet destroyed
- Louis XVI summons States-General for 1789
- New York City federal capital of the US
- Pitt proposes abolition of slave trade
- *The Times* begins publication
- George III ill

1789

In January 1789 Mozart turned thirty-three. This was in most respects a difficult year. Between 8 April and 4 June Mozart undertook a substantial tour to Berlin, but rather little is known about the journey, and many anecdotes and rumours have been supplied to fill the gap. Most revolve around Mozart's turning down offers of work out of his faithfulness to the Emperor back home, a fundamentally unconvincing picture. Mozart travelled with Prince Karl Lichnowsky, a close friend who had ties with Berlin and who belonged to his Masonic lodge.

It appears that the invitation to travel to Berlin came from Lichnowsky, and Mozart accepted on the grounds that to have such an expensive journey paid for would be a great benefit, particularly as he had few professional ties in Vienna. But there seem to have been conflicts and difficulties even over this arrangement, and the latest research has uncovered evidence that in 1791 Lichnowsky was suing Mozart for the repayment of debts. Together the two travelled first to Prague, and then stopped on 12 April at Dresden, where a concert took place at the Hôtel de Pologne. The following day he played for the wife of Elector Frederick Augustus III of Saxony, and also performed on the organ.

Then he visited Leipzig, where he improvised on the organ of St Thomas's Church, where J. S. Bach had been Cantor. Once again stories surround this visit (novels were written in nineteenth-century Germany about it), perhaps the most convincing of which is Rochlitz's tale of Mozart hearing the choir sing, discovering the parts of Bach's motet *Singet dem Herrn* and laying them out on the floor, murmuring, 'Here's something from which one can learn!' Mozart's manuscript of Bach's motet survives, with some markings for orchestrating it. Then he went to Potsdam, where a contemporary note survives from officials to King Frederick William II saying that 'one named Mozart reports here that he was brought hither in the company of Prince Lichnowsky, that he desired to lay his talents before your Sovereign Majesty's feet and awaited the command whether he may hope that Your Sovereign Majesty will receive him.'

Then there is silence, and we do not know whether Mozart was seen by the King or not. A note on the document instructs 'Directeur Du Port' to deal with the matter: Jean-Pierre Duport, director of the royal chamber music, was scarcely Mozart's favourite musician, but Mozart evidently bit his lip to the extent of writing a set of keyboard variations on a tune of Duport's. It seems that Potsdam did not quite work out as Mozart had hoped: first Lichnowsky went off and left him on his own, incurring expenses, and then Mozart decided to go back to Leipzig and give a concert there with his friend the singer Josepha Duschek. It was an artistically successful concert, apparently, but financially unprofitable, with a rather small house. The programme, as usual, consisted of a mixture of symphony movements, piano concertos, concert arias, and piano solos.

Then Mozart went to Berlin, where he did appear at court on 26 May; once again, there are stories of Mozart receiving a royal commission to write quartets and sonatas, and being given a hundred gold coins in a gold snuff-box, but although Mozart mentions the snuff-box, the rest may well belong in the realms of fantasy. Mozart certainly began to write string quartets (see the year 1790) but maybe only in the hope that the King, to whom he now had an introduction, would consider playing them at court. His business dealings continued when he made an arrangement with a music publisher to distribute his music in Northern Europe. On 28 May Mozart left Berlin and travelled back to Prague, again calling at Dresden. By 4 June he was back in Vienna, not much the richer. His letters to Constanze during his absence had been touchingly desolate, and with more than a slight feeling of guilt at having been away at a time when she was unwell.

But his letters to Michael Puchberg, from whom he was borrowing money, following his return from the tour are even more desperate than the ones which preceded it. Mozart outlines a situation which must indeed have been financially calamitous; what is difficult is to establish how far it was typical of the times. He is feeling ill, and Constanze had become seriously ill with an infected leg (necessitating possibly expensive treatment), 'but in spite of my wretched condition I decided to give subscription concerts at home in order to be able to meet at least my present great and frequent expenses. But even this has failed. Unfortunately Fate is so much against me, though only in Vienna, that even when I want to, I cannot make money. A fortnight ago I sent round a list for subscribers and so far the only name on it is that of the Baron van Swieten!'

This plan – subscription concerts at home? – seems on the face of it surprising. But there seems to have been a trend towards small-scale concert-giving at this period, and we know from his letters that Mozart once gave a carnival ball at home. It also brings back into the picture as his primary supporter at this time the good Baron, who assumed an even greater importance as a patron during this year. However, towards the end of the year Mozart was increasingly busy with his new opera *Così fan tutte*, which was to be performed at the Burgtheater in January. He also found time to write his sublime Clarinet Quintet for his friend Anton Stadler, which was first performed on 22 December. Constanze gave birth again in November, but the child, named Anna Maria, died after an hour.

- Goethe *Torquato Tasso*
- Burney *A General History of Music* completed
- Haydn Symphony No. 92, cantata *Arianna a Naxos*
- Wranitzky *Oberon*, Vienna
- Salieri *La cifra*, *Il pastor fido*, Vienna

- Prince of Wales takes over as Regent but George III recovers
- George Washington becomes President of the United States
- States-General meets at Versailles
- Third Estate declares itself a National Assembly

- Fall of the Bastille
- Austria and Russia defeat Turkey at Focshani
- Austrian troops take Belgrade
- Austrian Netherlands declare independence as Belgium

1790

In January 1790 Mozart turned thirty-four. The year started well, with the premiere of *Così fan tutte*. Haydn was in Vienna and attended a rehearsal, as did Michael Puchberg. The first performance took place on 26 January, of which the dedicated diarist Count Zinzendorf recorded: 'The music by Mozart is charming, and the subject rather amusing,' a judgement which the nineteenth century was not, on the whole, to share. Mozart was apparently paid 200 ducats for his composition, a generous fee, and the opera was more successful in Vienna than historians have usually acknowledged.

But it did not ease his financial difficulties, and the succeeding months added many more problems. Musically, it was one of the most unproductive years of his life in terms of finished compositions, and his opportunities for performance in Vienna were limited. So he undertook another tour, this time with his brother-in-law Hofer to Frankfurt for the coronation festivities of Leopold II. It was an ill-advised, ill-planned trip, and it produced very little by way of financial advantage because the concert Mozart gave clashed with court festivities ('some Prince was giving a big dejeuner and the Hessian troops were holding a grand manoeuvre,' reported Mozart). There is a long and entertaining account of the concert, which started at 11 a.m., by Count Ludwig von Bentheim-Steinfurt, which ends with the comment that 'the last Symphony was not given because it was almost 2 o'clock and everybody was sighing for dinner. The music thus lasted three hours which was due to the fact that between all the Pieces there were very long pauses. The orchestra was no more than rather weak with 5 or 6 violins but apart from that very accurate . . . There were not many people.'

The letters that Mozart wrote home to his wife during this trip are rather different from those he wrote on his previous journey in 1789. He is now more paranoid about her activities and her health, more unrealistic about his future. He claims to derive little pleasure either from composing or from seeing people. Only the idea of his absent wife brings any consolation. 'I am as excited as a child at the thought of seeing you again. If people could see into my heart, I should almost feel ashamed. To me everything is cold – cold as ice. Perhaps if you were with me I might possibly take more pleasure in the kindness of those I meet here. But as it is, everything seems so empty.'

Money continues to be an obsession, and in the other side of the correspondence (which has disappeared) she is reporting back on various financial problems which he has asked her to sort out. Mozart writes:

> Well, I shall begin to give little quartet subscription concerts in Advent and I shall also take pupils. There is a struggle going on between my yearning and longing to see and embrace you once more and my desire to bring home a large sum of money. I have often thought of travelling farther afield, but whenever I tried to bring myself to take the decision, the thought always came to me how bitterly I would regret it, if I were to separate myself from my beloved wife for such an uncertain prospect, perhaps even to no purpose whatever. I feel as if I had left you years ago.

Was Mozart depressed? The simple answer would be to say that he was, obviously, dismayed at the turn of events, which seemed to trap him into being unable to work, unable to earn a living by either playing or composing, and thus unable to pay his debts. But was he clinically depressed, and were the sudden swings of his activity a symptom of manic depression? The case has been argued in recent years by the Australian doctor Peter J. Davies, who distinguishes the normal alternation of moods of elation and sadness from the 'bipolar affective disorder' from which he believes Mozart suffered. In positive mood, 'the composer's hypo-manic swings were characterised by elevated or expansive moods, decreased need for sleep, excessive energy, inflated self-esteem, increased productivity, extreme gregariousness, physical hyperactivity, inappropriate joking and punning, and indulgence in frivolous behaviour without appreciation of the consequences.' In contrast, his depressions were characterised by illness and inability to work.

1790 certainly seems to fit the description of a depressive period for Mozart: it is almost completely devoid of substantial musical products. He arranged more Handel for van Swieten, but with what degree of enthusiasm we cannot tell. He was often troubled by illness during the year; his letters to Puchberg are full of perhaps exaggerated reports of his problems: 'I would have gone to see you myself in order to have a chat with you, but my head is covered with bandages due to rheumatic pains, which make me feel my situation still more keenly' (April). 'I am very sorry that I cannot go out and have a talk with you myself but my toothache and headache are very painful and altogether I still feel very unwell' (May). 'Whereas I felt tolerably well yesterday, I am absolutely wretched today. I could not sleep all night for pain. I must have got overheated yesterday from walking so much and then without knowing it has caught a chill. Picture to yourself my condition – ill and consumed by worries and anxieties. Such a state quite definitely prevents me from recovering' (August).

The appeal to Puchberg's sympathy and his pocket is clear, but so too is the state of Mozart's health. He refers quite often to the quartets and sonatas which he is writing, which he began in the previous year: 'I must have something to live on until I have arranged my subscription concerts and until the quartets on which I am working have been engraved.' In May he says that worry 'had prevented me all this time from finishing my quartets'. But in fact he never completed an entire set either of piano sonatas or of quartets. Instead he 'gave away' the quartets for 'a trivial sum simply in order to have the cash in hand to meet my present difficulties', and had them published by Artaria.

On 14 December Haydn held a dinner before his departure for London, and Mozart was encouraged to make the same journey. It was not the first time that a visit to London had been proposed to him as an attractive option, and in the years after his death many of his singers were to find work in the city (see below p. 115–25, 'Mozart's singers'). If Mozart had accepted an invitation to London at this point, much might have changed.

- Haydn String Quartets Op. 64
- Grétry *Pierre le Grand*, Paris
- Boccherini Quintets Op. 43
- Burke *Reflections on the Revolution in France*
- Kant *Critique of Pure Reason*

- Joseph II dies in February
- Coronation of Emperor Leopold II in Frankfurt
- Death of Adam Smith
- Feudal rights in France abolished
- Louis XVI accepts constitution
- End of Swedish–Russian war

1791

In January 1791 Mozart turned thirty-five. It was to be his last year, viewed too often by posterity as a tragic slide towards a death that gave no hint of his true worth. But on the contrary, viewed against the picture of the composer in his later years, 1791 appears an astonishingly active year. Once again Mozart was writing a large amount of great music; once again he was in demand for commissions and public concerts; and this is the only year of his life in which he managed to complete two major operas.

His financial situation can only have been improving as well, and depending on the arrangements for payment for performances of *Die Zauberflöte*, which was running when he died, he might have stood to repay his debts within a short time. He found time to petition for the post of Kapellmeister at the cathedral and was appointed assistant there (it would never have been thought that the aged occupant of the post would outlive him). His output was remarkable in so many different genres: he wrote many lavish dances that were need-ed for the balls at the Redoutensaal in the carnival season at the start of the year (not at all major works, but splendidly orchestrated dances of great impact and verve), a string quin-tet (and perhaps sketches for some others), a tremendous piece for mechanical organ in F minor, piano variations and a concert aria for friends in Schikaneder's theatre company, the completion of the gentle Piano Concerto K595, miniatures for glass harmonica and ensemble – an astonishing list . . .

The future was viewed realistically, not sentimentally. In 1791, the cultured Viennese did not depend on Mozart. They had a new monarch, Leopold II, who believed in restoring the enlightened values of the city, and had music and the the-atre close to his heart. In the short reign of Leopold II from 1790 to 1792 much was changed, much was transformed, and as John Rice has pointed out, this was a period which began to create the musical life of early nineteenth-century Vienna:

> The debuts of Leopold's Italian ballet and *opera seria* troupes less than a month before Mozart's death intro-duced the Viennese to new genres and new musicians. A decree promulgated by Leopold in March 1791 permit-ting the performance of orchestrally accompanied church music was one manifestation of a revival of church music, of which Mozart's Requiem, commissioned a few months later, was but one product. The year of Leopold's death saw the arrival in Vienna of two musicians who would do more to shape Viennese music during the next decade than any others. Haydn, still to write his late masses and oratorios, returned from his first trip to London, and Beethoven arrived from Bonn.

So there was a profoundly forward-looking atmosphere in the city. And for Mozart, the year was filled with activity. To write two operas at once must be difficult at the best of times, but in the middle of 1791 Mozart found himself under enormous pressure to deal simultaneously with two pressing commissions. The operas could scarcely have been more different: a German opera with spoken text in the tradition of the Singspiel, for a raucously popular house in the Vienna suburbs; and an *opera seria* for the coronation of the new Emperor in Prague, dealing with a historical story in elevated terms, and attempting to modernise the whole apparatus of ancient opera. It seems that Mozart crammed the writing of *La clemenza di Tito* into a very short period in interludes of writing *Die Zauberflöte*; on 2 July he reminds Constanze in a letter to tell 'that idiot Süssmayr' to send him back the outline score of the first act 'so that I can orchestrate it'. After the premiere of *Tito* on 6 September, which was poorly received, he rushed back to Vienna to complete *Zauberflöte*, and entered the final two numbers, the opening march of Act II and the overture, in his thematic catalogue for 28 September. The premiere took place on Friday 30 September, and Mozart could feel confident that the piece was an enormous success. Songs from the opera were advertised for publication. He took friends to subsequent performances, including Salieri and Cavalieri. There followed the Clarinet Concerto, and on 15 November a small Masonic cantata. According to Mozart's own catalogue of his works, because the Requiem was never finished, the rest is silence. He rehearsed some parts of the score with friends at his bedside on 4 December. On Monday 5 December, at 12.55 a.m., Mozart died.

- Haydn *L'anima del filosofo* composed London (not performed until 1951); Symphonies Nos. 93–96
- Czerny born
- Meyerbeer born
- Boswell's *Life of Johnson*

- Mirabeau, French President, dies in April

- Louis XVI stopped at Varennes and brought back to Paris
- Leopold II asks countries to support Louis XVI
- Austria's and Prussia's Declaration of Pillnitz
- National Assembly dissolved
- United States Bill of Rights confirmed
- *The Observer* first published

Mozart's singers

Mozart, like any good eighteenth-century composer, wrote specific music for specific singers. Time and again we read of his need to adjust his music to those who were going to perform it, and this was a natural task, not an unwelcome one. As Patricia Gidwitz has written, 'Every opera composer and poet during the late eighteenth century was a pragmatist, continually reworking his conceptions to fit constantly fluctuating conditions.' 'If a singer was incapable of singing the piece, or uncomfortable with it in any way, most late eighteenth-century composers willingly changed it.' The 'vocal profiles' of Mozart singers are hence extremely important, for it was their idiom that helped to create his style, their range that gave him the limits within which to work, their expressive abilities that coloured what he could write. Mozart wrote of Anton Raaff, his first Idomeneo: 'I'll change the aria for him so that he will enjoy singing it, for I like an aria to fit the singer like a well-made garment.'

In the case of his piano concertos Mozart was the creator; in the case of his vocal music Mozart worked tirelessly with his singers to be the co-creator, to realise something that they could both own. Here are a few of the singers for whom Mozart wrote, usually more than once, with the roles or arias they created:

JOHANN ADAMBERGER (1743–1804)
Belmonte (*Entführung* premiere), Vogelsang (*Schauspieldirektor*
premiere), arias K420 and K431, tenor in *Davidde penitente*
A light, somewhat nasal tenor, who also sang in operas by Gluck, Sacchini and Righini. A fellow Freemason with Mozart, he later sang in England at the King's Theatre, London. Mozart admired him, but Charles Burney said damningly that with a better voice he would have been a fine singer.

FRANCESCO ALBERTARELLI (?1760–?1820)

Don Giovanni (*Don Giovanni* Vienna premiere), 'Un bacio di mano'
K541 for an Anfossi opera

He also sang in Italian operas by Salieri and Paisiello in
Vienna, and then went to London in 1791 to sing for Johann
Salomon.

ANNA LUCIA DE AMICIS (1733–1816)

Guinia (*Lucio Silla* premiere)

'Elegant and graceful', according to Burney. 'She sings and
acts like an angel,' wrote Leopold Mozart. She was at the
King's Theatre in London in 1762, singing Galuppi and J. C.
Bach, and then moved to Italy where the Mozarts met her;
they became friends and Mozart created for her a fine imposing role in his *opera seria Lucio Silla*.

ANTONIO BAGLIONI (1760–?1820)

Ottavio (*Don Giovanni*), Tito (*La clemenza di Tito*)

A Prague singer, also well known as a teacher, praised by Da
Ponte but, perhaps surprisingly, not mentioned by Mozart

LUIGI BASSI (1766–1825)

Don Giovanni (*Don Giovanni* premiere), Count (*Figaro* Prague)

He also sang in Martín y Soler's very popular *Un cosa rara*,
which is quoted in *Don Giovanni*. He sang in Leipzig, Vienna
and Warsaw, and then moved to Dresden.

FRANCESCO BENUCCI (?1745–1824)

Guglielmo (*Così* premiere), Figaro (*Figaro* premiere), Leporello
(*Don Giovanni* Vienna premiere)

He joined the Italian opera company in Vienna and sang in
operas by Salieri, Paisiello and Sarti. A *buffo* baritone praised
by Mozart; Michael Kelly recalled in later years Benucci
rehearsing 'Non piu andrai' in *Figaro* to Mozart's delight.

CATERINA BONDINI (?–?)

Zerlina (*Don Giovanni*), Susanna (*Figaro* Prague)

She was the wife of the impresario Pasquale Bondini who presented *Figaro* in Prague and then commissioned *Don Giovanni*. A story from the double-bass player of the *Giovanni* orchestra says that Mozart got her to scream convincingly as Zerlina by pinching her violently.

DOROTEA SARDI BUSSANI (1763–1810)

Cherubino (*Figaro* premiere), Despina (*Così* premiere)

She was a comic *buffa* soprano, successful in the Italian company in Vienna singing Martín y Soler, Cimarosa and Paisiello. She then travelled to Italy and Lisbon, and appeared at the King's Theatre, London, though she was by then past her prime.

FRANCESCO BUSSANI (1743–1807)

Don Bartolo/Antonio (*Figaro* premiere), Commendatore/Masetto (*Don Giovanni* Vienna premiere), Alfonso (*Così* premiere)

A successful baritone/bass who sang in many Italian operas in Vienna by Salieri, Paisiello and others, and also managed the double bill of Salieri and Mozart staged for the visiting ambassadors at Schönbrunn. He is blamed by Da Ponte for the attempt to suppress the dance in Act III of *Figaro*, which may be fictional but provided the basis for a good scene in *Amadeus*.

VINCENZO CALVESI (?–?)

Ferrando (*Così* premiere), and two ensembles written by Mozart for Bianchi's *La villanelle rapita*, K479 and K480

A lyric tenor in the Vienna company, who had great success in operas by Paisiello, Salieri, Bianchi and Martín y Soler.

CATERINA CAVALIERI (1755–1801)

Constanze (*Entführung* premiere), Silberklang (*Schauspieldirektor* premiere), Elvira (*Don Giovanni* Vienna premiere), Countess (*Figaro* Vienna 1789), soprano in *Davidde penitente*.

Cavalieri was an outstanding soprano who sang first in the

German company in Vienna, and then in the Italian repertory. Mozart wrote some of his most brilliant music for what
he called her 'supple throat', but she was extremely demanding and especially for her he had to add a new scene to *Don
Giovanni* and rewrite 'Dove sono' in *Figaro*. She was Salieri's
pupil and mistress, but there is nothing to support the notion
in *Amadeus* that she was also Mozart's mistress.

FRANCESCO CECCARELLI (1752–1814)

Recitative and aria 'A questo seno deh vieni' K374

A Salzburg castrato who sang in Mozart's church music and at
concerts for the Archbishop; he later sang in Italy and settled
in Dresden.

CELESTE COLTELLINI (1760–1829)

Ensembles for Bianchi's *La villanelle rapita*, K479 and K480

A soprano, the daughter of one of Mozart's Italian librettists,
especially prized for her acting by Joseph II. She was the
soprano in the Bianchi opera for which Mozart wrote new
ensembles, and she subsequently married a friend of the
Mozarts from Lyon.

VINCENZO DAL PRATO (1756–1828)

Idamante (*Idomeneo* premiere)

A Munich castrato, for whom Mozart did not have a good
word. He said he had to sing along with him 'for he needs to
learn his whole part as if he were a child . . . quite hopeless . . .
no intonation at all'.

JOSEPHA DUSCHEK (1754–1824)

Arias 'Ah lo previdi' K272, 'Bella mia fiamma' K528

The Duscheks had connections in Salzburg and became close
friends of the Mozarts, welcoming them to Prague in 1787.
Mozart wrote the fine concert aria 'Bella mia fiamma' for
Josepha there, and she toured with him to Leipzig and
Dresden in 1789. The Duschek house in Prague is now a
Mozart museum.

GUGLIELMO D'ETTORE (?1740–71)
Mitridate (*Mitridate* premiere)
An Italian tenor who caused the Mozarts a great deal of
trouble; he had to have his music rewritten several times,
with virtuosic top Cs, and apparently intrigued against
Mozart. (Leopold recalled this in a letter to his son much
later, so it must have been especially bad.)

ADRIANA FERRARESE DEL BENE (?1755–?99)
Susanna (*Figaro* Vienna 1789), Fiordiligi (*Così* premiere), arias 'Al
desio' K577 and 'Un moto di gioia' K579 (both new for the Vienna
revival of *Figaro*)
She was seen in London, and sang in Gluck and Soler operas.
She was a fine singer but reportedly a very static actress;
Daniel Heartz has pointed out how the new arias Mozart
wrote for her in *Figaro* are significantly less dramatic and
action-filled than the ones they replace. In *Così* he made a
virtue of her rock-like stature. She became Da Ponte's mistress and they had to leave Vienna in 1791 after a scandal;
even he said she had a 'somewhat violent character'.

JOHANN [KARL] LUDWIG FISCHER (1745–1825)
Osmin (*Entführung* premiere), arias 'Non so d'onde viene' K512
and 'Così dunque tradisci' K432
The most famous bass in Germany, with an exceptionally wide
range, which Mozart used to the full. 'One must make good use
of such a man, especially as he is such a favourite with audiences
here,' Mozart wrote on 26 September 1781. Fischer came to
Vienna and had great success, and then sang around Europe.

FRANZ XAVER GERL (1764–1827)
Sarastro (*Zauberflöte* premiere), aria 'Per questa bella mano' K612
He was a bass member of Schikaneder's company, who
joined Mozart at his deathbed for a sing-through of parts of
the Requiem. Also sang Osmin in *Entführung* with great
success, and both Giovanni and Figaro in German versions
of those operas after Mozart's death. His wife Barbara Gerl

was Papagena (*Zauberflöte* premiere).

ANNA GOTTLIEB (1774–1856)

Barbarina (*Figaro* premiere), Pamina (*Zauberflöte* premiere)

She was a young soprano from a theatrical family who was only twelve when she sang Barbarina, and went on to appear in the first performance of *Zauberflöte* with Schikaneder's company. She was still alive when the first Mozart memorial in Salzburg was unveiled in 1842, but cut such an eccentric figure that people thought she was mad when she claimed to have been the first Pamina.

MICHAEL KELLY (1762–1826)

Curzio/Basilio (*Figaro* premiere)

Kelly is one of Mozart's most famous singers, yet sang in only one of his premieres. A *buffo* tenor from Ireland, he found success in Vienna and later in England. He sang in Salieri's *La scuola de gelosi*, at the launch of the Italian opera company, and in operas by Cimarosa, Sarti and Paisiello. Though his connection with Mozart was limited to one opera, his *Recollections* of 1826 have preserved a fund of enjoyable but not totally reliable stories about the composer. 'Madame Mozart told me that great though his genius was, he was an enthusiast in dancing, and often said that his taste lay in that art ... He was a remarkably small man, very thin and pale, with a profusion of fine hair, of which he was rather vain.' We can blame Kelly for the prevalence in England of stories about Mozart's fondness for billiards, and punch, 'of which beverage I have seen him take copious drafts'. He is amusing on the discussions over Curzio's stutter in the *Figaro* ensembles.

ALOYSIA LANGE (1760–1839)

Mme Herz (*Schauspieldirektor* premiere), Anna (*Don Giovanni* Vienna premiere), arias 'Alcandro, lo confesso' K294, 'Popoli de Tessaglia' K316, 'Nehmt meinen Dank' K383, 'Mia speranza adorata' K416, 'Vorrei spiegarvi' K 418, 'No, no, che non sei capace' K419, 'Ah se in ciel' K538

Aloysia or Aloisia Weber was the elder of the Weber daughters whom Mozart met in Mannheim, and his first serious love. She was the inspiration of some of his finest music. The concert arias make use of her silvery, perfectly focused voice which could rise above the stave to unparalleled heights. He wanted to marry her but she rejected him, and he turned instead to her sister Constanze.

She also took over the part of Constanze (*Entführung*) in Vienna and probably the soprano part in Mozart's Handel arrangements, certainly that of *Messiah*. She married Joseph Lange, whose unfinished portrait of Mozart is probably the best likeness we have, but they separated in 1795. She remained poor, and claimed to the Novellos that Mozart had loved her until he died.

LUISA LASCHI-MOMBELLI (?1766–?90)

Countess (*Figaro* premiere), Zerlina (*Don Giovanni* Vienna premiere)

She was the daughter of a singer for whom Mozart had written in *La finta semplice*, and became a much-praised singer of Italian opera in Vienna. 'What other singer is capable of producing such melting, marvellously smooth singing with such simplicity and genuine emotion?' wrote one review. She sang a surprising combination of Mozart roles, for the Countess was generally sung by *seria* singers like Cavalieri, and Zerlina by *buffa* singers.

STEFANO MANDINI (1750–?1810)

Count (*Figaro* premiere)

Although the role of the Count is a baritone, Mandini had first cultivated tenor roles in Vienna, including Almaviva in Paisiello's *Il barbiere di Siviglia* (which Michael Kelly also sang), and indeed it seems that the crossover between the two voices was more frequent than today; the ranges were restricted and it has even been suggested that 'tenor' described a vocal colouring rather than a precise range. His wife Maria Mandini was Marcellina (*Figaro* premiere).

GIOVANNI MANZUOLI (?1720–82)
Ascanio (*Ascanio in Alba* premiere)

An Italian castrato who had great success in operas by J. C.
Bach and others at the King's Theatre, London, in 1764–5;
there he met the Mozarts on their travels. Later in Italy he
came out of retirement to sing Ascanio for Mozart, but there
was a dispute over money and he flounced off, behaving, as
Mozart wrote, 'like a true castrato'.

MARIA MARCHETTI-FANTOZZI (1767–?1807)
Vitellia (*Tito* premiere)

She sang in Naples, Milan and then in Prague for *La clemenza di Tito*, in which her performance was approved by
Leopold II; she had one of Mozart's finest obbligato arias
with clarinet.

FRANCESCO MORELLA (?–?)
Ottavio (*Don Giovanni* Vienna premiere)

A lyric tenor, he had sung, like other Mozart singers, in
Paisiello's *Il barbiere di Siviglia*; but he lacked coloratura, so
when *Don Giovanni* was performed in Vienna, Mozart
replaced 'Il mio tesoro' with the simpler 'Dalla sua pace':
tenors today tend to want to include both arias.

JOHANN JOSEPH NONSEUL (1742–1821)
Monostatos (*Zauberflöte* premiere)

A theatre manager and actor as well as singer, he was first a
member of the Burgtheater company and then became part
of Schikaneder's theatrical circle. It is interesting that the part
of Monostatos should have been designed for someone who
was more an actor than a singer.

ANTON RAAFF (1714–97)
Idomeneo (*Idomeneo* premiere), aria 'Se al labbro mio' K295

A close friend and supporter of Mozart's, who may have been
influential in obtaining the commission for *Idomeneo*. Mozart
wrote the grand title role in the opera for him, by which time

Raaff's voice was past its best. Leopold described him as a 'god-fearing and honest man'; Mozart recognised that his voice was past its peak, but said that 'in bravura singing, longer passages and roulades he is superb'. He wrote for him in *Idomeneo* without restraint, and Mozart enjoyed his work even though his acting was poor. He also sang in Paris at the concert which included Mozart's 'Paris' Symphony.

VENANZIO RAUZZINI (1746–1810)

Cecilio (*Lucio Silla* premiere), *Exsultate jubilate* K165

He is the Milan castrato for whom Mozart wrote one of his most popular pieces. The motet, with its famous concluding 'Alleluia', followed his success onstage in *Lucio Silla*. On that occasion he apparently engineered extra applause by claiming he suffered stage-fright. Later he settled in England, where he sang at the King's Theatre and then ran concerts in Bath.

TERESA SAPORITI (1763–1869)

Anna (*Don Giovanni* premiere)

She was a member of Bondini's company who sang in Leipzig and Dresden as well as in Prague. She then worked in Italy and St Petersburg, and lived for over a century.

BENEDICT SCHACK (1758–1826)

Tamino (*Zauberflöte* premiere)

A minor composer of sacred music as well as a singer, Schack was part of Schikaneder's company and appeared as Ottavio in the German *Don Giovanni* after Mozart's death. He sang through parts of the Requiem with Mozart on his deathbed. He wrote warmly of Constanze's relationship with her husband in a later letter to her. His wife Elisabeth Schack was the Third Lady (*Zauberflöte* premiere).

EMANUEL SCHIKANEDER (1751–1812)

Papageno (*Zauberflöte* premiere)

The ebullient librettist of *Zauberflöte*, and the manager of the company that commissioned and produced it. He began his

career as an actor, but moved into management and presented Singspiels and operas at the Freyhaustheater in Vienna,
where he created a genuinely popular company. He said that
he and Mozart worked closely together on the opera, and
they were certainly drinking companions. In the *Zauberflöte*
premiere, his older brother Urban sang the First Priest and
Urban's daughter Anna sang the First Boy. He was a great
impresario, who suffered later in life from mental illness.

NANCY (ANNA) STORACE (1765–1817)
Susanna (*Figaro* premiere), aria 'Ch'io mi scordi di te' K505
She was an English singer who studied in London with the
castrato Rauzzini and then enjoyed huge success in Italy. She
came to the Vienna Burgtheater as part of the newly formed
Italian company, which was launched with Salieri's *La scuola
di' gelosi*, and sang in operas by Cimarosa, Sarti and Soler as
well as in two operas by her brother Stephen Storace. She
returned to London, where she sang at the King's Theatre.
Her private life was unhappy; she left her husband and had an
affair with her Figaro, Benucci; she toured with another
lover, the tenor John Braham, but they too separated. Mozart
remained on friendly terms with the family.

GIOVANNI VALESI (1735–1816)
Priest (*Idomeneo* premiere), perhaps Contino del Belfiore (*Finta
giardiniera* premiere)
A German tenor and teacher who adopted an Italian name;
he worked in Munich and taught Adamberger and also Carl
Maria von Weber; Mozart praised both his singing and his
teaching.

LOUISE VILLENEUVE (?–?)
Dorabella (*Così* premiere), arias 'Alma grande' K578 for a Cimarosa
opera, 'Chi sa, qual sia' K582 and 'Vado ma dove?' K583 for a
Martín y Soler opera.
Sometimes thought to be the sister of Ferrarese del Bene, the
first Fiordiligi, she had a distinctive style which Mozart

explores to perfection in Dorabella's music and the insertion arias. She was credited in one review with 'charming appearance, refined expressive acting . . . beautiful, stylish singing'. She was also rumoured to be beloved by Leopold II.

DOROTHEA WENDLING (1736–1811)
Ilia (*Idomeneo* premiere), aria 'Basta vincesti' K295a

The Wendlings were a highly musical family whom Mozart got to know in Mannheim. Dorothea came from a family of professional musicians and married the flautist Johann Baptist Wendling. For Ilia in *Idomeneo* Mozart wrote a special aria with beautiful concertante wind parts, one of which would have been played by her husband. She was highly praised for 'true singing: the language of the soul and the heart'. For her daughter Elizabeth Augusta Wendling, Mozart wrote two songs, 'Oiseaux si tous les ans' K307 and 'Dans un bois solitaire' K308.

Mozart's patrons

ARCHBISHOP SIEGMUND CHRISTOPH, COUNT SCHRATTENBACH (1698–1771)

Mozart's first patron and supporter in Salzburg, his father's employer. A supporter of the arts who encouraged the Mozart family travels, but was lavish with the court resources and left large debts. Appointed the young Wolfgang as assistant Konzertmeister of the court, an unpaid post.

ARCHBISHOP HIERONYMOUS, COUNT COLLOREDO (1732–1812)

Mozart's far less sympathetic employer in Salzburg from 1772, for whom he wrote mainly church music; subject of many furious Mozartian complaints. Mozart dismissed himself from his service in 1781. Outside the demonology of Mozart biography, he is regarded as an enlightened and strong ruler who restored financial stability after the excesses of his more artistic predecessor.

COUNTESS MARIA WILHELMINE THUN (1744–1800)

She was one of Mozart's keenest patrons in his early years in Vienna; he often visited the Thuns' home, played through operas to her as he was composing them, and dedicated the 'Linz' Symphony to her father-in-law. 'She is the most charming and delightful lady I have met in my whole life, and she also thinks highly of me,' wrote Mozart. However after 1782 she features less often in his activities.

BARON GOTTFRIED VAN SWIETEN (1733–1803)

One of the Mozart's most tireless supporters in Vienna and a musical connoisseur whose taste was highly regarded. He was a diplomat and director of the court library in Vienna from 1777 until the day of Mozart's death. He reintroduced Mozart to the music of Bach, which was heard at Sunday-morning gatherings at his house. When Mozart had few commissions at the end of the 1780s, van Swieten asked him to rescore pieces by Handel for his performances. He later became close to Haydn, and was involved in compiling the texts of *The Creation* and *The Seasons*.

COUNT KARL JOSEPH FIRMIAN (1716–82)

Austrian resident in Italy, exceptionally learned diplomat, who took care of the Mozarts when they arrived in Italy and introduced them in social circles. Mozart wrote arias for a concert at his house, and Firmian ensured him the commission for *Mitridate*.

CARDINAL COUNT LAZZARO OPIZIO PALLAVICINI (1719–85)

Ensured the young Mozart his Order of the Golden Spur and an audience with the Pope.

SIEGMUND HAFFNER (1699–1772)

Salzburg friend and city mayor until his death in 1772, whose family became close friends of Mozart. When his daughter married in 1776, Mozart wrote the 'Haffner' Serenade, and when his son was ennobled in 1782 he wrote the 'Haffner' Symphony. But Siegmund did not live to see either occasion or hear either piece.

COUNTESS MARIA LODRON (1738–86)

Commissioned divertimenti for family occasions; Mozart wrote the Concerto for three pianos for her and her daughters to play.

COUNT JOHANN BAPTIST ESTERHÁZY (1748–1800)

A Vienna Freemason and friend of van Swieten's, he was the imperial and royal chamberlain and court councillor. His palace was the scene of some of Mozart's most successful subscription concerts in 1783 and 1784. Mozart's Handel arrangements were also heard there in 1788 and 1789.

PRINCE DIMITRI GALITZIN (1721–93)
The Russian ambassador in Vienna, at whose house Mozart often performed. He reported that the Prince always sent a coach to collect him and take him home.

BARON FRIEDRICH MELCHIOR VON GRIMM (1723–1807)
Important supporter of Mozart, with whom he had a turbulent relationship. He had helped the family during their early stay in Paris and wrote enthusiastically of Mozart's skills. But when Wolfgang and his mother returned in 1778 he found Grimm far less congenial and said that he was able to help 'children but not grown-up people'. Grimm complained to Leopold in immortal words that he wished Mozart had half as much talent and twice as many social skills.

EMPEROR JOSEPH II (1741–90)
Controversial ruler of the Austrian people, eventually worn down by the lack of success of his ambitious reforms. He was a keen musician, and took a great interest in singers. He knew Mozart throughout his life, from the early appearance in Vienna in 1762, and may have recommended him as an opera composer in 1768. After Mozart settled in Vienna, he attended performances and eventually appointed Mozart as *Kammermusicus* in 1787. But this was a modest post, for which Mozart wrote dances for the court balls. Joseph's operatic reforms and the balance between German and Italian opera in Vienna had a major influence on Mozart's work. He appreciated Mozart's work with reservations; the oft-repeated line 'too many notes, my dear Mozart!' may well sum up both his affection and puzzlement at Mozart's complexities. But his relationship with Mozart was not as close as it is entertainingly portrayed in *Amadeus*.

PRINCE CARL VON LICHNOWSKY (1756–1814)
A pupil of Mozart's, who supported him and invited him in 1790 to travel with him to Prague, Dresden and Leipzig, where Mozart gave largely unsuccessful concerts. There

seems to have been some financial problem between them, for Mozart lent him some money on the trip, and it recently emerged that Mozart was sued by him in court and ordered to pay 1,435 gulden and 32 kroner to the Prince on 12 November 1791, less than a month before his death. Lichnowsky, who subsequently became an important patron of Beethoven, was rumoured to live beyond his means, so his trip with Mozart may have been a case of the blind leading the blind. The debt was not pursued after Mozart's death.

COUNT JOSEPH NEPOMUK VON DEYM (1752–1804)
The Count who commissioned the fantasias for mechanical organ from Mozart, to grace his waxwork museum in Vienna. Mozart hated writing them, but nonetheless produced masterpieces.

COUNT FRANZ WALSEGG-STUPPACH (1763–1827)
The mysterious Count who commissioned the Requiem from Mozart in memory of his recently deceased wife. He used to commission works which he either passed off as his own, or performed anonymously, hoping that those who heard might think he wrote them.

Mozart's composer contemporaries

CARL FRIEDRICH ABEL (1723–87)
Part of the London scene when the Mozarts visited in
1764–5; friend of J. C. Bach, with whom he collaborated on
the Bach–Abel concerts, and a viola da gamba player. His
music in the early galant symphonic style taught Mozart a
great deal: Mozart's K18 symphony is a revised version of
Abel's symphony Op. 7 No. 6.

ANTON ADLGASSER (1729–77)
Court organist at Salzburg from 1762. His third wife, Maria,
sang in Mozart's early works. He supplied the third part of
the oratorio *Die Schuldigkeit des ersten Gebots* K35, for which
Mozart and Michael Haydn wrote the other two parts.
Mozart described him to his Bologna mentor Padre Martini
as 'an excellent master of counterpoint'.

JOHANN ALBRECHTSBERGER (1736–1809)
Mozart knew and admired him in Vienna and considered his
organ playing the standard by which others should be judged.
He was a great admirer of J. S. Bach and copied out the '48'
Preludes and Fugues, music which Mozart also kept by him.
It is said that he arranged for Albrechtsberger to succeed him
as assistant Kapellmeister at St Stephen's after his death;
Albrechtsberger then became full Kapellmeister in 1793.

C. P. E. BACH (1714–88)
Admired by Mozart and his father, and by Baron van Swieten,
especially for his fugues. But unlike Johann Christian,
Mozart did not know him personally. It is actually in Mozart's
smaller keyboard pieces, especially the fantasias, that one
senses the impact of Bach's dramatic, improvisational style.

JOHANN CHRISTIAN BACH (1735–82)

Probably the composer (apart from Mozart's father) who had the most influence on Wolfgang's distinctive early style. His symphonies and concertos are closely reflected in Mozart's early works in those genres, and Mozart also admired his arias. They met in London on the Mozarts' first visit: Nannerl much later told the story that Johann Christian sat Wolfgang between his legs and they combined to improvise a sonata. Mozart then heard his music in Mannheim and they met again in Paris in 1778. 'You can easily imagine his delight and mine at meeting again; perhaps his delight may not have been quite as sincere as mine . . . there is no doubt he has praised me warmly, not only to my face, but to others also.'

LUDWIG VAN BEETHOVEN (1770–1827)

In 1787 Beethoven reportedly came to Vienna and played to Mozart, but is there any real evidence that they met? Mozart may have heard him play, but in any case Beethoven did not stay in the city longer than two weeks. The Mozart biography by Otto Jahn, who knew Czerny, says that Beethoven improvised and Mozart said to his friends, 'Keep your eye on him; one day he will give the world something to talk about.' And Beethoven later said to Czerny that Mozart's keyboard playing was 'choppy', better suited to the harpsichord than the fortepiano.

GEORG BENDA (1722–95)

The Bendas were an outstanding family of Bohemian musicians. Georg Benda left Bohemia for Prussia and became the Kapellmeister to Duke Friedrich III of Saxe-Gotha. He was in Vienna briefly in 1778–9 and also visited Mannheim, where Mozart saw his innovative melodramas, which consisted of spoken speech over or alternating with dramatic orchestral music. Mozart was so taken with *Medea* that he wrote to his father that all recitative ought to be composed thus, and carried the piece around with him.

FRANZ XAVER BRIXI (1732–71)

The Brixis were another extensive family of musicians, and Franz Xaver was active in Prague, where he wrote a huge amount of music and was widely respected. It is said that the influence of the family helped to ensure Mozart a favourable reception in Prague in the 1780s, and we know that Mozart improvised on themes from his organ music when in the city.

DOMENICO CIMAROSA (1749–1801)

One of the most influential and successful composers of Italian opera in the second half of the eighteenth century. His works were often performed in Vienna, and had a crucial influence on the development of operatic style. *Il matrimonio segreto* sounds extremely close to Mozart's mature style and Mozart wrote an aria for his opera *I due baroni* in 1789. Cimarosa's concertos also follow the Mozartian model. The story is told that when a painter told Cimarosa he was a greater composer than Mozart, he replied, 'Sir, what would you say to a man who told you that you were greater than Raphael?'

MUZIO CLEMENTI (1752–1832)

A brilliant pianist whose talents were recognised by Joseph II; a competition took place between him and Mozart in December 1781. Mozart rated his piano playing, up to a point ('he has great facility with his right hand. His star passages are thirds'), but thought he lacked all taste and feeling: 'he is a mere *mechanicus*.' He later declared Clementi's sonatas 'worthless', though they were very important in developing the English piano idiom inspired by Broadwood pianos (which Mozart, who liked Stein's Viennese pianos, did not explore).

JOHANN ERNST EBERLIN (1702–62)

Admired Salzburg composer of church music, who was court and cathedral Kapellmeister during Mozart's early youth in Salzburg. He was friendly with Leopold Mozart, who did not, however, succeed him when he died in 1762. Wolfgang continued to refer to and learn from his contrapuntal church music, but having asked for some fugues to be sent to Vienna for possible use at Baron van Swieten's gatherings, then decided they were too trivial to stand beside Bach and Handel.

JOHANN GOTTFRIED ECKARD (1735–1809)

The Mozarts came to know him on their visit to Paris in 1763–4, and Wolfgang made use of his style in some of his early works, including Eckard's Op. 1 No. 1 in his accompanied sonata K6. He was one of the composers whose music Leopold suggested Wolfgang orchestrate in his early keyboard concertos.

JOSEPH EYBLER (1765–1846)

He was distantly related to the Haydns, and studied in Vienna, where Joseph Haydn supported him and he served Mozart as an assistant in preparing the premiere of *Così fan tutte*. He also helped Mozart in his last illness, and was the first composer whom Constanze asked to complete the Requiem. But though he made a start, he gave up after adding a few notes to the incomplete Lacrimosa. He wrote large-scale music of his own and eventually succeeded Salieri as Hofkapellmeister in 1824.

CHRISTOPH WILLIBALD VON GLUCK (1714–87)

The major influence in reforming opera in the eighteenth century, whose works had a huge influence on the course of operatic development. Mozart would have seen *Alceste*, which clearly lies behind *Idomeneo*, and the *Iphigénie* operas, but he may have been ambivalent about the older man's music, for he never praises it in his letters. Leopold tried to get Gluck's support for a commission for the young Mozart, but it is not clear whether Gluck actually supported the project. Mozart's biographer Niemetschek says that when Mozart was in Vienna his 'intercourse with [Gluck] and ceaseless study of his exalted works gave Mozart much sustenance and influ-

enced his operas'. We know that Gluck attended at least one
Mozart concert, praised the music, and invited him to lunch,
and that Mozart wrote variations on a theme of Gluck, K455.

FRANÇOIS-JOSEPH GOSSEC (1734–1829)

'He is a very good friend of mine and at the same time a very
dull fellow,' wrote Mozart to his father. An important figure
in Parisian musical life, whose works were widely performed,
he was closely associated with the opera and the Concert
Spirituel.

JOHANN ADOLF HASSE (1699–1783)

One of the greatest opera composers of his day, but almost forgotten since. He was born in Hamburg, and worked in
Dresden and then extensively in Italy. He is thus a link between
J. S. Bach, whose music was known in Dresden, and the young
Mozart. After having written many operas, he came out of
retirement to compose the opera *Il Ruggiero* for the same occasion as Mozart's *Ascanio in Alba* K111, the wedding of Archduke
Ferdinand to Beatrice d'Este. But it was not a happy experience, as it 'had on the first evening all those mishaps that could
possibly occur to damage a theatrical production': Leopold
Mozart reported home that 'Wolfgang's serenata has killed
Hasse's opera more than I can say.' And Mozart's operas have
continued to kill Hasse's in the repertory.

JOSEPH HAYDN (1732–1809)

The relationship between Haydn and Mozart is a very rare
example of mutual and unfeigned admiration between two of
the leading composers of the day, each of whom learnt from
and respected the other. From symphonic works to operatic
finales to piano pieces, the interchange of ideas can be
explored. Mozart especially admired Haydn's string quartets,
and dedicated his six 'Haydn' Quartets to him. It was on the
occasion when some of these works were played through that
Haydn praised Mozart to his father, as the latter proudly
recalled (see p. 225).

MICHAEL HAYDN (1737–1806)

Joseph Haydn's younger brother and Mozart's favourite contemporary in Salzburg. He was a choirboy in Vienna and became Hofmusicus at Salzburg in 1763, where he would have had constant contact with the young Mozart, and then succeeded him as cathedral organist when Mozart left for Vienna. Wolfgang played his music often, and wrote to his sister Nannerl from Italy: 'I like Haydn's six minuets better than the first twelve. We have often had to perform them.' He admired Michael Haydn's church music: when he became involved in Baron van Swieten's concerts in Vienna, he asked for copies of masses and vesper music. Two of the violin and viola duos seem to have been written by Mozart as a favour to Haydn when illness prevented him completing a commission. (Haydn also drank excessively, which was the cause of hilarity to Wolfgang and scandal to Leopold.) Finally, Haydn's fine Requiem in C minor contains significant pre-echoes of Mozart's Requiem.

IGNAZ HOLZBAUER (1711–83)

Holzbauer was a composer and conductor, and Kapellmeister at the Mannheim court; he stayed in Mannheim when the court moved to Munich. Mozart admired the music of his most famous opera, *Günter von Schwarzburg* ('what surprises me most of all is that a man as old as Holzbauer should still possess such spirit'), and also adapted one of his sacred works, a 'Miserere', for performance in Paris. Mozart liked his masses and fugues, which he interestingly described to Leopold as 'quite in our style'; Holzbauer also wrote progressive symphonies in the Mannheim idiom.

LEONTZI HONAUER (1737–?1790)

Alsatian harpsichordist and composer whose work the Mozarts encountered during their stay in Paris. Mozart adapted four movements from his Opp. 1 and 2 in his first four keyboard concertos, K37 and K39–41.

NICCOLÒ JOMMELLI (1714–74)

One of the most important composers of eighteenth-century opera. Mozart saw *Armida*, his last opera, and thought it was 'much too clever and old-fashioned for the theatre'.

LEOPOLD KOZELUCH (1747–1818)

He was a Czech composer who, according to Niemetschek, intrigued against Mozart in Prague (where he was based until his death). But Mozart wrote warmly of him in 1781 when he heard that Kozeluch would not take a job with the Archbishop of Salzburg because of the way he had treated Mozart. He was one of the first successful Vienna freelance composers. Some of his symphonies have been revived, and are lively and convincing works.

VICENTE MARTÍN Y SOLER (1754–1806)

A Spanish composer of Italian opera who worked in Italy, and moved to Vienna in 1785. He wrote three highly successful operas with Da Ponte, of which the most popular was *Una cosa rara*, briefly quoted in the finale of *Don Giovanni*. Several singers who sang in Mozart's operas also sang in his. Martín y Soler also worked in London and St Petersburg, where he died.

JOSEF MYSLIVEČEK (1737–81)

One of the composers about whom Mozart was most enthusiastic. He first met the family in 1770, and stayed in touch afterwards, even after Mysliveček was ill with venereal disease and disfigured by surgery. Mozart said he would always wish to visit him, and 'if it were not for his face, he would be the same old Mysliveček, full of fire, spirit and life . . . All Munich is talking about his oratorio *Abramo ed Isacco*.' This work is so close to Mozart's in style that it was attributed to him for some time. Mozart also recommended his keyboard sonatas as 'quite easy and pleasing to the ear'.

GIOVANNI PAISIELLO (1740–1816)

The most successful and influential composer of Italian opera in the second half of the eighteenth century. He wrote over eighty operas, working in St Petersburg and then in Naples, where he was extremely powerful. His works were popular in Vienna and he visited the city in 1784, according to Mozart: 'I am fetching Paisiello in my carriage, as I want him to hear both my pupil and my compositions.' His hugely successful *Il barbiere di Siviglia* had a clear impact on the development of Mozart's operatic style, especially on *Figaro*, though Mozart admitted to chatting throughout another of his operas. *Il re Teodoro in Venezia* was written for Vienna in 1784.

HERMANN RAUPACH (1728–78)

One of a German family of musicians. Though he spent most of his time in St Petersburg, he met the young Mozart in Paris; four movements from his sonatas were arranged by Mozart in his early keyboard concertos, K37 and K39–41.

ANTONIO SALIERI (1750–1825)

The most notorious composer to feature in Mozart's biography. His power and influence in Vienna during Mozart's time there was unchallenged, and he was called the 'musical pope'. Mozart refers more than once to intrigues by Salieri against him, but in the last weeks of his life Mozart took Salieri and his mistress to *Die Zauberflöte*, which he reported they much enjoyed. Salieri's operas were rather more successful in Paris than in Vienna, where he felt unfashionable and neglected after the death of Joseph II. It was the rumours of his last years, reported in Beethoven's conversation books, though publicly denied in the Viennese newspapers, that gave rise to the idea that Salieri guiltily claimed to have poisoned Mozart – doubtless just an exaggeration of the fact that he did little to support him, probably intrigued against him, and may later have felt mildly guilty at Mozart's untimely death. This then provided the fictional inspiration for Pushkin's duo-drama *Mozart and Salieri*, Rimsky-Korsakov's one-act opera, and

thence Shaffer's play. None of his music has securely established itself in the repertory, though it is quite frequently
revived, and some of the operas are performed; most recently, his *L'Europa riconosciuta*, the first work produced at La
Scala, Milan, was chosen by Riccardo Muti for the reopening
of the same theatre in 2004.

GIUSEPPE SARTI (1729–1802)

'Sarti is a good honest fellow; I played many pieces for him
and finally some variations on an aria of his, which pleased
him greatly,' wrote Mozart. In his last year Mozart wrote a
final chorus for Sarti's opera *Le gelosie villane*, K615, and
entered it in his catalogue for 20 April; but it has completely
disappeared. Sarti later violently criticised Mozart's 'Haydn'
Quartets for their barbarisms and dissonances (see p. 13), but
it is not clear if he knew who they were composed by when he
penned his denunciation.

JOHANN SCHOBERT (c.1735–1767)

One of Mozart's earliest works is an arrangement of a sonata
by Schobert, and he particularly liked his D major Sonata
Op. 3. Mozart continued to admire his music when in Paris;
his A minor Sonata K310 seems to quote Schobert. Leopold
Mozart was not impressed by him personally ('flatters to one's
face and is utterly false'); he died at about thirty-two from
eating poisonous mushrooms.

JOSEPH SCHUSTER (1748–1812)

Composer and conductor at the Dresden court; he made a habit
of acquiring new music from Vienna and so came across
Mozart's music. Mozart heard his music in Munich, and
Schuster's divertimentos for harpsichord and violin inspired
Mozart to try something in the same 'gusto' in 1777. One string
quartet he wrote was even attributed to Mozart for a time.

FRANZ XAVER SÜSSMAYR (1766–1803)

Mozart's pupil and friend who completed the Requiem, wrote

the recitatives for *La clemenza di Tito*, and also finished Mozart's Horn Concerto in D 'No. 1'. He came to Vienna in 1788 and assisted Mozart in the last couple of years of his life. He was a not inconsiderable composer, and it has always been a matter of controversy how much of the missing parts of the Requiem he wrote himself; Constanze Mozart, anxious to protect the authenticity of the work, maintained that he worked from Mozart's sketches and instructions, and her sister too claimed that Mozart told Süssmayr how to finish the piece, in which case it is odd that it was Eybler who was first asked to complete the score.

IGNAZ UMLAUF (1746–96)

Few composers roused Mozart to such contempt as the Viennese composer Umlauf, who was Kapellmeister to the German Singspiel company: 'execrable . . . the music is so bad I do not know whether the poet or the composer will carry off the prize for inanity' (which remark *The New Grove* describes as 'somewhat intolerant'). He must have been favoured by Van Swieten: he was continuo player in Mozart's performance of C. P. E. Bach's *Resurrection Oratorio* and then conducted Mozart's *Messiah* orchestration.

JOHANN BAPTIST VANHAL (1739–1813)

A successful Czech composer who lived in Vienna from 1780, and according to Michael Kelly played quartets with Mozart, Haydn and Dittersdorf. Mozart had played one of his violin concertos to great applause (according to him) in Augsburg in 1777. Vanhal's symphonies represent an important development in the form, particularly the forceful minor-mode works, and Mozart probably learnt from them.

ABBÉ GEORG JOSEPH VOGLER (1749–1814)

A very serious composer, organist and theoretician, who had considerable stature in Mannheim and Munich, but whom Mozart found to be 'a fool, who imagines that he is the very pitch of perfection'. Mozart accused him of being very clever at pulling strings, and said he was 'a trickster, pure and simple', whose organ playing produced 'an unintelligible muddle'.

GEORG CHRISTOPH WAGENSEIL (1715–77)

Mozart learnt some of his keyboard pieces in his earliest years, and their galant style influenced his early work. When Mozart visited Maria Theresa in 1762, he played a Wagenseil concerto and reportedly asked for the composer to come and turn pages for him because 'he understands'.

Performing Mozart today

> Pianists peep out from every corner. To a man, and at all
> ages, they are occupied with what seems to be the central
> aesthetic problem in music today: the creation of an
> acceptable style-convention for performing Mozart.
> Virgil Thomson

Mozart was above all a performer, and his music grew out of
that fact. This was not unusual in the eighteenth century:
indeed it was the normal experience for composers. But for
Mozart, the intensity and single-mindedness of his early
experiences as a child performer surely coloured all his subsequent composing life, and the way in which his composing
emerged from his much-praised keyboard playing is one key
to understanding his music. Whereas you can argue with
some composers (but not many) that their music has an
abstract nature which makes the question of performing
forces secondary, with Mozart everything grows from the
changing materials he had at his disposal: the superb wind
instrumentalists of the Mannheim court immediately stimu-
late a new independence for those lines in *Idomeneo*, the voice
of Aloysia Weber creates a new style in the stratospheric concert arias he wrote for her, and every new orchestral situation
Mozart found himself in created a new challenge and a new
way of writing, which is why the 'Paris' Symphony is perfectly crafted for Parisian taste, and the 'Prague' Symphony for
the players who would perform *Don Giovanni*.

Over recent generations Mozart has been at the focus of
changes in performing style that have radically affected the
whole of classical music. In the beginning, the 'early music
revival' was devoted to recreating forgotten instruments and
reviving forgotten repertory. But it soon moved on, and in
Mozart's case this meant a radical change: the prospect of
performances which did not assimilate him into the perform-

ing conventions of the nineteenth century but treated him as an eighteenth-century composer whose style grew out of the conventions of the baroque. With Mozart and then Beethoven, as with Bach and Handel, the period-instrument movement took on something the audience knew: familiar pieces that sounded radically different.

Ironically, the appeal to the public of new Mozart performances on modern instruments was considerable – for instance in the vivid piano concerto performances of Daniel Barenboim and the English Chamber Orchestra in the mid-1960s, just as the new wave of period-instrument playing was taking off. It was in the smaller-scale Mozart performances by artists such as Colin Davis, Neville Marriner and others that a glimpse of a new approach could be heard. But in a standard guide to Mozart recordings published as late as 1970 (by Brian Redfern, in Alec Hyatt King's *Mozart: A Concertgoer's Companion*), the natural recommendation for the complete symphonies was the Berlin Philharmonic conducted by Karl Böhm.

I can recall the first recordings that made me realise the benefits of a new approach to Mozart, just before we had classical-instrument orchestras that could grapple with these stylistic challenges. One was the oboist Michel Piguet's lovely recording of the Oboe Quartet on Telefunken's Das Alte Werk label, which appeared in 1977. That featured Jaap Schroeder's Esterhazy Quartet, whose 1973 recordings of Haydn's Op. 20 Quartets were revelatory. Already by that time Nikolaus Harnoncourt's Concentus Musicus Wien was making pioneering recordings of some early classical chamber repertory (by Mozart contemporaries such as J. C. Bach, Ignaz Holzbauer, Johann Stamitz and Franz Xaver Richter, a recording still available on Teldec 8.41062), and these recordings seemed to offer a breath of fresh air. I knew little about the actual historical basis of the sounds and playing techniques I heard: I was simply responding to the lightness, grace and passion of the playing, which was totally disarming. Quite quickly one became dissatisfied with the creamy, sustained sounds of orchestras treating the Mozart symphonies as if they were only upbeats to the Romantic repertory, and one longed for more air in their textures, more sharpness in the playing. The familiar long legato lines in the strings, gently sustained wind chords, and deftly moulded textures (Mozart from Vienna and Berlin, from Herbert von Karajan to Karl Böhm) sounded increasingly inadequate to match our contemporary understanding of Mozart.

The more one looked at Mozart's original scores, with their phrasings and articulations, the less like present-day performances they sounded. (George Barth has shown how profoundly nineteenth-century editions of Mozart with their added slurs and expression marks affected our understanding of his music.) This was not just a matter of historical accuracy; it was a matter of taste. But it was a taste that seemed to suit the music, and the temper of the times. Of course there were recordings of the time which modified the traditional style with verve and skill, but they did not have at all the same impact on the public. Following the experiments of the 1970s with baroque orchestras, the right moment had come to attempt to play Mozart's orchestral music on the instruments of the time.

Some of the most interesting early experiments came in the operatic field: in 1980 Harnoncourt recorded *Idomeneo*, not with his period-instrument Concentus Musicus but with the 'modern' musicians of the Zurich Opera House, in what turned out to be a hugely influential and original performance, with its emphasis on fierce attack, strong dynamic contrasts, and reduced vibrato in the strings, so that the impact of dissonances was increased. This was vivid, powerful music-making, which restored Mozart's status as more than a miniaturist. The first Mozart symphony cycle on original instruments, by the Academy of Ancient Music at the start of the 1980s, jointly led by Jaap Schroeder and Christopher Hogwood, cleverly began with the less well-known symphonies, but quickly (perhaps too quickly) moved on to the late masterpieces. Harnoncourt himself chose to work instead with the Concertgebouw Orchestra in Amsterdam (producing some thrilling large-scale accounts of the later symphonies) and then with the Chamber Orchestra of Europe (for smaller-scale accounts of those same symphonies, nothing quite beats the final trilogy recorded live during Mozart's bicentenary in 1991), moving back to record the earliest symphonies with the period instruments of Concentus Musicus.

The period-instrument groups were quick to follow Hogwood's lead, and already in the richer accounts of the early symphonies by Trevor Pinnock and the English Concert there is more of a link towards a traditional sound; Roger Norrington's early-1980s recordings with the London Classical Players were fiercely original and provocative; John Eliot Gardiner waited a while until the skills of the players had developed, and then produced arguably some of the finest performances of the middle and late symphonies later in the 1980s with his English Baroque Soloists. Another breakthrough was the revival of the early piano: the achievements of piano builders in creating copies of eighteenth-century instruments gave rise to a new generation of players who could make these instruments speak, as Malcolm Bilson's recordings of the sonatas for Nonesuch in the late 1970s were followed by Robert Levin's. From 1983 to 1988 Malcolm Bilson and John Eliot Gardiner recorded all the piano concertos together for DG Archiv, and then Levin began a series with Christopher Hogwood and the Academy of Ancient Music which unfortunately coincided with the end of the CD boom and was never finished.

The operatic dimension to these innovations continued with Decca's decision to record operas in performances from the Drottningholm Court Theatre under Arnold Östman from 1987 (I had seen *Figaro* there under him earlier in the decade and it was a revelation), and Glyndebourne's bold decision to use the new Orchestra of the Age of Enlightenment for its Da Ponte cycle with Simon Rattle from 1989 onwards. Norrington conducted *Idomeneo* for the

Boston Early Music Festival and *Zauberflöte* in London in 1989 on period instruments, and Gardiner made a whole series of opera recordings in the early 1990s, with orchestras that sounded more confident and brilliant than ever. In the United States, period-instrument orchestras began to experiment with the classical repertory, and there was a period-instrument *Figaro* in New Jersey in 1989, though the ambitious record-company project to set up a New York-based Classical Band to record under Trevor Pinnock never took off. Nevertheless, period-instrument performances quickly took their place among the preferred recordings in *Gramophone* magazine recommendations and BBC Radio 3's 'Building a Library' choices. The fashion of the times had changed very quickly. Doubtless my own choices of recordings in the pages that follow are influenced by the prevailing taste, and by the feeling of newly-minted discovery offered by period-style performances.

During the following decade and a half up to the present, as more and more 'traditional' orchestras and conductors have come to absorb, consciously or unconsciously, the insights of the period-instrument movement, and that movement has itself become much freer in its use of historical evidence, a new approach has begun to emerge. The Vienna Philharmonic, playing Mozart with Nikolaus Harnoncourt, Roger Norrington, John Eliot Gardiner or Simon Rattle, have decisively modified their style. (Of course they can still revert when certain other conductors stand in front of them, but that is their unequalled skill.) Under Rattle, the Berlin Philharmonic played Mozart's last three symphonies at the Salzburg Easter Festival in 2005, and Rattle will perform the same symphonies with the Vienna Philharmonic on the anniversary of Mozart's death in 2006. The future of Mozart performance may indeed be a new synthesis which brings the best of the new 'old' style to bear on the best of the old 'modern' style. We shall see.

MOZART: THE MUSIC

Symphonies

Mozart's symphonies (there are more than sixty of them, in spite of the last being known as No. 41) take us on an enthralling journey from the symphony as overture, entertainment and display to the symphony as complex, deeply argued expression – a development that opened the door to the nineteenth century's conception of the symphony as the pinnacle of abstract musical art. Across the course of Mozart's composing life the function of the symphony changed, and Mozart's technical skill and resourcefulness also developed. In contrast to the notion of the composer writing for his art alone, we can be sure that, as in the rest of his output, Mozart rarely if ever wrote a symphony for which he did not have a direct, immediate need and a likelihood of performance.

There are many difficulties with the transmission and authenticity of the earlier Mozart symphonies – some symphonies are attributed in manuscript copies to different composers or to none, and continue to drift in and out of the canon of accepted works, while others have been lost: modern discoveries such as K19a can be authenticated, while the 'Odense' symphony K16a has not been (see below). Another symphony perhaps by Mozart turned up early in 2005, and was to be performed in Vienna. Those still doubted by the leading scholar Cliff Eisen are listed here with a question mark, but they will sometimes occur on record credited to Mozart. There are other symphonies by Mozart not listed here, but recorded and occasionally played these days, including reductions of multi-movement serenades to four-movement symphonic form.

Symphony No. 1 in E flat K16*
Symphony No. 4 in D K19
Symphony in F K19a
Symphony No. 5 in B flat K22
?Symphony in F K76
Symphony No. 6 in F K43
Symphony No. 7 in D K45*

The conductor Nikolaus Harnoncourt, a veteran of Mozart performance, recently wrote how 'astounded – flabbergasted, in fact' his ensemble was when they came to record Mozart's earliest symphonies for the first time; their quality and originality shone through every page, and the poise and subtlety of the part-writing was immediately evident. However, others have suggested that in purely musical terms Mozart's early music is less mature than, say, Mendelssohn's at the same age. It is difficult, as the Mozart scholar Neal Zaslaw has emphasised, to disentangle the development of the symphony as a form from Mozart's own personal development as a composer. What is clear is that Wolfgang had a magpie-like ability to pick up and transform the ideas of others: his earliest symphonies show how perfectly he absorbed the style of composers whose music he would have heard while on tour – Johann Christian Bach and Carl Friedrich Abel in London, for instance.

Another factor in assessing these early works is the extent to which Mozart's father Leopold was active in encouraging, assisting and editing his son's earliest compositions. Symphony No. 1, dated London 1764, came from their stay in Ebury Street on their visit to London. According to Mozart's sister Nannerl, the first symphony was written while Leopold was confined to bed ill, yet it still shows signs of their father's hand in the scoring of the exuberant, confident music. The scoring does not quite match either, so maybe she was recalling one of the later works. In the E flat first movement, the contrast between the opening fanfare and subsequent quiet chord sequence begins a long line of such contrasted statement-and-reply openings in his major works, while the final presto has a surprisingly angular chromatic line. Symphony No. 4 sounds like an opera overture, with a central Andante which briefly tries imitation, first between two lines and then between all four – Mozart's baroque heritage, though it was to emerge more fully later in life, was never far away. The F major symphony K19a (which was known to exist from Leopold's catalogue of his son's early work) turned up in Munich in 1981 just in time to be incorporated into the New Mozart Edition.

The B flat symphony K22 buzzes with life, with a first movement propelled by trills in the violins, a dark G minor Andante (the key and mood of Pamina's lament in *Die Zauberflöte* over thirty years later) and a triple-time finale which also derives its energy from upward turns. The (perhaps authentic) F major symphony K76, which Eisen thinks is neither by Mozart nor his father, has the first appearance of a minuet and trio – soon to be indispensable in the four-movement symphonic form – in which the minuet is conventional, but the trio is distinctly quirky. The F major K43 includes a lovely slow movement taken from Mozart's early Latin opera *Apollo et Hyacinthus*, with muted first violins singing over pizzicato seconds and divided violas, a ravishing effect. The D major symphony K45 is dated 16 January 1768, and was adapted as the overture to his opera *La finta semplice*, making the link between early symphony and opera overture explicit (though the symphony's minuet and trio was not included in the opera version). The energy of the first movement is derived from its sharp contrasts and bounding bass lines, while the finale's dotted rhythms and relentless triplets give it an elated air of perpetual motion.

(The symphony K16a in A minor, which was listed with its initial theme in Breitkopf's catalogue and hence given a Köchel number, disappeared in the nineteenth century but turned up in Odense in 1983. It's a fine work, and was recorded by Hogwood in his Mozart symphony series which also included some other dubious symphonies, with a note by

Neal Zaslaw saying it almost certainly was not by Mozart. It is now agreed to be spurious, but is well worth hearing.)

🎧 *Complete Symphonies*
Academy of Ancient Music / Christopher Hogwood
Decca Oiseau-Lyre 452 496–2 (19 CDs)

Symphony No. 7a in G K45a*
?Symphony in B flat K45b
Symphony No. 8 in D K48
Symphony No. 9 in C K73

We don't need to worry here about the controversies that have surrounded the authorship of the G major symphony – if the opening sounds like anything to us, it will be the Schubert of 'Who is Sylvia?'! The three-movement structure is conventional and the music propelled by its harmonies. The B flat symphony K45b exists only in a copy and has tentatively been assigned by Neal Zaslaw to Salzburg around 1767 (the New Mozart Edition prefers Vienna 1768): its lilting triple-time Allegro points forward to the much more famous Symphony No. 39 in E flat. Because its opening movement is in triple time, the finale is not; it is a rather gracefully energetic Allegro. The D major symphony K48 is dated Vienna 13 December 1768, and is a ceremonial work with trumpets and drums. The C major symphony K73 is not so secure in its origin or dating, but Salzburg or Italy 1769–70 is the current consensus, and once again there are baroque echoes in the walking bass lines that strongly propel the first and last movements.

🎧 *Early symphonies (with readings of the letters)*
Concentus Musicus Wien / Nikolaus Harnoncourt
BMG DHM 82876 587066 2 (3 CDs)

Symphony No. 10 in G K74*
Symphony in F K75
?Symphony in D K81
?Symphony No. 11 in D K84
?Symphony in D K95
?Symphony in C K96
?Symphony in D K97

The G major symphony K74 seems to have been written in April 1770 during Mozart's visit to Rome (Alan Tyson showed it is written on the same paper as an aria composed there). It is full of sheer energy, driven by offbeat syncopations (like the opening of the fast section of the 'Prague' symphony) before it subsides into the quiet and untroubled central movement. There is something hypnotic about the repeated notes of the finale's rustic dance, with its echo of a pastoral bagpipe's drone. The Symphony in F K75 oddly has its minuet and trio as the second movement, for no evident musical reason; more fun is the folky finale. Musicologists have doubted but generally accepted K75 (and excluded K76); they are much less certain about K81, which is attributed to Leopold in some sources (though it gains admittance to the New Mozart Edition and thence to complete recordings of Mozart's music), and one is forced to admit there is little special about its suave and effective progress. The same is true of K84, which boasts varying attributions to Wolfgang, Leopold and Dittersdorf. Cliff Eisen urges caution about assuming K95–7 are Mozart's, because there are no autographs: K95 is less original than K96, where a lilting but forceful 6/8 Andante with off-beat accents is a pastoral movement and so might be intended for Christmas use (like, for example, that in Corelli's *Christmas Concerto*). Finally in this group of non-autograph works, another cheerful D major symphony, K97, perhaps from 1770, whose finale might have given Beethoven an idea for his Seventh Symphony, had he ever heard the piece.

🎧 *Early symphonies* English Concert / Trevor Pinnock
DG Archiv 471 666 2 (4 CDs)

Symphony No. 12 in G K110
Symphony No. 13 in F K112
Symphony No. 14 in A K114**
Symphony No. 15 in G K124
Symphony No. 16 in C K128
Symphony No. 17 in G K129*
Symphony No. 18 in F K130*
Symphony No. 19 in E flat K132

With this group of works, written from 1771 onwards, Mozart's symphonies are painted on a larger canvas and achieve a greater individuality than his earlier exuberant pieces. K110 in G, with horns, has a noisy opening Allegro – longer than any movement he had written so far – whose second section starts by contrast in gentle imitation. Imitative writing unusually also animates the final Allegro, with arpeggios tossed between the strings. K112 in F is still in conventional mode, and Leopold wrote the minuet into the score, which he also labelled. But from K114 onwards we are in the beginnings of a different world: this A major symphony is dated 'Salzburg 30 December 1771', and all the following group of eight were written there. Mozart had not written anything instrumental quite so wonderfully worked out as this symphony, with its subtle opening and huge leaps in the first violins around harmonic surprises, all contained in a firm framework – a really compelling symphonic argument. In the trio of the minuet Mozart puts all the activity in the second violins while letting the firsts play an almost single-note tune. By 21 February 1772 he had moved on to K124 in G, with its triple-time first movement and finely contrasted minuet and winsome trio, followed by a finale with enough ending jokes to bring the house down.

One of the things that Mozart begins to demonstrate in these symphonies is how to develop his musical material, and the first movement of K128 in C has a development section which starts very surprisingly in E flat and races round several keys before returning to C. There is no minuet, and the finale is in the style of a gigue. K129 in G with oboes and horns includes the sort of crescendo that Mozart must have learnt from his Mannheim colleagues; the Andante sounds as if it will be conventional, but the material is briefly developed in the second half into a lovely descending, offbeat imitation, while the bouncing final Allegro also contains two quiet, unexpected imitative sections for the strings. Mozart finds more and more he can do with his material, and the impression persists in K130 in F, from May 1772, a work of great subtlety. It gets going gradually with a characteristic bouncing rhythm that recurs throughout the first movement. The minuet sets violins against basses, and the trio bizarrely adds very high horns. The finale is a real step forward, thoroughly worked out with maximum contrast and development, with touches of chromaticism – a movement that can stand beside many of his later ones. In July 1772 Mozart returned to the key of his first symphony for K132 in E flat, also with four horns, where the musical material is less striking but the scoring and sonorities are beautiful. The extended slow movement was later replaced: was that because the first one made the special point of apparently quoting a Christmas tune (which Mozart knew because he heard it in the chimes of Salzburg), or simply because it was too long? Again there is a substantial finale, which starts with a gavotte-like half-bar and includes some sidesteps into remote keys (there is an almost chilling moment as the strings slide into A flat and the horns hold a single note – moved down an octave on the repeat – against the violins' D flat!) before racing to the rumbustious finish.

🎧 *Symphonies Nos. 14–18* Prague Chamber Orchestra / Charles Mackerras
Telarc 80242
🎧 *Symphonies Nos. 17–19, 22, 32* Amsterdam Baroque Orchestra / Ton Koopman
Erato 45714

Symphony No. 20 in D K133*
Symphony No. 21 in A K134
Symphony in D K161 and K163
Symphony in D K111a and b
Symphony No. 22 in C K162
Symphony No. 26 in E flat K184*
Symphony No. 27 in G K199
Symphony No. 23 in D K181**
Symphony No. 24 in B flat K182

Mozart now knew how to write symphonies that were not only brilliantly effective but musically substantial. K133 in D was composed in Salzburg in July 1772. Stanley Sadie in *The New Grove* draws attention to the way the extrovert opening movement combines influences from Italy and from Mannheim (the easeful build-up of the theme also recalls Johann Christian Bach), and how cleverly Mozart keeps the quiet opening in reserve, bringing it back only at the very end of the movement. Then there is a muted Andante, with solo flute partly doubling the violins an octave higher, a vigorous minuet and winding trio, and then something really special: a finale in 12/8 time – a gigue, but with four rather than two beats in the bar. This enables Mozart to indulge in some dazzling effects, shooting scales and braying wind chords, as well as a possibly unconscious echo of the work's opening: exhilarating.

The A major symphony K134 is more restrained, using pairs of flutes and horns to fine effect in the Andante which pre-echoes the Countess's aria 'Porgi amor' from *Le nozze di Figaro*: you could not possibly predict which little fragment Mozart would pick up on for his development, nor the short, imposing coda he adds. The final Allegro's deft opening looks back to the opening movement of the earlier A major symphony, but veers in all sorts of unexpected directions before finishing with a new bold gesture. The D major symphony K161 and 163 is a version of the overture to *Il sogno di Scipione* (the movements run continuously), while K111a and b was used for *Ascanio in Alba* (where it had an ending which ran into the start of the opera, most unusual for the time).

A group of Salzburg symphonies from March to May 1773 (the precise dates have been altered or defaced in the autographs for reasons that remain unclear) show total confidence in the form, perhaps renewed by his third visit to Italy, but actually marked the end of a period when symphonic composition would be central to Mozart's activity. K162 in C with horns and trumpets is relatively conventional: a majestic first movement, eloquent triplets in the Andante, and then a hunting finale. The opening of the E flat K184 (probably dated under the scratchings March 1773) strikingly pre-echoes the Sinfonia Concertante for violin and viola in the same key, though that should not let us ignore the twisting dissonant note that then provides a mainspring of the movement's argument. Wonderfully, it just evaporates into thin air, and the Andante takes over before leading straight to the triple-time finale. Whether or not this symphony was originally designed as an overture, it was used as one during the 1780s for a play by the Berlin playwright Plumicke, along with movements from Mozart's music for *Thamos, King of Egypt*.

The G major symphony K199 (now dated Salzburg April 1773) has a dance-like feel, with an effect in the first-movement development that would be used in the *Idomeneo* ballet music. The Andantino grazioso allows itself a few bars of chromatic intensity before fading into the transparent, almost fugal opening of the finale. You would search in vain for a melody in the opening movement of the dazzling D major symphony K181, my personal favourite among these early works (though Mozart scholar Jens Peter Larsen calls it 'somewhat characterless'): this is music totally created out of gestures, harmonies and brilliantly paced development. A few bars of intricate writing for four-part strings (including an expressive viola part) show how good a string-quartet composer Mozart had now become, but they are soon overtaken by rushing scales that pile on top of each other: this is the apotheosis of the J. C. Bach style. The central movement is an operatic aria or serenade for solo oboe, and the finale includes the two-part string writing that is such a success in the 'Paris' Symphony and the very end of *Don Giovanni*. K182 in B flat offers more to those in search of symphonic argument; in the Andantino grazioso Mozart again uses a flute to double the violins an octave higher, before oboes return for the bouncy finale.

🎧 *Symphonies Nos. 21–41*
Academy of St Martin-in-the-Fields / Neville Marriner
Philips 422 502–2 (6 CDs)
🎧 *Symphonies Nos. 19–23*
Prague Chamber Orchestra / Charles Mackerras
Telarc 80217

Symphony No. 25 in G minor K183***

Mozart's first surviving symphony in a minor key, and a masterpiece. It was completed in Salzburg on 5 October 1773, and though it has laboured under the shadow of the 'great' G minor symphony, No. 40, it has now found a secure place in the repertory (especially since it was used as the title music for the film of Shaffer's *Amadeus*). 'The urgent tone of the repeated syncopated notes at the start represents something new, and so do the dramatic falling diminished seventh and the repeated thrusting phrases that follow' (Stanley Sadie). The combination of bold instrumental gesture, which Mozart had thoroughly mastered, with newly trenchant and darkly effective thematic material, gives this remarkable movement its power. A more recent writer, Simon Keeffe, emphasises on the other hand the continuity between this movement and earlier Mozart symphonies, and says the result here owes less to the use of the minor mode than to the fact that Mozart 'combined pre-existent stylistic practices in an especially taut and concise fashion'.

Mozart may have heard Haydn's Symphony No. 39, also in G minor and also including four horns, and also J. C. Bach's Op. 6 No. 6; but Mozart's writing for solo horn in this movement is uniquely eerie. He may have heard symphonies in this so-called *Sturm und Drang* style ('storm and stress', a term derived from a contemporary German literary movement), and appears to have absorbed their spirit immediately. The finale, as daring in its exploitation of unison as Haydn's 'Trauer' Symphony No. 44 (which also relies on a bold use of a diminished seventh at the close), sustains an almost terrifying power which the development section unrelentingly exploits. As Alfred Einstein asked: 'What purpose of the day can this document of impetuous expression have served?'

♫ *Symphonies Nos. 25 and 40*
Concertgebouw Orchestra / Nikolaus Harnoncourt
Teldec 242 970–2

Symphony No. 28 in C K200*

Although the date is again not clear – 17 (or 12) November 1774 (or 1773) – this was the last of the symphonies that Mozart wrote in Salzburg during this fertile period. For a C major symphony with trumpets and horns it is rather delicate in style, with pert exchanges between the violins, and a soaring tune which shows how Mozart could increasingly integrate melody into his orchestral gestures. The Andante initially sounds foursquare, but that is deceptive; as the second half starts, Mozart becomes utterly whimsical, inserting a pause, a single wind note, and then developing a coda figure. In the minuet and trio Mozart saves his most angular outburst for the second half of the trio, while the Presto finale tests the agility and precision of the violinists to their utmost.

♫ *Symphonies Nos. 25, 28, 29*
Prague Chamber Orchestra / Charles Mackerras
Telarc 80165

Symphony No. 29 in A K201***

So it arrives, completed on 6 April 1774 in Salzburg: a symphony in which Mozart, without abandoning any of the élan and extroversion of his earlier works, brings an utter memorability of line and melody to every bar of the work. In an earlier symphony the shape of its beginning might have been pure harmony, but in this justly more famous work the winding line, rising through expressively decorated octaves, is almost as singable as an aria. The contrast with the G minor symphony could hardly be stronger: in place of storm and stress is a serene inevitability. Which is not to say that the symphony lacks power: the development takes over the last throwaway linking phrase of the first section to heighten the tension. When the same phrase returns at the end of the recapitulation, Mozart contradicts every expectation by asking a question: string and wind exchange puzzlement, and strings almost drift up and out of sight before the theme returns. The Andante too is not different in type from those in earlier symphonies, just more profoundly haunting, with the strings' mutes coming off only in the final bars for a positive outcome to the yearning quest. Did Mozart ever write a more uncomplicatedly effective finale than this rip-roaring hunting movement? Here the witty modulations do sound like Haydn, and Mozart keeps his horns somewhat at bay until unleashing them to cap the unison strings in the coda. A swoosh upwards, a dramatic pause, a single cadence, and it's over.

🎧 *Symphonies Nos. 29, 31, 34, 35, 36, 38, 39, 40, 41* London Philharmonic Orchestra / Thomas Beecham
EMI References CHS 7 63698 2
🎧 *Symphonies Nos. 29 and 34* Vienna Philharmonic Orchestra / James Levine
DG 419 189–2
🎧 *Symphonies Nos. 29, 33, 40* Orpheus Chamber Orchestra
DG 453 425–2

Symphony No. 30 in D K202
Symphony in D K196 and K121
Symphony in D K208 and K102

Nothing so striking here, and indeed the symphony K202 is much more rarely played these days than those that come before or after: perhaps a symphony for a special Salzburg occasion which was meant to do its job (in May 1774) and no more. Mozart's biographers have worried over the seeming regression this work represents: it certainly sounds like a reversion to his earlier style, in which gesture predominates over melody. The D major symphony K196 brings together the overture to *La finta giardiniera* with a specially composed finale written in Salzburg, while K102 is a finale to make a new symphony out of the overture and first aria from *Il re pastore*. Around this time the Serenades K204 and K250 were also revised and shortened to make four-movement symphonies.

Symphony No. 31 in D, 'Paris' K297**

In 1777 Mozart left the service of the Prince-Archbishop of Salzburg in high dudgeon and embarked on a trip to Munich, Augsburg, Mannheim and Paris – with his mother, but without his father. This was to have fateful consequences which coloured Mozart's relationship with his father for ever: Mozart's mother died in Paris in July 1778 and Mozart found it extremely difficult to communicate the news to his demanding father. Instead, in a wild and gossipy letter he distracted his father (and himself) with extended accounts of his musical experiences. It now seems unlikely, for example, that Mozart wrote two new symphonies for Paris as he claimed, but this one would be enough. Mozart wrote: 'I was very nervous at the rehearsal, for never in my life have I heard a worse performance. You have no idea how twice they scraped and scrambled through it. I was really in a terrible way and would gladly have had it rehearsed again, but as there was so much else to rehearse, there was no time left. So I had to go to bed with an aching heart and in a discontented and angry frame of mind.' Nothing new there for composers hearing their work for the first time! But the performance on 18 June 1778 turned out to be a great success (according to the composer), prompting applause in mid-movement which has been the subject of much comment since. What is more indicative is Mozart's suggestion that he wrote certain passages, especially for the violins alone at the start of the finale, especially for the Parisian taste: this may be true, but he had written in this manner in previous symphonies for Salzburg. One aspect that was certainly due to Paris, however, is the presence of clarinets in a symphonic score.

The 'Paris' Symphony is a work of cinematic vividness, in which contrasting material is juxtaposed with all the skill of a master cameraman focusing in on different pictures and then combining them. A unison statement and sweeping upward scale. A gentle falling dotted sequence. A striding bass line. Wispy first-violin ideas with second-violin triplets. Unison hammerings for full orchestra. The electric way in which these ideas are played with and brought together provides the mounting excitement of this opening movement: no wonder the Parisians clapped. The Andante was famously replaced because the promoter of the Concert Spirituel persuaded Mozart that it was too elaborate for his audience. Both versions seem innocuous enough (it is faintly amusing that the greatest Mozartians cannot be sure which was the original and which the substitute movement). The brilliance of the symphony is however epitomised in the finale with its bustling, offbeat opening, leading to the eruption that had the Paris audience applauding. As the movement progresses, its contrapuntal elegance and wit becomes astounding. We end almost breathless from excitement at the array of devices Mozart has effortlessly strewn in our path.

Symphony No. 35 in D, 'Haffner' K385***

> I am up to my ears in work . . . And now you ask me to
> write a new symphony too? How on earth am I to do so?
> Well, I must spend the night over it, for that is the only
> way; and to you, dearest father, I sacrifice it. I shall work
> as fast as possible, and as far as haste permits, I shall write
> something good.

This is the new Mozart, appearing busy and over-committed
in Vienna, living the new life of the freelance musician, and
resenting any demands made on him by his father back home.
But the occasion for which Leopold wanted celebratory
music was connected to one of Wolfgang's oldest friends,
Siegmund Haffner, and so he obliged with a piece which during the Mozart revival of the twentieth century became one
of his most popular, particularly with larger-scale chamber
orchestras. It is so memorable that the music is difficult to
forget, but Mozart did just that, if we are to believe his letter
to his father when he retrieved the score the following year:
'My new Haffner symphony has quite astonished me, for I
had forgotten every single note of it. It must certainly make a
good effect.' And so it does, from its initial arresting octave
leaps and whispered answering string figures, through rushing upward scales and tense passages where the octaves, now
suppressed and quiet, are heard over ever-pulsing running
bass lines that keep the tension growing and growing. A magical return through a chromatic wilderness to the open spaces
of the main theme adds to the excitement, and after the rising
unison figure bursts into the final climax, Mozart takes the
violins to the very top of their register. The second movement could only be a relaxation, while the Minuet and Trio
are remarkably conventional, probably a reflection of the serenade-like nature of the occasion. But the finale is another
tour de force: here rhythmic energy and natural power take
on an almost Dionysian exuberance, and many have heard
echoes here of Osmin's music from *Die Entführung aus dem
Serail*. Mozart said it should be played 'as fast as possible'.

🎧 *Symphonies Nos. 35, 36, 32*
Scottish Chamber Orchestra / Jukka-Pekka Saraste
Virgin VC7 90702–2
🎧 *Symphony No. 35 etc.*
BBC Symphony Orchestra / Arturo Toscanini
BBC Legends 4016–2

Symphony No. 36 in C, 'Linz' K425***

This symphony is called 'Linz' because Mozart wrote it 'at breakneck speed' for a concert in the city on 4 November 1783: he was travelling through the city, was asked by his hosts to give a concert, but did not have a symphony with him. (Was it really easier to write a new symphony than to remember an old one? Probably, for as with the 'Haffner', Mozart had difficulty remembering his old music without his scores.) This is really a Viennese symphony, however: the effect of Vienna on Mozart's musical development can scarcely be over-estimated, and we can immediately hear the new complexity and intricacy of the musical argument. Here the importance of the symphony as a vehicle for serious discourse is apparent, one in which all the instruments are given equal place, with a new prominence for the wind, and the treatment of the material is of unprecedented subtlety. The Adagio slow introduction is a new feature for Mozart, as if to warn us of the music's impending seriousness. Hans Keller justly called the themes of the outer movement 'elatingly urgent', and they take off with barely suppressed power. What is notable is the spareness of texture in so much of the first movement – thrice-repeated unaccompanied sevenths in the strings, surrounded by pauses – which gives the surrounding C major pomp so much greater effect. The beautiful F major siciliano is also broken by strange scale passages, this time highlighting the interval of the ninth before serenity returns. After the noble minuet and trio, the Presto finale combines its forward propulsion with simple, eloquent melodies. There are two heart-rending sequences, not quite paralleled anywhere else in Mozart's output, as the strings dialogue in aching sequence under wind chords, reaching a height of intensity before subsiding chromatically to nothing, after which the celebrations get going again – one of those marvellous Mozartian moments which leave you wondering where in his imagination that music can have come from.

𝄞 *Symphonies Nos. 36 and 38*
Prague Chamber Orchestra / Charles Mackerras
Telarc 80148
𝄞 *Symphonies Nos. 36 and 38*
Columbia Symphony Orchestra / Bruno Walter
CBS MYK 44826

Symphony No. 38 in D, 'Prague' K504****

The spirit of *Don Giovanni* hovers over this glorious symphony, completed in Vienna on 6 December 1786 for a visit to Prague the following January, which counted among the happiest and most successful of all his late tours. Mozart was respected, much in demand, and created a huge success with *Le nozze di Figaro* in the city; his personal appearance playing the piano 'at a large concert in the opera house' on 19 January, was by all accounts a triumph. 'When at the end of the concert Mozart improvised alone on the piano for more than half an hour and had transported us to the highest degree of rapture, this enchantment dissolved into a loud torrent of applause,' wrote his friend Franz Niemetschek. In his reminiscences Niemetschek very clearly indicated the status he expected a symphony to reach by the end of the eighteenth century, when he praised the 'Prague' as 'full of unexpected transitions . . . so that they immediately incline the soul to expect something sublime'. That expectation is immediately created by the D minor opening of the symphony, portentous and dramatic, full of violent contrasts and chromatic lines. It disappears, to be succeeded by the Allegro in which a breathtaking array of material is presented and developed: a quiet first-violin syncopated line with a little rising tag, a wind fanfare with a falling phrase, a solo oboe hovering around the flattened seventh of the scale, and an exuberant sequential figure with offbeat wind chords. Mozart's imagination darts among these fragments, rearranging them as if shaking a kaleidoscope, building an extraordinarily complex structure from them. Keller believed this symphony was the triumph of sonata form, and hence could contain no minuet; the real reason for the absence of that movement is more likely to be pragmatic, but it is certainly true that the extended Andante – where the chromatic lines of the symphony's introduction suddenly become transformed into unthreatening beauty – provides all the contrast necessary before the finale. This uplifting movement finds sheer enjoyment in playing off the contrasts between strings and wind, giving each demanding writing, piling invention on invention while giving no moment of respite in its forward movement – the sort of effect which Beethoven later achieved in the finale of his First Symphony. There is no more purely exhilarating Mozart symphony.

🎧 *Symphonies Nos. 38 and 39*
Academy of Ancient Music / Christopher Hogwood
Decca Oiseau-Lyre 410 233–2
🎧 *Symphonies Nos. 38 and 39*
English Baroque Soloists / John Eliot Gardiner
Philips 426 283–2
🎧 *Symphonies Nos. 38 and 39*
Chamber Orchestra of Europe / Nikolaus Harnoncourt
Teldec 4509 90866

Symphony No. 39 in E flat K543****

It is still not completely clear why Mozart wrote three symphonies in the summer of 1788, but of one thing we can be sure: he intended them for some specific concert or tour, and did not simply write them out of what Alfred Einstein called 'an inner impulse', representing 'an appeal to eternity'. Neal Zaslaw, in an entertaining paper entitled 'Mozart as a working stiff', has laid to rest the idea that Mozart ever wrote purely in the abstract, and has made convincing suggestions of occasions during his last years – in Vienna, Dresden, Leipzig, Frankfurt and Mainz – on which these symphonies could well have been performed. They were probably intended for a subscription series in Vienna in June and July 1788, which never took place.

Zaslaw says 'Mozart did not compose because he was inspired, although inspiration may be why he composed so well.' He certainly never composed better or to greater effect than in these three masterpieces. One of their remarkable features as a trilogy is that they are as different in mood and emotion as, say, *Figaro*, *Giovanni* and *Zauberflöte* – and it is the last of these, with its predominance of E flat, that is inevitably recalled in Symphony No. 39. The influence of Haydn on Mozart's last three symphonies can be traced to the fact that Haydn's first three 'Paris' symphonies, Nos. 82–84, were published in Vienna in 1787, and so would undoubtedly have been studied by Mozart.

The slow introduction, extremely grand with French-style dotted rhythms and rushing scales, builds up tension and ends with a passage where the world gapes uncertainly open at our feet – a moment that left that great analyst Donald Tovey struggling: 'one of those sublimities that are incomparable with each other and with everything else'. The tension is then released in the warm triple-time Allegro. Though the Allegro has its moments of force in the tutti sections (with scales echoing those in the introduction), its main attraction is the sonority of the quieter sections, which recall the purified world of *Zauberflöte*, with the pizzicato bass line to the upper strings' tender second subject. The Andante begins in untroubled mood in A flat but is soon darkened by two episodes in F minor that unleash something of the power felt in the slow movement of Haydn's 'London' Symphony.

Mozart manipulates his melodic lines cleverly, with four-bar sections split into uneven portions of one-and-a-half and two-and-a-half bars, with the middle two half-bars unaccompanied! The lovely codetta rises up from the bassoon in imitation, over a pedal note from the horn, and the clarinets intertwine as the theme returns. The minuet's solid dancing strength and the trio's refined popular melody and hurdy-gurdy-like accompaniment both owe much to the innovations which Haydn made in his symphonies. What is Haydnesque about the last movement is not so much its mere cheerfulness, but that like so many Haydn movements (and so few Mozart ones) it is based on only one subject. The pleasure the composer takes in the key relationships is intense, and the development explores to the full the fun that can be had with the tiny subject. When the theme is heard for the last time it is presented in unison over a drone bass, in a homage to the pastoral tradition (also echoed in Haydn's 'London' Symphony). In one of the wittiest endings Mozart wrote, the theme is tossed aside in the final cadence.

🎧 *Symphonies Nos. 39, 40, 41*
Chamber Orchestra of Europe / Nikolaus Harnoncourt
Teldec 9031 74858–2 (live, 5 December 1991)
🎧 *Symphonies Nos. 39 and 41*
London Classical Players / Roger Norrington
EMI 7 54090 2
🎧 *Symphonies Nos. 39 and 41*
NDR Sinfonie Orchester / Günter Wand
BMG RD60714

Symphony No. 40 in G minor K550****

There are few works more difficult to approach freshly than Mozart's Fortieth, familiar to us through jazzed-up, simplified, rearranged versions of all shapes and sizes. And it has been one of the few works of Mozart to have remained secure in the repertory through the nineteenth century. That has given rise to a huge variety of conflicting interpretations, from Schumann's famous description of 'a work of Grecian lightness and grace' to those who have described it as the apogee of Mozart's tragic character. Emotional ambiguity can scarcely go any further, and it is vital that we hear the piece openly and without prejudice for it to reveal its marvels. There could be few more ambiguous openings than that of this symphony: an accompaniment, then a melody which is hardly a melody (linked to Cherubino's first outpouring of emotion in *Figaro*?). Contrast and unity are rarely so closely woven as in this symphony's first group of themes: there is no formal opposition, as in the 'Jupiter', but rather a fluctuation between materials that shows its fullest expression in the development section. Here Mozart removes nearly all feeling of stability, for through the two-part fugatos, bass-less reworkings of the theme's semitone fragment and final chromatic collapse, there is always the feel of a home key to steer towards.

The Andante (so often played too slowly to reveal its true beauty) is the real successor of all those little imitative movements in Mozart's early symphonies, but deepened a hundredfold – the way that the simple theme becomes clothed in descending wind figures and extended in sequences is miraculous. The predominantly two-part minuet suddenly expands in its second section into a fully argued web of counterpoint, against which the harmonious trio in G major provides a moment of unearthly repose before the torrent of the finale. This movement can be seen as the successor of all those implacably forward-moving Mozartian symphonic finales, but with added depth and substance – notably in the development section, where the simple chord sequence of the opening is suddenly distorted into a line with no fewer than ten of the twelve chromatic notes. This moment, beloved of those twentieth-century dodecaphonists who took it as a symbolic message from history, is matched by the way the music is dragged back to its tonal framework. The rest of the symphony sounds like an escape from this moment of trauma, right up to the stormy final coda with upward rushing bass lines, one of Mozart's finest moments of last-minute intensification.

🎧 *Symphonies Nos. 40 and 38*
English Chamber Orchestra / Benjamin Britten
Decca 430 494–2
🎧 *Symphonies Nos. 40 and 41*
Prague Chamber Orchestra / Charles Mackerras
Telarc 80139

Symphony No. 41 in C, 'Jupiter' K551****

Mozart's last symphony is dated 10 August 1788, and was completed soon after Nos. 39 and 40. Together they make an incredibly imposing set, but whether they should be performed together is doubtful: hearing them in succession can be rather like seeing three cathedrals piled on top of each other. The 'Jupiter' is deliberately the grandest of the three: it is also the most formal in the balance and contrast of its themes. It is almost foursquare at its opening: fanfare, gentle answer, fanfare, gentle answer. The wind leads the integration and overlapping of these themes, and a new subject in the strings not only sounds like an operatic aria but actually is one ('Un bacio di mano' K541, which Mozart wrote to insert in an Anfossi opera). The development leads the fanfare figure so far astray chromatically in the strings that a few bars of steadying wind are necessary to restore the equilibrium before the recapitulation. The muted Andante cantabile explores its elaborated way not as a set of variations as does Beethoven's Ninth, though there is something of that symphony's increasing elaboration and intensity, both worrying yet consoling: Zaslaw has expressed well its 'mysterious reverberations of unease'.

After the unusually chromatic minuet and a trio which cleverly begins with a cadence, the famous finale unfolds. It is not by any stretch of the imagination 'a fugue with four subjects' – that description can only apply to the coda where four subjects are indeed, very briefly, combined fugally. But it is more a triumphant combination of sonata-form development with an imitative texture. The movement is the culmination of those imitative string-quartet textures in the early symphonies, and it makes this the first symphony whose emotional weight falls firmly on its last movement as the resolution of a journey (as would happen, for example, in Beethoven's Fifth). The suggestion has been made that the use of an 'ancient' tag in the finale marks Mozart's re-engagement with church music. Whether or not this is true, the consciously antique theme certainly looks back to his youth. But combined with this backward-looking source is the astonishingly forward-looking development, which takes the dislocation of the themes to new heights, with real four-part imitation under striding wind chords.

Just as we think normality has returned with the harmonious recapitulation, one of the most unnerving moments in Mozart's music takes the ground from under our feet, as chromaticism returns with renewed force, leaving the violas struggling for their lives in the middle of the texture. That is the perfect set-up for the even greater surprise of the fugal coda. Just as we think the argument of the work is over, it suddenly combines directly the themes which have been presented. This is the apotheosis of the learned exercises that Mozart was familiar with from his youth, triumphantly reworked as a miracle not just of construction, but of expression. The combination is brilliantly, tantalisingly brief, before Mozart sweeps the whole learned panoply aside with the insistent braying of trumpets and drums.

'The veritable symphonic testament of Mozart', said Georges de Saint-Foix. Inevitably so, but the fact is that these incredibly adventurous final works point forward quite as much as they point backwards. As Hans Keller nicely put it: 'it is a little facile to say that after the finale of the "Jupiter" no further symphonic thought was possible or necessary for him . . . by all means, let us be wise after the event, so long as we are sure that we are being wise.' The last symphonies make the unfinished business of Mozart's creative life painfully clear, for there is everything to indicate that had Mozart lived longer, he could have written symphonies that would have pushed music decisively into the nineteenth century.

🎧 *Symphonies Nos. 40 and 41*
Orchestra of the 18th Century / Frans Bruggen
Philips 434 149–2
🎧 *Symphonies Nos. 40 and 41*
English Baroque Soloists / John Eliot Gardiner
Philips 426 315–2
🎧 *Symphonies Nos. 40 and 41*
New Philharmonia Orchestra / Carlo Maria Giulini
Decca 452 889–2
🎧 *Symphonies Nos. 39, 40, 41*
Chamber Orchestra of Europe / Nikolaus Harnoncourt
Teldec 0630 18957–2

Concertos

Piano concertos

If one had to pick a single genre which perfectly encapsulates Mozart's distinctive work as a composer, then (for all that it would be absurd to set aside the operas) it would have to be the piano concerto. Because that was the genre he made wholly his own, the most personal of his creations: arias he wrote for himself to sing, symphonies for himself to play. And also because it is the piano concertos that show most exactly the balance in Mozart's creativity between performer and composer: the two were indivisible. He started, as ever under his father's direction, to understand the form by recreating the music of his contemporaries, and went on to develop by leaps and bounds his own instinctive understanding of the possibilities. One of the finest modern players of this repertory, Robert Levin (whose understanding of Mozart's style is so complete that he improvises cadenzas and indeed whole pieces in Mozartian idiom), has referred to the impact of Mozart's increasing skill as a composer of opera on the piano concerto. It's a fascinating thought, linking Mozart's ability in symphonic work to order and juxtapose themes, with that of his operatic writing, in which that juxtaposition serves a precise rhetorical function in setting the libretto. As Levin puts it: 'greater complexity of thematic exposition in instrumental works could parallel the specific dramatic situation dictated by a text.' In the piano concertos this is achieved by means of figuration that is essentially non-vocal: arpeggios across the range of the piano, for instance. But perhaps this thought helps to account for the immediately understandable and approachable narrative of these concertos: they do indeed seem to tell a wordless story.

Piano Concerto No. 1 in F K37
Piano Concerto No. 2 in B flat K39
Piano Concerto No. 3 in D K40
Piano Concerto No. 4 in G K41
Piano Concerto in D K107/1
Piano Concerto in G K107/2
Piano Concerto in E flat K107/3

In 1767, when Mozart was eleven, his father gave him some sonata movements by composers whose names have since faded from our minds, including Raupach, Honauer, Schobert, Eckard, and C. P. E. Bach, with the instruction to turn them into miniature concertos. Mozart had met some of these composers in Paris and admired and learnt from their music. It must have been a stimulating exercise: the solo parts replicate the sonata movements, but the young Mozart adds orchestral ritornelli to set off the solo sections. The exercise was evidently carried out in close collaboration with his father, and was repeated a few years later (1771 or 1772) with three complete sonatas by Johann Christian Bach (Op. 5, Nos. 2, 3, 4), whose music Mozart grew to admire while in London. These arrangements survive as K107.

🎧 *Piano Concertos K37, K39–41*
Ingrid Haebler / Capella Academica Vienna / Eduard Melkus
🎧 *Piano Concertos K107*
Ton Koopman / Amsterdam Baroque Orchestra
Philips Complete Mozart Edition Vol. 7 422 507–2 (12 CDs)

Piano Concerto No. 5 in D K175 / Rondo in D K382*
Piano Concerto No. 6 in B flat K238
Concerto No. 7 in F for three pianos K242
Piano Concerto No. 8 in C K246

The Fifth Concerto, usually referred to as his first original one because it follows the series of concertos based on the music of other composers, was written in Salzburg in December 1773, just before Mozart turned eighteen. He seems to have toured it widely, and later said of a Mannheim performance, 'I played my old concerto in D major, because it is such a favourite here.' For a revival in Vienna in 1782, he replaced the finale with a new Rondo. Even though it's a sparkling and original work, it tends to be neglected today in favour of later works, as is the lighter B flat Concerto, written in January 1776, which both Mozart and his sister Nannerl played in Salzburg and on tour.

The Concerto for three pianos, from the following month, is more often brought out these days for special collaborations between pianists, whether virtuosi or prime ministers: it was written for the Lodron family of Salzburg, with two reasonably tricky parts complemented by one very easy part for the youngest daughter of the family. The musical material is modest, no match for the later Concerto for two pianos. The C major Concerto K246 was also revived by Mozart in Mannheim, Paris and then in Vienna in the heyday of his concerto performances in the 1780s, but it was originally written in April 1776 for a Countess Lutzow, who was the niece of the Archbishop of Salzburg. It demands elegance and facility, little more, and the finale is a pretty dull rondo in minuet tempo.

♀ *Piano Concertos K365, K242, K466* András Schiff, Daniel Barenboim, Georg Solti / English Chamber Orchestra / Georg Solti
Decca 430 232–2
♀ *Piano Concertos K175/382, K238, K246, K271, K365, K413, K415* Mitsuko Uchida / English Chamber Orchestra / Jeffrey Tate
Philips 473 889–2

Piano Concerto No. 9 in E flat K271*

Mozart hits his stride as a concerto composer with this highly original work which dates from January 1777. It has long been called the 'Jeunehomme' Concerto, as if it referred to the youth of Mozart himself, but has now been linked with a young lady, Victoire Jenamy, the daughter of Mozart's friend the ballet master Noverre. Its audacious opening, abandoning an orchestral introduction and bringing in the piano after the first bar, is only one of many masterstrokes in the piece. The central Andantino is in a dark C minor, with much elaboration for the soloist, while the finale is the first example in his concertos of the perpetual-motion movement created out of rhythm and harmony without noticeable melodic content. But as the music whisks along, a cadenza for the soloist suddenly leads us to a lovely minuet, with muted and pizzicato accompaniment, as if the serenaders from *Così* had just walked in. Another cadenza, and the bustle returns unabated.

🎧 *Piano Concertos K271, K456* Leif Ove Andsnes / Norwegian Chamber Orchestra
EMI 57803
🎧 *Piano Concertos K271, K503* Richard Goode / Orpheus Chamber Orchestra
Nonesuch 79454

Concerto No. 10 for two pianos in E flat K365**

One of the most important relationships of Mozart's early years was with his sister Nannerl, with whom he made all his early tours and who was herself a fine pianist. But as his genius overtook her talent, their relationship became strained, and fatally so after the death of their father. We can only presume that this magnificent concerto was written, like some of the piano duets, for brother and sister to play together, and Leopold's intervention in writing out part of the cadenzas probably supports that (though Mozart also played it with his pupils, as he did in Vienna in 1781 in a performance with Josepha Auernhammer).

The original date of the piece is not clear: estimates have ranged from 1775–7 to Köchel's 1779, which seems convincing. Extra trumpet and drum parts were added, possibly by

Mozart for the 1781 concert, more likely for the nineteenth-century Breitkopf publication. Musically this concerto inhabits the world of the Sinfonia concertante in the same key, which definitely is 1779, and it is equally mature though perhaps not quite as adventurous. The interplay of the two musical characters is so equal that you cannot tell them apart: the first movement is propelled by its energetic interplay between the soloists, while the central movement is far more relaxed. The finale is a witty Rondeau with a taxing cadenza.

🎧 *Piano Concertos K365 etc.* Friedrich Gulda, Chick Corea / Concertgebouw Orchestra / Nikolaus Harnoncourt
Teldec 8.44154
🎧 *Piano Concertos K242, K365 etc.*
Malcolm Bilson, Robert Levin, Melvyn Tan / English Baroque Soloists / John Eliot Gardiner
DG Archiv 463 111–2 (9 CDs)
🎧 *Piano Concertos K365, K242, Variations K501* Murray Perahia, Radu Lupu / English Chamber Orchestra
Sony Classical 44915

Piano Concerto No. 11 in F K413
Piano Concerto No. 12 in A K414*
Rondo in A major K386
Piano Concerto No. 13 in C K415*

These three concertos form a group written in Vienna in 1782–3, after Mozart's move there, and intended for his own series of concerts with which he was establishing his career in the city. At this optimistically entrepreneurial stage in his life, he proposed in an advertisement in January 1783 to sell manuscript copies of the works as well – to whom, it is not quite clear. Perhaps to ensure their saleability, the wind parts were dispensable and the concertos could be played with only string quartet accompaniment, making them quite suitable for domestic use. Incidentally, the bass lines of the solo piano parts are written with thorough bass – figures that show the intended harmonies – throughout the score, demonstrating that the piano was expected to play all the time and emerge as a soloist, rather than remaining silent as the orchestra plays. These were the concertos of which Mozart famously said to his father that they were designed both for amateurs and connoisseurs: they 'are a happy medium between what is too easy and too difficult; they are very brilliant, easy on the ear and natural, without being vapid. There are passages here and there from which connoisseurs alone can derive satisfaction, but these passages are written in such a way that the less learned cannot fail to be pleased, without knowing why' (letter of 28 December 1782). Scholars could write a whole theory of late eighteenth-century music around this fascinating sentence, which reveals an acute awareness of audience taste, rather than the refined and remote awareness of a rarefied future so often attributed to Mozart.

All three concertos have an intimate feel, and the A major has an especially lyrical mood. The concertos of Johann Christian Bach are an influence here (and the central movement seems to be based on an actual theme of his), but the language has developed rapidly and the interplay of ideas is subtly managed. The lovely Andante has Mozart's evening serenade feel to it, and there is a fully decorated repeat for the pianist – presumably the sort of thing Mozart would have played himself in all his concertos, but here he wrote it out because the work was to be sold. The perky finale is a Rondeau showing how he can find musical inspiration even in a little unison bass line. The first movement of the F major concerto is more extrovert, with some showy hand-crossing for the soloist, but the Larghetto, with sotto voce violins and pizzicato basses, is dreamy, and the final minuet is elegant, almost suave. The C major concerto, beginning with an imitative fanfare-like figure for strings, in some ways prefigures the mood of the 'Jupiter' Symphony, though the piano part never expands emotionally beyond brilliance and, in the final Rondeau, witty playfulness.

The Rondo in A major has been the subject of extensive Mozartian sleuthing in recent years, since the autograph was split up into numerous fragments and the end of the music lost altogether (though it was imaginatively reconstructed by the English composer Ciprani Potter as long ago as 1838). Then it was spotted in 1980 among a miscellany of music by Süssmayr in the British Library by the great English Mozartian Alan Tyson. What a nice feeling that must have been . . . The piece seems to have been a discarded attempt at a finale for the A major Concerto, but it is sometimes played on its own.

Piano Concerto No. 14 in E flat K449*
Piano Concerto No. 15 in B flat K450*
Piano Concerto No. 16 in D K451
Piano Concerto No. 17 in G K453**
Piano Concerto No. 18 in B flat K456*

These fine concertos date from the height of Mozart's success in Vienna as a composer and performer, and show him revelling in the opportunities presented by the interplay between piano and orchestra – especially the increasing emancipation of the wind players as soloists of almost equal status to the pianist. Mozart's new-found confidence is perhaps shown by his starting a new thematic catalogue of his music, of which K449 is the first entry, completed 9 February 1784 (for a performance by Barbara Ployer on 17 March). The first movement is in triple time, as was to be the opening movement of Symphony No. 39 in the same key, while the central Andantino is a lilting sotto voce melody heavily decorated by the soloist. The finale starts as an entrancing quasi-baroque movement in which the soloist exuberantly elaborates the simple theme until it cannot be confined any longer and skips away to the close in triple time. This has a smaller orchestra than those that follow, and Tyson believed the opening was written as early as 1782, being abandoned and then revisited at the start of 1784.

The B flat concerto of 15 March 1784 expands the palette still further with independent bassoons as well as oboes and

horns, and the solo part sounds demonstratively virtuosic, as
if Mozart is demonstrating everything he can do. A flowing
central movement and skipping final Allegro (with a prominent part for the first oboe) lead to a flamboyant hand-crossing cadenza which takes the left hand right down three
octaves of semiquavers in its opening bars. The concerto
almost manages to end quietly, but not quite. The D major
concerto, completed just a week later on 22 March, is equally extrovert, making much use of dotted rhythms, and by way
of contrast quiet syncopations over a walking bass which are
familiar from earlier symphonies. The Andante is one of
those Mozartian movements whose chromatic inflections can
sound maudlin if played too slowly, while the final Rondeau
bustles its little melody along with no respite, and like K449
decides to end in hectic triple time.

The G major Concerto was also written for Barbara
Ployer, completed in April 1784, and performed at a private
concert in Dobling in June (at the same concert Mozart
played his own piano and wind Quintet, and the two of them
played the great two-piano sonata K448). It's famous for the
fact that Mozart claimed his pet starling could sing the theme
of the finale (albeit with one wrong note and one pause,
which he wrote down on 28 May 1784 in his account book, a
very short-lived attempt at domestic organisation). Certainly
it's a simple and memorable tune, as is the ingratiating succession of varied themes in the opening movement, which are
combined and reordered in magical sequences as the movement progresses. It seems unlikely that Mozart finished the
B flat concerto as late as 30 September, when he entered it in
his catalogue, as it was written for the blind pianist Maria
Theresia Paradis to play in Paris, and her last concert there
was on 2 October. Whatever the truth, Leopold Mozart
heard his son play the work in February 1785, when he 'had
the great pleasure of hearing the interplay of the instruments
so clearly that for sheer delight tears came into my eyes'. It is
an unpretentious piece, in which string and wind groups are
set against each other in a way Leopold could have admired,

and they also have their distinct roles in the central G minor movement, especially in the interlude in G major.

⋒ *Piano Concertos K449, K537* Maria João Pires / Vienna Philharmonic Orchestra / Claudio Abbado
DG 437 529–2
⋒ *Piano Concertos K453, K467* Maria João Pires / Chamber Orchestra of Europe / Claudio Abbado
DG 439 941–2
⋒ *Piano Concertos K175/382, K449, K451* Robert Levin / Academy of Ancient Music / Christopher Hogwood
Decca Oiseau-Lyre 458 285–2

Piano Concerto No. 19 in F K459****

This concerto is not among the canonic group of Mozart's last piano concertos, but it is at least their equal; it never ceases to amaze with its depth and power. In contrast to the gentle colours of the G major concerto K453, the F major is a work of the highest seriousness, and it is a measure of the difference between the two concertos how their similar dotted-rhythm openings lead in different directions. (The piece was entered by Mozart in his thematic catalogue with trumpets and drums in the scoring, but this may well be a mistake and no parts survive.) The wind spring to prominence as soon as the soloist enters, and Mozart writes five-part imitative figures for them while the pianist employs newly expressive figurations, far more chromatic than the tonal arpeggios and runs of the earlier concertos. Impressive suspensions in the bass line underline the theme when it returns, giving it remarkable grandeur. The central movement, so reminiscent of Susanna's yet-to-be-written Act IV aria in *Le nozze di Figaro*, 'Deh vieni', is a perfect example of Mozart's ability to let his wind soloists fly freely in the texture against the soloist's lines: indeed they have the last word here as the soloist ends with the very first thing he played. The finale is wholly deceptive, starting as one of those chirpy exchanges between piano and orchestra with which we have become familiar, and developing along similarly busy lines. But this suddenly gives way to the most strenuously worked and impressive contrapuntal section, which starts in the minor, culminating in a magnificent cadenza pounding right down to the bottom of the piano. It must have been breathtaking in Vienna in 1785, and it still is. Busoni arranged this movement for two pianos.

♫ *Piano Concertos K459, K488* Maurizio Pollini /
Vienna Philharmonic Orchestra / Karl Böhm
DG 413 793–2
♫ *Piano Concertos K459 etc.* András Schiff /
Salzburg Camerata Academica / Sándor Végh
Decca 448 140–2

Piano Concerto No. 20 in D minor K466****

Like the G minor symphony, this profound minor-key work fulfilled all the expectations of the nineteenth century about Mozart's tragic genius, and so remained in the repertory during that period at a time when all Mozart's other supreme concertos and most of his symphonies lay forgotten. You can immediately tell why it would appeal to the Romantic sensibility: from the eerily uncertain opening bars and intricate string part-writing, this is a piece that proclaims its emotional content from the start, and points forward to the D minor of *Don Giovanni*. There is a rhythmic fluidity which gives the concerto its oddly floating, loose quality. If we are to believe Mozart's catalogue, it was completed on 10 February 1785, just one day before he played it. If it was indeed this concerto that Leopold heard in the concert the next day, he declared himself more than satisfied with the standard of playing. When he took the piece back to Salzburg to perform it there, he reported that 'we had to practise the rondo three times before the orchestra could manage it'. The first movement, interrupted by the piano with a completely new melody which it then integrates into the developing structure, ends – very unusually – in total quiet, *pianissimo*. The central Romanza sings chromatically at first, but then gives way to a fierce and turbulent central section full of piano triplets. The finale, whose material is clearly linked to that of the first movement, I always find one of Mozart's oddest: it starts as a powerful rondo in D minor, but then turns into the major, with the chirpy trumpets and horns at the end making fun of us all, and inducing the same eerie quality, though this time jovially, with which this remarkable concerto began.

🎧 *Piano Concertos K466, K595*
Murray Perahia / English Chamber Orchestra
Sony SACD SS42241
🎧 *Piano Concertos K365, K459, K466* Martha Argerich /
Orchestra di Padova e del Veneto / Alexandre Rabinovitch
Teldec 98407

Piano Concerto No. 21 in C K467****

Famous for the wrong reason (the sentimental use of the central movement in the film *Elvira Madigan* gives a totally misleading impression of the piece), this concerto deserves to be famous for the right reason: it is a glorious, highly original piece of work whose central movement is astonishingly innovative. It was the product of a hectic period, when Leopold Mozart was still in Vienna embroiled in his son's activities, and it is from him that we learn of this concerto's success when given at the court theatre on Thursday 10 March 1785. His testimony, supported by an advertisement for that concert, also reveals that Mozart took not only his own fortepiano but also a special pedal attachment which 'will be used by him in improvising'. This fascinating organ-like device has caused much controversy over the years: did Mozart also use it in playing the concertos, for the bass line?

Nowhere more happily than in the first movement of K467 did Mozart combine so cleverly the conventions of the

opening unison fanfare with the easeful melody that was now
his trademark. The opening flows naturally; the soloist
enters, unusually, with a cadenza (maybe a second thought, to
judge from the pagination of Mozart's autograph) before
elaborating the C major theme and then a darker minor-key
subject which looks forward to the G minor symphony. The
sequential writing for piano and wind is both exciting and
expressive, and the truly symphonic argument of the movement ends quietly. The famous Andante (not slow: it pulses in
triplets throughout) is bold and experimental in its use of
continual dissonances which resolve. The inner parts of the
textures are strengthened by first bassoon doubling muted
second violins, the muted first violins echoing the pianist's
aching solo, which periodically plunges beneath the accompaniment to the bass clef. What a mysterious, magical movement! The finale is a version of the scampering perpetual-
motion movement Mozart has tried before, but this is better
than ever, as wind and piano bass line vie for supremacy, and
chromaticism resolves into resonantly open C major scales as
the work tumbles to its conclusion.

🎧 *Piano Concertos K467, K503* Stephen Kovacevich /
London Symphony Orchestra / Colin Davis
Philips 426 077–2
🎧 *Piano Concertos K467 etc.* Géza Anda /
Salzburg Camerata Mozarteum
DG 447 436–2
🎧 *Piano Concertos K467, K595* Murray Perahia /
Chamber Orchestra of Europe
Sony Classical SK 46485

Piano Concerto No. 22 in E flat K482***

By the end of 1785 in Vienna it seemed that Mozart could do
no wrong. His music was in demand, his concerts had subscribers, and he was already planning the next Lenten concert
series for 1786 when he completed this E flat concerto on 16

December. It was probably performed on 23 December.
Clarinets are included alongside flutes, and horns, trumpets
and timpani combine to give the piece a martial air, though
its E flat colouring is always mellow and subtle. The first
movement's piano part is full of ideas that are not developed,
inventiveness spinning cheerfully out of control; the C minor
Andante is highly decorated. The 6/8 finale begins like a conventional gigue, with much independent writing for solo flute
and bassoon, and energetic clarinet accompaniment figures.
My favourite moment is a tiny seven-note fragment for the
solo piano, repeated five times over the quietest of accompaniments, perky yet wistful. Then, as in K271, the movement
stops and a beautiful serenade takes over, here hymned by
clarinets, bassoons and horns. The helter-skelter returns, but
just as crashing tonic chords make you feel it's all over, back
comes the seven-note fragment, this time under quiet sustained wind chords, somehow unbearably poignant, as if
Mozart cannot quite let go of the miracle he has created.

🎧 *Piano Concertos K482*, *K595* Alfred Brendel /
Scottish Chamber Orchestra / Charles Mackerras
Philips 468 367–2
🎧 *Piano Concertos K482 etc.* Robert Levin /
Academy of Ancient Music / Christopher Hogwood
Decca Oiseau-Lyre 452 052–2

Piano Concerto No. 23 in A K488***

Along with the D minor concerto K466, this concerto has
been among Mozart's most popular creations, perhaps
because it conforms to ideas of Mozart's sunniness and lack of
complication as much as the D minor did to clichés about his
tragic spirit. In neither case is the over-simplification true, for
this A major work has a central movement of unusual depth.
The piece was completed as Mozart's popularity in Vienna
seemed at its height, but was just about to decline, and was
included in his Lenten concerts in 1786. (Tyson pointed out

that the opening is written on late 1784 or early 1785 paper, before the scoring included clarinets.) The gentle nature of the opening Allegro, with wind and strings given equal prominence in the opening, is not broken by the soloist, who, rather surprisingly for Mozart, enters with the theme of the orchestral opening. Mozart's own cadenza, short and unthematic, survives for this movement. The central Adagio is unusual both in its marking – which this time does imply a slow tempo – and in its key of F sharp minor: this is Mozart's only movement in this key. The large leaps in the piano part are highly expressive, but the issue of whether Mozart would have filled them in with elaboration is a tricky one to solve musically, especially where they dart across bare pizzicato accompaniments for the strings. In the second group of material the wind soloists lean into their wonderful dissonances across the bar-line, extending them right up to the final cadence, where Mozart transforms the beginning into an ending. The final movement is Allegro assai, a chattering, busy exchange which never loses either its high spirits or its command of musical logic.

𝄞 *Piano Concertos K488, K491*
Richard Goode / Orpheus Chamber Orchestra
Nonesuch 7559 79489–2
𝄞 *Piano Concertos K488, K491* Clifford Curzon /
London Symphony Orchestra / István Kertész
Decca Classic 452 888–2

Piano Concerto No. 24 in C minor K491****

This concerto, now recognised as one of Mozart's greatest, may have marked his turning-point with the Viennese public. We know nothing from contemporary accounts of its first performance, which is presumed to have taken place in Mozart's concert of 7 April 1786. It has been argued that it might have puzzled or alienated a public expecting a cheerful display piece; yet he had already explored a serious character in earlier works, and this is simply the most serious of them all. Although its uses Mozart's largest orchestra for a concerto, with one flute, pairs of oboes, clarinets, bassoons, trumpets, horns, timpani and strings, it is a dark work which rarely escapes from its minor-key intensity. The chromatic lines of the opening, the fragmentary nature of the piano part, full of uncertain pauses, and the brooding power of the movement's coda which ends with hushed chords – all these are what give the work today its powerful appeal (and which drew Beethoven to this work in particular). The central movement in E flat major temporarily eases the pain, and includes some of Mozart's most free-flowing writing for wind ensemble (listen to how the bassoon is active right to the end of the coda). But where you might expect a move to the major for the finale (as Beethoven was to do in his Fifth Symphony), Mozart stays in the minor for a fine set of variations that is only once allowed into C major. Even the fast triple-time ending is firmly, darkly, even despairingly in the minor.

🎧 *Piano Concertos K491 etc.* Alfred Brendel /
Scottish Chamber Orchestra / Charles Mackerras
Philips 462622–2

Piano Concerto No. 25 in C K503****

Whatever the Viennese reaction to his C minor concerto K491, it was not enough to put Mozart off writing another magnificent concerto, this time in C major, later in the same year, completing it on 4 December 1786. As Robert Levin points out, it is the longest of all his concertos (432 bars in the first movement, 382 in the last). But it turned out to be the final instalment of this series of concertos for himself to play, and his Advent concerts that year appear to have been cancelled. This work was perhaps first heard on 7 March 1787. As if to contradict criticisms of K491's darkness, this is a light-filled, triumphant work whose orchestral opening is the grandest of any in his concertos. The material of the first movement, too, is amazingly varied and fluently developed. Though 1786 was the year of *Figaro*, it is Papageno who lurks around both the second theme of the first movement and the innocent theme of the rondo finale (others have noted a likeness to the *Idomeneo* gavotte, and the movement is certainly dance-like). In the central movement, on the other hand, as David Wyn Jones has written, 'the orchestra sets the scene for the disconsolate prima donna . . . but no prima donna could match the range and agility of the decoration found in Mozart's piano writing.' No one either could fail to be swept away by the exuberance and brilliance of the finale, which is partly due to the lightness of the material, but also partly due to Mozart's dazzling writing for himself to play. Did it convince the Viennese? We do not know, but Mozart's concerts came to an end soon after.

🎧 *Piano Concertos K503 etc.* Stephen Kovacevich /
London Symphony Orchestra / Colin Davis
Philips 426 077
🎧 *Piano Concertos K503, K271* Richard Goode /
Orpheus Chamber Orchestra
Nonesuch 79454

Piano Concerto No. 26 in D, 'Coronation' K537**

This is the neglected sister among Mozart's late piano concertos, for it is far less often played than its companions. Indeed it does not even seem to be fully worked out in the score, which makes one think that Mozart played it himself, prepared it in a hurry, and as so often in these cases, improvised a good deal as he went along. Alan Tyson said that much of the piece was 'partially written' early in 1787. We know it was performed on 14 April 1789 at a special concert for the coronation of Emperor Leopold II in Frankfurt. But as it was entered in his catalogue on 24 February 1788, it is generally supposed that he also played it in a Viennese concert, and H. C. Robbins Landon made the ingenious suggestion that it was used in the interval of a performance that Mozart arranged a couple of days later of a C. P. E. Bach oratorio. Whatever the uncertainties of the piece, it can make a fine effect if played with the freedom and elaboration which Mozart himself doubtless brought to his material.

🎧 *Piano Concertos K537 etc.* Clifford Curzon /
BBC Symphony Orchestra / Pierre Boulez
BBC Legends 4020–2
🎧 *Piano Concertos K537 etc.* Murray Perahia /
English Chamber Orchestra
Sony SK39224

Piano Concerto No. 27 in B flat K595****

One of the most revealing scholarly advances of recent years in looking at Mozart's manuscripts has been the study of both his changing handwriting and the paper on which he wrote. In particular, the work of the late Alan Tyson showed just how often Mozart started a work, put it aside because he had no reason or impulse to finish it, and then returned to it some time later. A key example is this last piano concerto, always thought to have been a product of his final year: it was certainly finished on 5 January 1791, but is now believed to have been begun perhaps in 1788, around the time of the three final symphonies. (This concerto does begin, just like the G minor symphony, with a disconcerting bar of accompaniment alone, a transition from nothing into the music.) Yet the work has a seamless continuity and unity of mood: its elegiac restraint has often been linked to the events of Mozart's last year, but there is no reason to assume Mozart could not have conjured up its particular spirit at any time. It is in no sense a demonstrative piece but an inward, almost introverted meditation. The opening movement is as serene as that of the G minor symphony is restless: its art conceals considerable art, especially when the second entry of the piano comes in the totally remote key of B minor, and with the unison woodwind calls now in the strings, this leads to another piano entry also in the remote key of C major. The Larghetto seems to concentrate a lifetime's experience into its simple theme – but even this movement has an eerie moment, when at the close flute and violin play the theme in bare octaves around the piano. The finale is a rondo, and although we can hear the echoes through the whole of his concerto-writing career of the skipping, hunting finales he loved, this is an almost ethereal transformation of that tradition. A couple of days after he completed the concerto Mozart used the finale theme again in a song whose title may perhaps give a clue to its meaning: 'Longing for spring'.

𝄞 *Piano Concertos K537, K595* Clifford Curzon /
London Symphony Orchestra / István Kertész
Philips 456 757
𝄞 *Complete Piano Concertos* Malcolm Bilson /
English Baroque Soloists / John Eliot Gardiner
DG Archiv 431 211–2 (9 CDs)
𝄞 *Complete Piano Concertos*
Murray Perahia / English Chamber Orchestra
CBS SX12K 46441 (12 CDs)

String concertos

Violin Concerto No. 1 in B flat K207
Violin Concerto No. 2 in D K211
Violin Concerto No. 3 in G K216*
Violin Concerto No. 4 in D K218*
Violin Concerto No. 5 in A K219*

Mozart played the violin from an early age, but as his father noted, 'many people do not even know that you play the violin, since you have been known from childhood as a piano player'. Leopold himself, as a violinist, was the author of a standard treatise on violin playing and would have taught his son to play. Mozart's five authenticated violin concertos (there are a couple of others, including the notorious 'Adelaide' concerto written by its supposed editor Casadesus, and ones which may include some real Mozart) were all written in Salzburg, initially for himself to play. Antonio Brunetti, the new leader of the orchestra in 1776, would have played them (indeed Leopold Mozart tells us that Wolfgang wrote for K219 'a new Adagio for Brunetti, as the first was too studied for him'). They were always supposed to have been written in a very concentrated period between April and December 1775, but the dates on the manuscripts have been erased and rewritten for some unknown reason. It now seems that No. 1 dates from 1773 and is therefore Mozart's first surviving original concerto. Their depth of expression is unequalled in Mozart's music up to this time except in the A major symphony K201 of 1774; the opera *Il re pastore*, which also dates from this period, includes some striking violin music including an aria with obbligato violin, and it seems as if Mozart was feeling his way towards a concerto style; another aria shares its theme with the opening of K216.

The first concerto, too rarely played, is thoroughly worked out and highly effective for the soloist, but musically uncomplex. The second, starting with a conventional Mozart fanfare, is more concise: Neal Zaslaw calls it 'tighter in structure and more organic in relationships between themes and sections'. It was published as a 'concerto facile' in 1802. The singing Andante and Rondeau finale have nothing musically unusual. The third concerto, the earliest to have found a secure place in the repertory, has a Mozartian sweetness on the surface, but beneath that is a compelling density of thought. In the central slow movement Mozart replaces the two oboes with two flutes (they were presumably played by the same Salzburg instrumentalists) and this gives a tender, serenade-like quality. Originality is saved for the final rondo, which is broken by contrasted episodes hinting at the language of a popular song, a style that Mozart used more than once when writing in G major.

The start of the D major concerto K218 goes back to cheerful fanfaring, and the movement maintains a very active role for the soloist. The middle movement, Andante cantabile, leads to another highly original finale which contrasts a poised Andante grazioso opening with a sudden Allegro ma non troppo 6/8 section. This alternation returns, giving a slightly stop–start feel to the movement. The fifth and last concerto, completed on 20 December 1775 – just a month before Mozart's twentieth birthday – once again takes us into the world of the Salzburg divertimento. The first movement is interrupted by the arrival of the soloist in a slow passage, while into the minuet rondo of the finale bursts a quick Turkish-style march which he adapted from some earlier ballet music, not unlike the famous 'Rondo alla turca' from the piano sonata K331, also in A. These references were all doubtless the source of much hilarity in Salzburg. But what really impresses here is the development of the composer through these concertos: Mozart matured musically at the speed at which the rest of us think.

♫ *Violin Concertos, Rondo K269, Adagio K261*
Christian Tetzlaff / Deutsche Kammerphilharmonie
Virgin Classics 45314 (2 CDs)
♫ *Violin Concertos Nos. 1, 3, 4*
Viktoria Mullova / Orchestra of the Age of Enlightenment
Philips 470 292
♫ *Violin Concertos* Arthur Grumiaux /
London Symphony Orchestra / Philharmonia /
Colin Davis / Raymond Leppard
Philips 438 323–2 (2 CDs)

Concertone in C for two violins K190
Adagio in E for violin K261
Rondo in B flat for violin K269
Rondo in C for violin K373

The Concertone for two violins was written in Salzburg when Mozart was eighteen, and taken with him on various tours. With its principal parts for two violins, with contributions for solo oboe and solo cello, it is very much in the fashion of the times for *sinfonie concertante*, and Leopold advised him to perform it in Mannheim. But neither here, nor in Paris, where the form was also popular, did it see performance. The other isolated movements for violin may have been written as replacements for movements in the violin concertos, for Antonio Brunetti to play, though the C major Rondo was performed by him on its own at a concert on 8 April 1781.

Sinfonia concertante in E flat for violin and viola K364****

This is one of the peerless, superbly original creations of Mozart's early maturity – it is a miraculous creation for someone of twenty-three, and it is safe to say there has never been a greater violin and viola concerto. In a superb passage in his book *The Classical Style*, Charles Rosen demonstrates how the whole work is characterised by the sonority of the viola part, which Mozart probably wrote for himself to play. 'The very first chord gives the characteristic sound, which is like the sonority of the viola translated into the language of the full orchestra. This first chord alone is a milestone in Mozart's career.' In order to give the viola part extra projection, Mozart cleverly wrote the part in D rather than E flat, and then instructed the player to tune up the strings by a semitone: confusing, but effective! The entry of the soloists, emerging stealthily out of the orchestral texture, is unique in the literature. The dark-hued central movement is in C minor, and Mozart never wrote a finer duet in all his operas. You would call it Bachian if there was any thought that Mozart could have heard Bach's Passions. The final Rondo is full of life and inventiveness, tossing ideas between the two soloists with abandon and reaching the very top of their registers. The written-out cadenzas survive in a fair copy but the autograph is sadly lost, so the date of 1779 is an estimate. Where on earth did the idea come from? It is true that on his visit to Paris he would have heard a variety of *sinfonie concertante* for various instruments, and might have thought he could do better. He experimented with a few other combinations of soloists (wind instruments, violin, viola and cello), and Philip Wilby has completed a version of another Sinfonia concertante for piano and violin, but this is the only such piece he finished apart from his two- and three-piano concertos.

🎧 *Sinfonia Concertante K364* Norbert Brainin, Peter Schidlof / English Chamber Orchestra / Benjamin Britten
BBC Legends BBCB8010–2
🎧 *Sinfonia Concertante K364* Gidon Kremer, Kim Kashkashian / Vienna Philharmonic Orchestra / Nikolaus Harnoncourt
DG 453 043–2
🎧 *Sinfonia Concertante K364* Frank Peter Zimmermann, Tabea Zimmermann / RSO Stuttgart / Gianluigi Gelmetti
EMI 7 54196 2

Wind concertos

It's an intriguing thought that Mozart wrote a trumpet concerto for church use as early as 1768, mentioned by Leopold Mozart in a letter but now lost. Perhaps other concertos which he gave to friends are also lost, like the three bassoon concertos supposedly for Thaddeus, Baron von Durnitz. Otherwise his output for solo wind instruments was modest, especially considering how gloriously he wrote for them in his symphonies, concertos and operas.

Bassoon Concerto in B flat K191**
?Flute Concerto No. 1 in G K313*
Oboe Concerto in C K271 / ?Flute Concerto No. 2 in D K314
Andante in C for flute K315*
?Sinfonia concertante in B flat for flute, oboe, bassoon and horn K297b/A9
Concerto in C for flute and harp K299

The Bassoon Concerto is an underrated, underperformed work which shows a real understanding of the lyrical character of the instrument. Apparently completed on 4 June 1774, its three movements complement each other well: the central movement (oddly marked Andante ma adagio) is an extended aria; the final rondo starts as a stately minuet but the bassoon bounces away in triplets.

Mozart surprisingly claimed to dislike writing for the flute (or more probably it was the particular flautist he had in mind, or even more probably it was his excuse to his father for not having finished the commissions in question). The first flute concerto was inspired by the players he heard in Mannheim, notably Johann Baptist Wendling, but was actually commissioned (with Wendling's help) by an amateur flautist Ferdinand de Jean. It's a charming work in which the artistry is concealed beneath a veneer of good humour, recreating the pastoral tone always associated with the flute. There is, however, no authentic source for this work, which was first published by Breitkopf in 1804. The second flute concerto K314 is now believed to be an arrangement, not by Mozart, of the Oboe Concerto in C, written in 1777 for the Salzburg oboist Giuseppe Ferlendis, another outstanding player, and mentioned in a letter of 14 February 1778. The single-movement Andante in C for flute is of such quality it seems a pity that it never made its way into a full-length concerto.

The history of the Sinfonia concertante K297b for wind is very complex, and the work has not come down to us in a genuinely Mozartian form, but it has been restored by editors including Robert Levin, and is an effective piece. Most famous in this group of works is the Concerto in C for flute and harp K299, one of the few works by Mozart to which I have never warmed: it sounds always determinedly superficial. Its origins in Paris in April 1778 clearly show it to be influenced by the vogue for *sinfonie concertante*, and like the flute works was born of necessity, in this case to please the flute-playing Comte de Guines and his harpist daughter, who seems to have been among Mozart's least talented pupils: as he wrote, 'she has no ideas whatever . . . nothing comes . . . so I write down four bars of a minuet and said to her "what an ass I am!" I then told her to finish the minuet.' He wrote a perfectly appropriate piece for her and her father, but was never paid.

🎧 *Flute Concerto No. 1, Flute and Harp Concerto*
Susan Palma, Nancy Allen / Orpheus Chamber Orchestra
DG 427 677–2
🎧 *Flute Concerto No. 1, Flute and Harp Concerto, Bassoon Concerto* Lisa Beznosiuk, Frances Kelly, Danny Bond /
Academy of Ancient Music / Christopher Hogwood
Decca Oiseau-Lyre 417 622–2
🎧 *Flute and Harp Concerto, Oboe Concerto, Bassoon Concerto*
Willem Hazelzet, Saskia Kwast, Marcel Ponseele, Marc
Vallon / Amsterdam Baroque Orchestra / Ton Koopman
Erato 91724
🎧 *Sinfonia concertante for wind K297b*
Orpheus Chamber Orchestra
DG 429 784–2

Horn Concerto No. 2 in E flat K417*
Horn Concerto No. 4 in E flat K495**
Horn Concerto No. 3 in E flat K447*
Horn Concerto No. 1 in D K412 (compl. Süssmayr)
Rondo in E flat for horn K371

Mozart's relationship with his performers is nowhere more amusingly in evidence than in his writing for the horn. All these concertos were written for his close friend Joseph Leutgeb, who was the principal horn in Salzburg and then followed Mozart from Salzburg to Vienna (with financial help from Leopold Mozart), where he joined his wife's cheese-making business but still played the horn. The relationship was clearly close, and based on the sort of Mozartian buffoonery that must either have been deeply heart-warming to Leutgeb or deeply irritating. The Concerto No. 2 (the first to be written) is inscribed 'Wolfgang Amadé Mozart takes pity on Leutgeb, ass, ox and fool in Vienna on 27 May 1783'. The next concerto to be written was the most famous, K495, whose score is written in different coloured inks, blue, red, green and black. (The earnest editor of the *Neue Mozart Ausgabe* suggested that this 'depicts refinements of dynamics and colouristic inflection', but we can also assume it is all part of manically distracting Leutgeb.) The finale has to modern ears in this country never quite recovered from the vocal version by Michael Flanders:

> I once had a whim and I had to obey it
> To buy a French horn in a second-hand shop
> I polished it up and I started to play it
> In spite of the neighbours who begged me to stop . . .

The 'first' Horn Concerto turns out to be the last, and to have been completed, like the Requiem, by his pupil Süssmayr. This entertaining piece of detective work by Alan Tyson (who also suggests that the fourth concerto is earlier than the third) has pointed out that the inscription on the manuscript 'Venerdi Santo li 6 Aprile' is followed by a year usually read as 1797 or as a slip for 1787. But since Good Friday also fell on 6 April in 1792, Tyson suggests that that was when Süssmayr completed and dated it, after Mozart's death – even incorporating a fragmentary quote from the Lamentations of Jeremiah which might have been among the composer's drafts for the Requiem. (Who knows? The date doesn't look like 1792 to me.) Still, this is a jolly and effective piece, though no performance has yet managed to fully include Mozart's increasingly hysterical instructions to his friendly soloist in the draft of the rondo: 'a lei Signor Asino . . . Animo . . . presto . . . su via . . . da bravo . . . Coraggio . . . e finisci gia? . . . a te . . . bestia . . . oh che stonatura . . . Ahi! ohime! . . . bravo poveretto.'

The Rondo K371 was presumed to be an isolated movement, but in 1988 sixty further bars turned up and Robert Levin combined this with his reconstruction of the movement K370b to form a Horn Concerto 'No. o'.

There is also a noble opening of a Horn Concerto in E major, K494a, with some contrapuntal writing for orchestra; this piece breaks off after less than a hundred bars, but has been recorded.

🎧 *Horn Concertos* Hermann Baumann /
Concentus Musicus Wien / Nikolaus Harnoncourt
Teldec 242 757–2
🎧 *Horn Concertos* Dennis Brain / Philharmonia /
Herbert von Karajan
EMI 61013
🎧 *Horn Concerto fragment in E major K494a* Anthony
Halstead / Hanover Band / Roy Goodman
Nimbus 7156

Clarinet Concerto in A K622****

Mozart's most famous wind concerto is rarely heard in the form Mozart may have intended. It was completed in the autumn of 1791, for his friend Anton Stadler who was pioneering the use of the basset clarinet, with an especially low range that extended the bottom of the instrument by a third. After Mozart's death the solo part of the work was adapted for conventional clarinet and that is how it was published. (A different hypothesis by Cliff Eisen is that though the work was begun for basset clarinet, its final form was for the normal instrument; as the autograph is lost, we cannot know.) It was not entirely a product of his last year, since Alan Tyson showed that the first 199 bars are identical with those of an earlier attempt at a basset-horn concerto: 'this fragment was probably written down a year or two earlier, possibly even as early as 1787.' Mozart's pupil Süssmayr, who travelled with him to Prague for the premiere of *La clemenza di Tito* (writing recitatives for Mozart en route), was also writing a basset clarinet concerto for Stadler, and this may have stimulated Mozart to trump him. And with what skill he does so, since this concerto has become one of the immortal masterpieces of the repertory. 'Never would I have thought that a clarinet could be capable of imitating the human voice as deceptively as it is imitated by you. Truly your instrument has so soft and lovely a tone that nobody who has a heart can resist it' – so wrote Mozart to Stadler, giving further expression of a warmth that had already been shown in the Clarinet Quintet of 1789. That responsiveness is at its deepest in the central movement, whose melody breathes a spirit of serenity and of resignation which seems entirely in tune with the spirit of Mozart's last year.

☊ *Clarinet Concerto*
Michael Collins / Russian National Orchestra / Mikhail Pletnev
DG 457 652–2
☊ *Clarinet Concerto, Clarinet Quintet* Eric Hoeprich / Orchestra of the 18th Century / Frans Bruggen
Philips 420 242–2

Other orchestral pieces

Over the course of his short but busy life Mozart wrote all sorts of occasional music, music to accompany celebrations in Salzburg and beyond, often out of doors. Early examples include so-called *Finalmusik* to mark the end of the Salzburg university year in August, when the performances were transitory around the town (using added marches while on the move) and – maybe because they were given standing up – using basses rather than cellos in addition to violins and violas. The university documents in 1769 record 'Ad noctem musica . . . ab ad adolescentulo lectissimo Wolfg. Mozart' – night music by the learned adolescent. The requirement in Salzburg was for large-scale serenades with an extended number of movements; following Mozart's move to Vienna, he wrote no more of these pieces but instead smaller serenades for wind, and some famous miniatures including the *Eine kleine Nachtmusik* and the Adagio and Fugue in C minor. In his final years his modest court position in Vienna took him towards the provision of dance music. All these pieces show Mozart pouring the very highest skill into the provision of entertainment music.

Divertimenti, cassations and serenades etc.

Galimathias musicum K32
Cassation in G K63
Cassation in B flat K99
Cassation in D K100 and March in D K62
Divertimento in E flat K113
Divertimento in D K131

What a jolly farrago is the *Galimathias musicum*: a collection of short bizarre pieces labelled by Leopold Mozart a 'Quodlibet' (that is, a piece bringing together diverse elements, usually popular songs) and put together in The Hague on tour in March 1766: Leopold clearly had as much of a hand in this as did the young Wolfgang, whose fugue was rejected in favour of a seriously boring version by his earnest father. The three early cassations, a term derived from 'gassatim gehen', performing on the move, are all *Finalmusik* from 1769: cheerful strings of mostly lively movements which would have accompanied the march across the Salzach River to the Mirabell Garden. More substantial are the pair of divertimenti, the E flat for Milan in 1771 (the first work of Mozart's to use the clarinet) and the D major, with its typical seven-movement sequence, one of a long line of Salzburg serenades.

♫ *Complete Serenades*
Academy of St Martin-in-the-Fields / Neville Marriner
Philips Complete Mozart Edition 422 503–2

Divertimento in D K136*
Divertimento in B flat K137
Divertimento in F K138*

These three lively string pieces from 1772 often find their way into chamber-orchestra programmes; they are much more short and concise than other divertimenti of the time, and are really miniature symphonies in the three-movement form of the Italian sinfonia. Alfred Einstein thought that they were originally intended for an Italian tour, and might have had wind instruments added to them, but they work equally well when played by string soloists. The D major work leads off with a curling theme propelled by its suspensions, with a very Italian Andante and a little fugue in the finale. The B flat work puts its slow movement first, with two contrasted fast movements to follow. The F major divertimento uses a familiar orchestral style with bustling scales and wide, bouncing leaps, and its final Presto includes both a minor-mode episode of some seriousness and a fugato which points forward to Mozart's later symphonic development.

🎧 *Divertimenti K136, K137, K138, K251*
Amsterdam Baroque Orchestra / Ton Koopman
Erato 2292–45471-2

Serenade in D K185 and March in D K189
Serenade in D K203 and March in D K237*
Serenade in D K204 and March in D K215
Serenade in D, 'Serenata notturna' K239*

Though the Serenade K185 was written in Vienna in the summer of 1773 (while Mozart was looking unsuccessfully for work there), it was intended for Salzburg, as were all the other works here. Its seven movements include what is virtually a mini violin concerto in its second and third movements; probably Mozart played it himself.

Back in Salzburg, some 1774 celebrations prompted the Serenade K203, with its fine dotted-rhythm March K237; it includes a lovely muted slow movement with buzzing, trilling second violins bearing an eloquent first-violin melody, almost literally showing buried emotion, as Fiordiligi was later to do. The 1775 work is again in D, with plenty for a solo violinist to do, and a little opportunity for the wind principals in the fifth movement. The most famous of this group is the 'Serenata notturna' of 1776, perhaps because it is relatively short. Is it complete? The March, which is one of Mozart's most subtle and elaborate, leads straight to a minuet and trio and thence to a Rondeau finale which seems to celebrate the bucolic side of the Salzburg character.

🎧 *'Serenata notturna' etc.* English Chamber Orchestra /
Benjamin Britten
Decca 430 495-2
🎧 *Serenade K185, Cassation K100*
Academy of St Martin-in-the-Fields / Neville Marriner
Philips 426 388-2

Divertimento in D K205
Divertimento in F, 'Lodron No. 1' K247 and March K248
Divertimento in D K 251
Divertimento in B flat, 'Lodron No. 2' K287
Divertimento in D K334 and March K445
Notturno in D for four orchestras K286*

These smaller-scale pieces are for mixed groups of wind and solo strings, maybe for outdoor use but certainly for entertainment purposes. K205 has been connected, for example, with the garden of Mozart's friend Dr Mesmer, but it seems more likely to be associated with the name-day festivities of Maria Anna Elisabeth von Andretter, on 26 July 1773. The D major Divertimento K251 was written in July 1776, perhaps for Nannerl's name-day, while the B flat K287 was composed in the following year for the Countess Lodron's name-day. The D major Divertimento K334 is the third to feature the combination of strings and two horns, this time written in 1780 for the Robinig von Rottenfeld family; this is a later and more mature work from 1779/80. It has an especially expressive associated march (of which Saint-Saëns owned the autograph). There is a fine set of variations in which the horns shine. The real oddity here is the Notturno for four orchestral groups, probably from 1776/7, where the attempts at echo effects through foreshortenings and some overlapping of phrases suggest a highly experimental work for Mozart. Having once heard it in performance I would have to admit it's almost completely unsuccessful, but it surely bore fruit in the visionary writing for different dance groups in the Act I finale of *Don Giovanni*.

♪ *Divertimenti K334, K136*
Stockholm Chamber Orchestra / Franz Welser-Möst
EMI 7 54055 2
♪ *Notturno K286, etc.*
Vienna Mozart Ensemble / Willi Boskovsky
Decca 458 310–2

Serenade in D, 'Haffner' K250 and March in D K249**
Serenade in D, 'Posthorn' K320 and Marches in D K335**

Both these splendid serenades take us far beyond the conventional achievements of the earlier works, and deserve the closest attention. The 'Haffner' Serenade is not to be confused with the 'Haffner' Symphony, which followed its success. It was written for the wedding of Siegmund Haffner's daughter to the Salzburg merchant Franz Xaver Spath, and Mozart (who had just turned twenty) seemed determined to excel himself, and wrote no less than eight movements of variety and splendour. There are at least three different pieces here: a three-movement symphony (formed by movements 1, 6 and 8), a small violin concerto (2, 3 and 4) and a group of minuets (3, 5 and 7). The work effortlessly sustains its hour's length.

The 'Posthorn' Serenade is equally imposing, and was completed on 3 August 1779. It's the last of the serenades Mozart wrote in Salzburg, but to suggest as Einstein did that the first movement dramatises the conflict between Mozart and his employer is maybe taking things a little far. Here the main parts in the third and fourth movements are for a wind group rather than a violin soloist (and these two movements were performed separately, at a Vienna concert in 1783, so Mozart must have thought well of them; and he also adapted movements 1, 5 and 7 into a popular symphony). The work plumbs depths of feeling in the Andantino, but Mozart, as so often, pulls back and inserts a joke: here the appearance of the Posthorn or 'corno di posta' itself in the minuet's second trio. Perhaps it was a reference to the university students returning home, though it has more fancifully been seen as Mozart's longing to escape Salzburg. The wind soloists have a cadenza in their concertante Andante, while in the first trio of the second minuet Mozart uses a piccolo to enhance the colour.

♫ *'Haffner' Serenade K250* Lucy van Dael /
Orchestra of the 18th Century / Frans Brüggen
Philips 432 997-2

🎧 *'Haffner' Serenade K250, Dances K600*
NDR Symphony Orchester / Günter Wand
BMG RD60068
🎧 *'Posthorn' Serenade K320, K185 etc.*
Vienna Mozart Ensemble / Willi Boskovsky
Decca 440 036–2

Masonic Funeral Music K477**
Ein musikalisches Spass **K522**
Eine kleine Nachtmusik **K525*****
Adagio and Fugue in C minor K546**

Four extremely characterful and contrasted works, three of which feature regularly in concert programmes. But how many of them are actually orchestral? (The New Mozart Edition oddly includes two of them in a volume called 'Symphonies'.) The Masonic Funeral Music is a bold and personal statement which Mozart revised for the funeral ceremony on 17 November 1785 of two masons, one from the family of Haydn's patrons, the Esterházys. Winds, including three basset horns, open the work ominously, like the oracle from *Idomeneo*, and winding string lines lead to a solemn statement of the Lamentations of Jeremiah chant. There was apparently a version from earlier in that year that included voices, but here the liturgical chant is given to the wind, over expressive strings. Almost as soon as it has started, the music expires.

The 'Musical Joke' is a heavy-handed parody of second-rate musical composition, deadly accurate in its parodies, but somehow not nearly as funny as Mozart's genuine musical jokes. It was presumably intended for some domestic gathering: it is really a chamber piece for solo strings. It was always thought to be the first piece Mozart composed after his father's death, giving rise to much speculation as to his motives; but Alan Tyson showed that most of it was written much earlier.

The 'Little Night Music' must be the most successful serenade ever written, and certainly features in any 'top ten' list of Mozart CD sales. Why? Its virtues are utter simplicity, memorability and perfect balance. Its initial fanfares and melody, really no different from those in so many other Mozartian openings, indelibly remain in the mind. And that is equally true of the Romance and especially of the final rondo, whose ascending opening echoes the start of the piece; apart from a questioning seventh just before the coda, there is little to disturb the perfect Mozartian equilibrium here.

The Adagio and Fugue is a fascinating piece, or rather pair of pieces. The Fugue started out as a duet for two pianos K426, composed in 1783. This dates from the time when Mozart was increasingly involved with baroque music: one of the tasks he may have undertaken was to score some preludes to precede transcriptions of Bach fugues. Five years later he returned to this piece and noted in his list of works for 26 June that year: 'A short Adagio [ein kurzes Adagio] . . . for a fugue which I had already written a long time ago.' So he transcribed this Fugue for strings and then added a new Prelude. It is an angular work, full of fierce dotted rhythms and leaping intervals, but translated into Mozart's own harmonic world: a most disturbing piece which seems to pre-echo Beethoven's *Grosse Fuge*. There is a part for double bass in the Fugue, suggesting that this arrangement is indeed for orchestra. (A BBC producer in search of the authentic Mozart did once mount a studio recording of the piece with the Adagio played on strings followed by the fugue on pianos, but the tape was lost and had to be replaced by extracts from two different records!)

🎧 *K525, K522, K251* Concentus Musicus Wien / Nikolaus Harnoncourt
Teldec 244 809–2
🎧 *Serenades and Divertimenti* Orpheus Chamber Orchestra
DG 431 689–2

🎧 *K525, K546, K239, K522*
The English Concert / Andrew Manze
Harmonia Mundi HMU 907280

Dances

Mozart's dance music has often been ignored because it consists of occasional pieces written to order, some of it late in his life as part of his duties as court composer, for balls at the Redoutensaal in Vienna. But it is a fundamental misunderstanding of Mozart to assume that just because he was writing for the dance he would produce music of secondary importance. Dancing was an absolutely integral part of normal life in Mozart's time, and the spirit of the dance runs throughout his music. Scholars have traced the impact of dance forms on his arias, and made links between the spirit of various dance movements and his own works. As always, Mozart worked productively within the forms he had available, and always stretched their boundaries. 'Whoever would know Mozart, must hear this music,' wrote Erik Smith, the record producer who committed Mozart's complete works to CD. It is, however, not so easy to encounter in the concert hall the collections of German dances and minuets that Mozart provided, as they do not lend themselves to concert performances. But some conductors have revived individual groups of dances with great success, and in 1991 Roger Norrington programmed those written in 1791 with a group of dancers, to revelatory effect.

Seven Minuets K65a
Nineteen Minuets K103
Six Minuets K164
Sixteen Minuets K176
Four Contredanses K101
Four Contredanses K267

From when he was just thirteen to the very last year of his

life, Mozart produced dances for all occasions, mainly in the three forms of the minuet, contredanses and the German dance. These early examples, rarely played these days, would have been written for celebrations in Salzburg and Italy, in particular during the frenetic days of the annual carnival. The simplest set, K65a, dates from 26 January 1769. In K103, from Salzburg 1771-2, oboes or flutes and trumpets are added to the orchestration, though usually omitted in the trio sections, as in K104. K164 dates from June 1772, and K176 from December 1773: already here there are more interesting musical effects, with pauses and sudden contrasts. The contredanses K101 for the 1776 carnival begin with a gavotte, while that dance comes second in the K267 contredanses for the 1777 carnival. (The two sets of six minuets K104 and K105 are actually by Michael Haydn.)

Ballet music, *Les petits riens* K299b

In Paris, during May–June 1778, Mozart wrote some items for a ballet by the French dancing master Noverre. There are twenty pieces and an overture, but not all these pieces are by Mozart and scholars have been unable to decide definitively which movements are by him. Mozart characterised the rest with typical directness as 'a lot of rotten old French airs . . . This ballet has already been done four times with great applause.' It seems the work was undertaken to help Noverre out, maybe in the hope of a future commission.

Three Minuets K363
Six Minuets K461
Six Contredanses K462
Minuets and Contredanses K463

By the time Mozart got to Vienna in the early 1780s, dances were ever more the rage: both large-scale court affairs and domestic gatherings. One of Mozart's letters back home describes a ball which he organised in his own apartments, with gentlemen paying two gulden to attend: 'We began at 6 in the evening and finished at 7 – what? only an hour? No, no – at 7 in the morning.' So there was plenty of call for dances such as these sets, where Mozart is as inventive as possible within the confines that the regular form demanded.

Six German Dances K509*
Six German Dances K536
Six German Dances K567
Twelve Minuets K568
Six German Dances K571
Twelve Minuets K585
Twelve German Dances K586
Three Contredanses K106

Apart from the first lively set, associated with Mozart's happy stay in Prague in early 1787 (and supposedly the result of a trick whereby he was invited to dinner and then locked in a room to compose), all these varied dances were written for Vienna from 1788 onwards. Even the contredanses with the early Köchel number 106 are now thought to date from Vienna in 1790. On 7 December 1787 Mozart was appointed Royal Imperial Chamber Composer and began composing dances with some regularity. He received 800 gulden a year, but as he (probably mythically) said, reported by Rochlitz, that is 'too much for what I do, too little for what I could do'. Erik Smith has written of the 'full wonder of the scoring of Mozart's late dances', and there is indeed much variety in evidence here.

🎧 *Deutsche Tanze K509, K536,567, K571, K586*
Tafelmusik / Bruno Weil
Sony SK 46696

Six Minuets K599
Six German Dances K600**
Four Minuets K601*
Four German Dances K602*
Two Contredanses K603*
Two Minuets K604*
Three German Dances K605**
Six German Dances K606**
Contredanses K607, K609, K610

These sets of dances were all composed during Mozart's remarkable last year, and give the lie to any idea that he was unproductive or underachieving during that time. These sets contain some of his richest and most imaginative scoring, with posthorns and sleighbells in K605, and most notoriously, in K602, the hurdy-gurdy – the instrument which enjoyed such a vogue in the heyday of Marie Antoinette's court. Start perhaps with the dances K600, completed on 29 January 1791, an infectious set right from the slanting melody of the first dance, and the cheerful flute descant of the second, the plunging fanfare of the fourth, and the imitation of a canary bird of the fifth. The varied dances of K601–6 make a wonderfully varied set, and 'Die Schillenfahrt' in K605 has become famous. The third dance of K601 was re-entered by Mozart as K611 in his catalogue as 'Die Leyerer' for 6 March, as if he had forgotten writing it, which given his extraordinary productivity at this moment, he might well have. The other famous tune is the first of K609, which is based on 'Non piu andrai' from *Figaro*, but that is likely to have been written earlier than 1791.

☊ *Dances and Marches:*
complete Vienna Mozart Ensemble / Willi Boskovsky
Philips Complete Mozart Edition Vol. 6 422 506–2 (6 CDs)
selection Decca 430 634–2
☊ *'A Little Light Music': K522, dances etc.*
Orpheus Chamber Orchestra
DG 429 783–2

Wind ensemble music

Just as Mozart wrote serenades for outdoor use in Salzburg, so too he wrote 'Harmoniemusik' for groups of wind instruments, probably first in Italy, then in Vienna where outdoor wind serenades were becoming more popular. The basis of these ensembles was pairs of wind instruments (clarinets and sometimes oboes, horns and bassoons), and these were the ensembles that the Emperor established as his *Harmonie* in Vienna in 1782. Royer Hellyer has speculated that this drove Mozart to compose for this combination in Vienna, but that he was overtaken by the vogue for operatic transcriptions. He probably made one of these himself, from *Die Entführung*, but there is no evidence it was ever performed at court. In the film of *Amadeus*, however, it is hearing the great Serenade in B flat at court that first alerts Salieri to Mozart's genius.

Divertimento in B flat K186
Divertimento in E flat K166
Divertimento in C K188

The first two works were probably written while Mozart was in Milan in March 1773, and unusually for the time include clarinets in their scoring. (K166 is dated Salzburg 24 March 1773, but we know that clarinets were not available there.) K188, from some time during 1773–5, is an altogether special and unusual work for two flutes, five trumpets and timpani, in the tradition of the outdoor fanfare music that sounded around Salzburg; probably involved would have been the court trumpeter Johann Schachtner, one of the Mozart family's closest friends, who later provided anecdotes of the young Wolfgang, including one that he was frightened of the trumpet. (K187 is an arrangement by Leopold and Wolfgang Mozart of music by Starzer and Gluck.)

Divertimento in F K213
Divertimento in B flat K240
Divertimento in E flat K252
Divertimento in F K253
Divertimento in B flat K270

These five works are all so-called *Tafelmusik* for entertainment during dinner: the exact context can be heard parodied by Mozart in the Act II finale of *Don Giovanni*, where Giovanni hears and rejects various operatic numbers played to him. These are lively and workmanlike pieces, with a notable 'Contredanse en Rondeau' at the end of K213 and an amusing folk tune at the end of K252, which translates as 'The cat won't give up chasing mice'. The B flat K270 is the most mature work, with an extended first movement, a gavotte with a gracious coda, a minuet with a Ländler trio, and a triple-time Presto to finish.

𝄞 *K213, K240, K252, K253, K270* Amadeus Winds
Decca Oiseau-Lyre 425 819–2
𝄞 *Wind Divertimenti and Serenades* Netherlands Wind Ensemble
Philips Complete Mozart Edition Vol. 5 422 505–2 (6 CDs)

Serenade in E flat K375***
Serenade in C minor K388****
Serenade in B flat K361****

Whatever objections people may have to Peter Shaffer's portrait of Mozart in *Amadeus*, and many of them are justified on historic if not dramatic grounds, you cannot fault him on one thing: his choice of music to illustrate Mozart's genius. The moment in the original play when Salieri hears the Adagio from the B flat Serenade K361 is one of the great musical descriptions in drama (it is completely bungled in the film, where two movements from the Serenade are grotesquely edited together), and serves to highlight what a unique work this is, recognised as such by Mozart's contemporaries. As

Schink wrote in his 1785 *Fragments litteraires*, 'Oh what an effect it made – glorious and grand, excellent and sublime!'

All these three serenades are classics of the repertory and show Mozart lavishing intense care and understanding on writing for wind instruments. The origin of the E flat Serenade K375 seems to have been as a sextet written for St Theresa's Day in 1781; it was performed at the house of Herr von Hickel, court painter. As Mozart recorded, 'The six gentlemen who executed it are poor beggars who, however, play together quite well. Particularly the first clarinet and the two horns . . . I wrote it rather carefully. It has won great applause too.' On 31 October, Mozart's name-day (his saint's feast day, not his birthday), the players came to serenade him, and 'placing themselves in the centre of the courtyards, surprised me, just as I was about to undress, in the most pleasant fashion imaginable with the first chord in E flat'. It is difficult to imagine the piece without the sound of the two oboes that Mozart added the following year; their dissonances on the opening page alone give the work its bitter-sweet quality.

There are few clues to the origin of the C minor Serenade, which bears the description 'Nacht Musique' (although this is not in Mozart's hand): the description seems more appropriate for this dark and gloomy piece than for the sunny string serenade with the same title. Indeed the whole piece almost seems to reflect the literary associations of night with hidden tragedy. It may be the work Mozart referred to on 27 July 1782: 'I have had to compose in a great hurry a serenade, but only for wind instruments,' though that may refer instead to the new arrangement of the E flat Serenade. The C minor's first movement opens with a solidly baroque theme (whose arpeggio and falling seventh links it to such baroque classics as Bach's *Musical Offering*). But in the clarinet's quiet echo of the theme the falling seventh assumes an expressive importance; the movement is at times extremely hesitant, as when the oboe eases up an octave into the second subject (wonderfully intensified in the recapitulation). Both here and in the finale the music seems to peter out before re-gathering its strength. The minuet and trio are written in strict canon, and the final movement's variations, anticipating those in the same key in the finale of the C minor piano concerto, are marvellous. The movement seems about to end in the minor, when the E flat of the horns 'falls like a gentle beam of light' (Einstein). Although the movement manages to end in C major, its reckless gaiety sounds like blind rejoicing.

The B flat Serenade, sometimes called the 'Gran Partita', for thirteen wind instruments (actually twelve wind instruments plus either contrabassoon or more appropriately double bass) is one of the greatest and most unusual of all Mozart's creations. It may have been stimulated by the skilled wind players from the Mannheim orchestra with whom he collaborated on *Idomeneo*, or it may have originated later in Vienna in conjunction with the clarinettist Anton Stadler (Stadler certainly played some movements from it on 23 March 1784). It has also been suggested that it might conceivably have been linked to Mozart's own wedding celebrations. Whatever the circumstances, the piece shows Mozart responding with incredible resourcefulness to the variety of wind instruments available to him, creating different combinations of sounds for the clarinets, horns and basset horns, all beautifully woven into textures for which there is really no precedent. Robert Levin suggests that the work has more in common with the piano concertos written earlier, in which the wind instruments began to be emancipated: perhaps this was one of the many pieces which Mozart started, but did not finish until later when an opportunity for performance arose. There is a stately opening Largo and a crisp opening, Molto allegro. The first of two minuets, each with two trios, features different wind instruments (the quartet of two clarinets and two basset horns in the first trio of minuet I for example), and then the sublime Adagio – the one so well described by Peter Shaffer – unfolds as a continuous line handed on from oboe to clarinet to basset horn over syncopated pulsation from the rest of the wind. (Dvořák was to directly copy this effect in his great D minor Serenade.) The variations are among the loveliest he wrote: varied, relaxed and always lyrical, again featuring pairs of instruments in relief, with singing triplets for the oboes. The finale is a rumbustious dance for the full ensemble which shows Mozart's mastery of writing dances transferred to a new and revolutionary medium.

♫ *Serenades K375, K388, Adagio K411*
Netherlands Wind Ensemble
Chandos CHAN 9284
♫ *Serenade K361* Octophorus / Barthold Kuijken
Accent ACC 68642D
♫ *Serenade K361* Orchestra of St Luke's / Charles Mackerras
Telarc 80359
♫ *Serenades K253, K270, K289*
London Wind Soloists / Jack Brymer
Decca 430 298-2
♫ *Serenades K361, K375, K388 etc.*
Amadeus Winds / Christopher Hogwood
Decca 458 096-2 (2 CDs)

?Five Divertimenti K439b
Adagio in F K410*
Adagio in B flat K411*
12 Duos for two horns K487
?Duo for bassoon and cello K292

The Five Divertimenti K439b are doubtful in origin, and have come down to us from Mozart's wind-playing friend Anton Stadler. They are unpretentious but effective instrumental experiments, whose date is uncertain. They were probably written for Stadler and his friends to play on three basset horns, though they have been published for other combinations of wind instruments. The two adagios for basset horns with clarinet or bassoon are beautiful miniatures for the Stadler circle, probably written in Vienna in 1782–3. Some of the duos written possibly for two horns survive in autograph, marked 27 July 1786 'while playing skittles'; this may have led to a confusion with the 'Kegelstatt' Trio of a week later: it would certainly have been easier to write these undemanding duets than that masterpiece of chamber music while in the middle of bowling.

♫ *Wind Divertimenti and Serenades* Holliger Wind Ensemble
Philips Complete Mozart Edition Vol. 5 422 505–2 (6 CDs)

Adagio in C for glass harmonica K356*
Adagio in C minor and Rondo in C major for glass harmonica quintet K617*

Two beautiful miniatures featuring a most unusual instrument. The glass harmonica was originally invented by Benjamin Franklin: it features glass bowls which rotate in water and can be played with the fingers, creating an unearthly sound. The instrument was further developed so that it was easier to play, but it was always a highly specialised beast. The solo piece, equally effective for organ, is a luminous Adagio of only twenty-eight bars, with all the refined simplicity of *Die Zauberflöte*. The ensemble, completed on 23 May 1791, has the spareness typical of Mozart's late style: clarity, no decoration, intense sounds from the combination of two winds and two strings with the glass harmonica. These pieces were written for the blind player Maria Anna Kirchgassner, whose playing was by report 'ethereally beautiful'; she later played the instrument in London in March 1794, but according to H. C. Robbins Landon, on that occasion the room was too large and the audience were too loud for the instrument.

♫ *K617, 356* Bruno Hoffmann et al.
Philips Complete Mozart Edition Vol. 14 422 514–2 (5 CDs)
♫ *K617, 356* Vienna Glass Harmonica Duo
LOTU LR9413

Chamber music

String quartets

For Mozart, the domestic performance of chamber music was central to his life and would have been so since his earliest days. One of the most attractive of the early stories told about Mozart by the court trumpeter (and violinist) Johann Schachtner concerns a performance in the Mozart household in which Leopold, Schachtner and Herr Wenzl played through some trios, and the tiny Wolfgang pleaded to join in on the violin, although he had not 'had the least instruction in the violin' (a little unlikely this, with his father the author of a renowned violin-teaching method). He was allowed to play the second-violin part along with Schachtner, who eventually stopped playing: 'I soon noticed with astonishment that I was quite superfluous, I quietly put my violin down, and looked at your Papa; tears of wonder and comfort ran down his cheeks at this scene, and so he played all 6 trios.' (see also p. 54)

As with his symphonies, one can trace through the sequence of string quartets both Mozart's own personal development as a composer and the deepening of the string quartet form – much of the latter accomplished by Joseph Haydn, in music that we know Mozart studied, admired, and learnt from.

String Quartet No. 1 in G K80
String Quartet No. 2 in D K155
String Quartet No. 3 in G K156
String Quartet No. 4 in C K157
String Quartet No. 5 in F K158
String Quartet No. 6 in B flat K159
String Quartet No. 7 in E flat K160
String Quartet No. 8 in F K168
String Quartet No. 9 in A K169

String Quartet No. 10 in C K170
String Quartet No. 11 in E flat K171*
String Quartet No. 12 in B flat K172
String Quartet No. 13 in D minor K173*

The first work here stands apart as Mozart's first surviving essay in the form, written during his first trip to Italy, and inscribed, 'Lodi, 15 March 1770 at 7 o'clock in the evening' – as if he wanted to remember the moment when he entered into this remarkable idiom. He took the score to Paris eight years later, recalling that it was the piece 'I composed one evening at the inn in Lodi'. The remaining twelve form two sets of six: in both sets, the keys are clearly related. In the first six, each key rises by the interval of a fourth, while in the second set they are in pairs of major thirds: F–A, C–E flat, B flat–D. All six of the first set (which date from Italy, mostly written in Milan between the end of 1772 and the start of 1773) are in three movements and show a broadly Italianate style.

Are they worth playing? Hans Keller, that champion of later Mozart, thought them 'quite abominable': as a quartet player himself, he wrote, 'Why play them at all and thus insult Mozart's genius?'

But by the second set, probably begun in Vienna in August 1773 and completed in September, there is far more contrapuntal writing and it is clear that he had been looking at Haydn's quartets, perhaps especially the Op. 20 set with their tightly argued fugal movements. If truth be told, Mozart's closing fugue in the F major quartet K168 is a bit stolid, but other moments of counterpoint are more effective: for example the Andante of K171 in the style of a double fugue, as well as the minuet of K172. Then there is the remarkable opening of the E flat quartet K171, with its angular slow introduction (which recurs at the end of the movement) and the quiet beginning to the Allegro, where you can't quite tell that it has moved into a faster tempo. There is something consciously experimental about the D minor quartet K173, as

Mozart toys with chromatic phrases and wide leaps, sudden pauses and Haydnesque modulations; in the last movement he writes an ultra-learned chromatic fugue to finish.

🎧 *Complete String Quartets* Amadeus Quartet
DG 423 300–2 (6 CDs)

String Quartet No. 14 in G K387***
String Quartet No. 15 in D minor K421***
String Quartet No. 16 in E flat K428**
String Quartet No. 17 in B flat K458*
String Quartet No. 18 in A K464**
String Quartet No. 19 in C, 'Dissonance' K465****

The six quartets which Mozart dedicated to Haydn were the 'fruit of a long and laborious effort', as he wrote in the eloquent dedication. Perhaps he thought when he completed the outstanding G major quartet K387, and dated it 31 December 1782 in Vienna, that it would be easy to complete a set of six; or perhaps, as Alec Hyatt King has argued, the idea of a set followed only later. (Mozart offered a set of six to a Paris publisher in April 1783.) Progress was slow, and others followed only fitfully; he completed the last two in January 1785. The last three were performed for Haydn himself in February, which was the occasion for Haydn's remark to Leopold: 'Before God and as an honest man I tell you that your son is the greatest composer known to me either in person or by name. He has taste and, what is more, the most profound knowledge of composition.' The set was published later that year; its dedication was written on 1 September 1785.

Whether or not Mozart had publicly admitted the hard work that went into these pieces, you would have to admire their supreme combination of learned skill and emotional directness. The problems raised by his earlier quartet compositions have all been solved. The G major K387 is rightly renowned for the final sonata-form fugue, with a four-note theme that is far closer in spirit to the 'Jupiter' Symphony

finale than many other supposed antecedents of that movement, since though the notes are not the same it rises and falls
in the same shape. Here Mozart is using counterpoint, as
Cliff Eisen puts it, 'not so much as a texture in and of itself,
but as a structural topic'. Thematic integration is also evident
here: the rising chromatic line of the finale's second section is
directly pre-echoed by the remarkable minuet.

The power of the D minor quartet is surely unsurpassed in
the quartet literature before Beethoven. The legend is that
Mozart wrote or completed it as his wife gave birth to their
first child in the next room: surely to make this direct equiv-
alence between labour pains and intense music is the most
naive form of musical biography imaginable, yet it is one of
those legends that uncannily fits the music. The insistence on
repeated notes and plunging octaves in all the movements is
clear, giving an almost obsessive feel to the whole work.
Although the F major Andante is more relaxed, the minuet is
unrelenting in the way it pushes dissonances across the bar-
line while the cello descends ominously in chromatic steps
(until the arrival of the airy D major trio). The final set of
variations, which looks like an innocent siciliano, is really
quite scary, with triplets hammering away at the top of the
texture till the very close, which consists of twelve repeated
high Ds for the violin, falling down an octave, strangely echoing the start of the piece.

The E flat quartet consciously draws on the model of
Mozart's earlier work in this key for its opening, but here the
chromaticism is more integrated, more at one with the rest of
the material. The minuet is in the self-consciously pastoral
style, with a prominent drone, while the finale seems to
attempt to outdo Haydn in witty pauses, shifts and earthy rum-
bustiousness. The B flat quartet K458 might be called the
apotheosis of the hunt, while the A major quartet is much more
gentle (a characteristic also attributable to the symphony K201
in the same key). This quartet finds room for interesting and
difficult-to-play chromatic lines in the finale; there are many
alterations in the autographs which seem to show Mozart

struggling with this work, and possibly a fragmentary rondo that survives (K464a) should be regarded as its rejected finale.

Mozart saves his greatest achievement, however, for the last of the set (dated Vienna, 14 January 1785), generally known as the 'Dissonance' on account of its slow introduction. The introduction seems calculated to build tension towards its release in what is a relaxed and lyrical first-movement Allegro. It does so by an astonishing, unprecedented canonic imitation of a winding chromatic line a beat apart between the upper three strings over a pulsing bass. You cannot be sure what key this is in or where it is going, until it somehow comes to rest on a dominant seventh. The Allegro seems by contrast simple, but how wonderfully it is intensified: the theme appears first accompanied simply by the upper strings, then repeated more forcefully (like the 'tutti' section of a concerto) by rising and falling arpeggios in the cello, and then laid out in imitation. The rising arpeggios then become a subject in themselves in the development, a brilliant idea. In the development of the Andante cantabile, there is some mysterious sense that both sections of the previous movement are fused in the aching imitation that unfolds over the cello's undulating figures – a motif that becomes ever more intense and important as the movement develops. As for the finale, it is amazing how much Mozart draws out of its theme, with the chromatic line returning to underpin the secondary theme (which turns out to contain a falling fifth): the argument of the falling fifth contains right to the final canonic flourish through the parts and the cadence. Exhilarating. Here, surely, Haydn heard something he could learn from and returned Mozart's compliment: it must be the opening of this quartet that lies behind his 'Representation of Chaos' at the beginning of *The Creation*.

🎧 *The 'Haydn' Quartets* Hagen Quartet
DG 471 024–2 (2 CDs)
🎧 *The 'Haydn' Quartets* Quatuor Mosaiques
Astree K8746 (2 CDs)

String Quartet No. 20 in D, 'Hoffmeister' K499
String Quartet No. 21 in D K575*
String Quartet No. 22 in B flat K589*
String Quartet No. 23 in F K590*

After the wonders of the six 'Haydn' quartets, Mozart did not return to quartet writing for a while, though he composed one isolated work for the publisher Franz Anton Hoffmeister (the publisher who had failed to issue Mozart's piano quartets on the grounds of their complexity). This work, completed 19 August 1786, is deliberately simpler, and Hoffmeister did issue it. The three 'Prussian' quartets come as something of an anti-climax, and though they are undeniably important I have never really felt that they represent Mozart at his best.

Mozart was taken by his pupil Prince Lichnowsky to meet Frederick William in Potsdam, and Mozart gave a concert there on 26 May 1789 (probably including the 'Coronation' Piano Concerto and perhaps one of the last three symphonies). There he would also have met the fine cellist who was director for the court concerts, Jean-Pierre Duport, as well as his younger brother Jean-Louis. It was not a very successful trip, but Mozart returned home with a commission for six piano sonatas and six quartets; perhaps sensing that they not really wanted, he only wrote one of each, later adding two more quartets. Perhaps too he was especially daunted by the problem in the quartets of giving the cello-playing Emperor a starring role. It's evident he succeeded in K575: dramatically leaving the cello altogether out of the opening, he then introduces it high in its register so it could hardly fail to be noticed. The Andante echoes a Mozart song, 'Das Veilchen', while the cello has another solo role in the trio of the minuet, and launches the finale with a theme clearly linked to that of the first movement. The cello is prominent again in the Larghetto of K589, but in K590 there are only a couple of places where the King's skills at playing in the tenor register are alluded to. For all the resourcefulness of these quartets, they never attain the eloquent heights of the 'Haydn' quartets, though Alec

Hyatt King wrote that they form 'a triumphant conclusion to Mozart's composition in this difficult form'.

🎧 *K499*, *K589* Salomon Quartet
Hyperion Helios CDH 55094
🎧 *K499 etc.* Leipzig Quartet
MDG 307 0936–2 (2 CD)
🎧 *K499*, *K589*, *K590* Hagen Quartet
DG 423 108–2

String quintets

String Quintet No. 1 in B flat K174*
String Quintet No. 2 in C K515**
String Quintet No. 3 in G minor K516**
String Quintet No. 4 in C minor K406*
String Quintet No. 5 in D K593*
String Quintet No. 6 in E flat K614**

These magnificent quintets are all too rarely played because their instrumentation is so unusual. H. C. Robbins Landon wrote that their music 'can only be described as alarming in the extreme', and they certainly contain some of Mozart's very greatest inventions – especially the C major K515 and G minor K516. (The C minor K406 is a transcription with some simplifications of the wind serenade in the same key, which is a great work in its own right.) Mozart apparently became interested in the string quintet with two violas through the influence of Michael Haydn, who had written a notturno for that combination in early 1773. Mozart's first work was begun that summer, and he completed it in December. It wasn't until much later, in April 1787, that he returned to the form, and we cannot be sure why. But the C major quintet (with its opening pre-echo of Leporello's shortly-to-be-written catalogue aria) is a perfectly formed masterpiece of supreme balance and poise, indeed the grandest and the longest of his chamber works for strings, in which the exchange of the opening phrase – cello arpeggio and violin turn – animates much of the first-movement conversation. The Andante pits first violin against first viola with great beauty, but most notable in the work is the absolute equality of all the instruments. The finale takes off from Haydn's sonata-rondo form, and develops it in the most imaginative way.

The contrast between the C major and G minor quintets of 1787 is uncannily like the contrast between the G minor and C major symphonies of 1788. The G minor's Adagio ma non troppo is said by H. C. Robbins Landon to be 'possibly the most personal and intimate music Mozart ever wrote', 'a mirror of Mozart's personal tragedy' because his father was ill and died two weeks after he finished it. True, Mozart was already beginning to be out of favour in Vienna and sliding into debt, but who is to say that that is what animates this extraordinary music? Cliff Eisen finds the movement equally extraordinary, but in musical ways, pointing in bars 13–14 to a 'moment of stillness punctuated by a succession of exploding mini-supernovas outlining the prevailing harmony. It is a unique moment, profoundly captivating for its sheer beauty and its preoccupation not with harmony or melody or rhythm but merely with sound.' If the work was biographical, how could the finale then be so cheerful (even though it is preceded by an eloquent Adagio introduction)? Mozart's feelings always seem broader and deeper than the biographical events to which they are sometimes attached.

Mozart returned to the string quintet at the very end of his life, and wrote the final two quintets in Vienna in December 1790 and April 1791. In their first publication in 1793 they were said to have been composed for an (anonymous) Hungarian amateur, but we do not know who this was. (Constanze Mozart later said that her husband had worked for Johann Tost of the Esterházy band, and this has sometimes been connected with this commission.) In K593 the Larghetto introduction returns to interrupt the first movement, while the finale is an essay in what can be done with a descending chromatic tag (though the first edition unaccountably changed it to a more winding shape). The E flat quintet, as Charles Rosen notes, 'makes a few musicians uncomfortable, perhaps because it lacks the expressive freedom of the other quintets, and seems to concentrate its richness'. Hans Keller was more dismissive: 'a bad arrangement of a wind piece in mock-Haydn style'. We have to beware of judging these pieces by the wrong standards, or as Cliff Eisen has written sternly, 'because of the unfulfilled expectation (or perhaps the unfulfilled desire) that they correspond to what was then (and still is) accepted as "the" Classical style'. My own reservation about K614 would be that in other works of his last year, Mozart's melodies were piercingly memorable; but here there is a strange absence of lyrical melody, and the spareness is to me oddly unattractive. However, the work is highly regarded by some Mozartians. There are also several quintet fragments, including a couple from his last year, which seem to show how tricky he found this form.

🎧 *Complete String Quintets* Hausmusik
Virgin 5 45169–2 (2 CDs)
🎧 *Complete String Quintets and Divertimento K563*
Grumiaux Trio
Philips 470 950–2 (3 CDs)

Ensembles with wind

Flute Quartet No. 1 in D K285*
Flute Quartet No. 2 in G K285a
?Flute Quartet No. 3 in C K285b
Flute Quartet No. 4 in A K298
Oboe Quartet in F K370**
Horn Quintet in E flat K407*
'Kegelstatt' Trio in E flat for clarinet, viola and piano K498**
Clarinet Quintet in A K581***

This is an attractively varied group of pieces for wind and strings: they were written at different times in Mozart's life but all bear witness to his enormous enjoyment of wind instruments and their potential. This even applies to the flute quartets, which he claimed to hate writing. They were composed to a commission from Mannheim; probably through the agency of his friend Johann Baptist Wendling, he received a request to write some flute music from a rich Dutchman, de Jean. Mozart was pleased by the commission, and started in good heart: 'one quartet for the Indian Dutchman, for that true friend of mankind, is almost ready'; the first was completed on 25 December 1777 and is the best of the bunch. Then Mozart became progressively dispirited; the first is better than the second, while the third may have been arranged by other hands and dates from the time of *Entführung*: the second movement is a transcription of one of the movements of the B flat Serenade; the other movements draw on music by Hoffmeister and Paisiello, so there is little that is original here.

The Oboe Quartet is also inspired by a great Mannheim player, the oboist Friedrich Ramm, and Mozart confidently takes the virtuoso player up to a high F, notably at the finale's close. (That finale also contains a very odd moment where the strings play in 6/8 but the oboe veers off in 4/4, giving a distinctively seasick effect.) The Horn Quintet was written, like all his solo music for that instrument, for his friend Joseph Leutgeb, who came from Salzburg to live in Vienna, where this was written probably around the end of 1782 (though the autograph, sold in London in 1847, has disappeared). The 'Kegelstatt' Trio, though I have heard its awkward phrase-lengths adversely criticised by a famous living composer, seems to me a little masterpiece, beautifully using the sonority of clarinet and viola to complement the piano. It was written for his piano pupil Franziska von Jacquin, and Anton Stadler the clarinettist; Mozart probably played viola himself. The first movement is monothematic, based on the little turn that begins it, while the finale is one of Mozart's most melodically inspired. The story of its being written while Mozart was bowling (hence the nickname) is most likely a confusion with the duos (possibly for two horns) scribbled down in the previous week (see p. 222).

The Clarinet Quintet was written for Anton Stadler, using his innovative basset clarinet (for which the 1791 Clarinet Concerto was also written), and its first performance was on 22 December 1789 in Vienna. But Stadler seems to have sold or lost the score, and so the form of the work as it has come down to us is the published rearrangement for normal clarinet. It doesn't seem likely that this makes as much difference as in the case of the concerto. The work is given the full symphonic apparatus of four-movement form, though the finale is a light set of variations. The highlight, as in the concerto, is the Larghetto, an exquisite melody spun out and elaborated by the clarinet, with some wonderful touches of bass-less writing in which the music seems to float aloft.

🎧 *Quintets, Quartets and Fragments*
Academy of St Martin's Chamber Ensemble
Philips *Complete Mozart Edition* Vol. 10 (3 CDs)
🎧 *Clarinet Quintet etc.* Eduard Brunner / Hagen Quartet
DG 419 600
🎧 *Oboe Quartet* Paul Goodwin / Terzetto
Harmonia Mundi HM907 220
🎧 *Clarinet Quintet, Horn Quintet and Oboe Quartet*
Antony Pay, Timothy Brown, Neil Black /
Academy of St Martin-in-the-Fields
Philips 422 833–2

Miscellaneous works for strings

Duo in G for violin and viola K423*
Duo in B flat for violin and viola K424*
?Preludes for string trio K404a
Divertimento in E flat for string trio K563**

There are a couple of early duos for violin and bass dated 1 September 1768 (K46d and K46e), a trio for two violins and bass (K266, 1777), and a fuller sonata for bassoon and cello K292, but the first pieces in this genre to be heard today are the ingenious duos for violin and viola – rather surprisingly not linked in time with the fine Sinfonia concertante with those soloists, but dated Salzburg 1783. The story in a biographical sketch of Mozart's fellow composer Michael Haydn suggests that these two duos were written by Mozart as a favour to complete a set begun with four by Haydn, and indeed that Mozart consciously adopted Michael Haydn's stylistic traits in the process. He had boasted to his father on 7 February 1778 that 'as you know I can more or less adopt or imitate any sort and any style of composition', and whether one can agree with H. C. Robbins Landon that Mozart actually tried to 'camouflage his authorship', these are certainly 'labours of love in every sense of the word' and show total mastery of the instruments.

The dubious Preludes K404a were written to preface Mozart's transcriptions of three Bach fugues from the '48' for chamber-music gatherings at the baroque-loving Baron van Swieten's. But who were they written by? Not necessarily Mozart. A large amount of music was written out for these fascinating gatherings, among which a surprising transcription by Mozart of a piece by Froberger that has recently surfaced. These Preludes are, however, the only work in the Mozart catalogue for string trio besides the wonderful E flat piece that follows. Lurking under the misleading title of a divertimento, and with the unusual string-trio instrumentation that makes it unpopular with quartets (even as an occasional piece in a concert, because it is long), K563 is one of Mozart's most marvellously inventive pieces. It is dated Vienna 27 September 1788, and was written for Michael Puchberg, the man who lent Mozart a considerable amount of money in his last years. Let us hope he realised what a priceless piece of music he had received in return: what would one give to have been at a really good read-through of this work!

None of the miscellaneous works has such formal perfection as here. The typical unison arpeggio opening is here gentle, not insistent, linked with rather than contrasted with the material that follows. The second movement is a beautiful A flat Adagio, and after the first Minuet there is a central set of Variations of great intensity, one of my favourites in all Mozart's output, with a misty, winding minor-mode episode and then a dazzling major-mode flurry to finish. A minuet with trios is necessary to wind down the tension; then the final Allegro launches a lyrical, lilting theme which is of the same family as the finale of the Piano Concerto K595 (which gives the lie to that piece being purely valedictory). This theme is contrasted with a figure that has all the instruments playing chords together; these are then, of course, taken apart and used imitatively, until they appear in a sort of stretto canon on the last page. There is a quality in Mozart's greatest works which is something to do with consistency of tone, feeling, sound and architectural argument: all these are here to the utmost, and it is one of his very finest creations, all the sadder for being so neglected.

☊ *K563* Jascha Heifetz, William Primrose,
Emanuel Feuermann
RCA 09026 51740–2
☊ *K423, K424* Szymon Goldberg, Paul Hindemith (K424),
Frederick Riddle (K423)
MUSI CD 665
☊ *K404a, K563* Grumiaux Trio
Philips 416 485–2
☊ *K423, K424* Gidon Kremer, Kim Kashkashian
DG 439 525–2
☊ *K563* Gidon Kremer, Kim Kashkashian, Yo-Yo Ma
Sony Classical 39561

Piano ensemble music

Divertimento in B flat (Piano Trio No. 1) K254
Piano and Wind Quintet in E flat K452****
Piano Quartet in G minor K478****
Piano Quartet in E flat K493***

The early B flat piano trio is an experimental upbeat to the later set six discussed below, in which the strings essentially accompany a piano sonata. Though the piano and wind quintet and the two piano quartets may also be called experimental because no one seems to have tried the form before, they are immediate successes. (The publisher Hoffmeister did not think so, abandoning his planned series of three piano quartets after the first. But Mozart thankfully had already persevered with the second.)

The piano and wind quintet was performed in a concert on 1 April 1784 (and was entered in the catalogue only two days earlier, which considering the concert was postponed from 21 March, was cutting it a little fine). Mozart was ecstatic about the work's reception, writing to his father, 'I consider it to be the best work I have ever composed.' Mozart's skill at balancing the solo instruments with the piano is evident throughout, from the first Largo introduction to the opening Allegro moderato on a graceful theme. You sense him relishing the different characteristics of each instrument and their textural combinations. Each makes the simple melody of the Larghetto into its own, and the final Allegro is again on a notably lyrical, dancing theme, which develops inexorably towards a cadenza in which all the instruments participate.

The G minor piano quartet is a titanic work, and it is difficult to think of another Mozart first movement which is so clearly and yet powerfully laid out formally so that any ear can grasp it. Hans Keller memorably wrote: 'The piano quartet in G minor furnishes conclusive proof, more than any other single masterpiece, that Mozart's was the only truly omniscient ear of which we know.' The first part of the movement, with its angular unison opening for the strings, must be repeated, both to clarify the structure and also to make the beginning of the development section sufficiently uplifting: here the piano takes the tiny coda phrase, and extends it into a fantastic flourish. The repeat also highlights the way in which the opening theme returns at the beginning of the coda, but with the piano's upward leap extended by a single note right up the keyboard, surprising us and showing that something extraordinary is going to happen. It does: the strings obsessively repeat the opening theme while the piano pounds in arpeggios around them, as the movement reaches a tumultuous conclusion. The finale is a song-like rondo: the naturalness with which it grows from its germinating theme and extends its tentacles has an air of, what could one call it, exalted gaiety. But as if to mirror the powerful coda of the first movement, there is a shock in store: the coda takes the innocent theme and slams it with a sudden chord into the key of E flat on the piano, with resultant shocks around the ensemble, before recovering itself to end in (still minor) G.

The E flat quartet is much quieter and more serene, but no less closely argued, with the instruments more integrated into one texture rather than setting piano against string trio. The opening emerges gently out of repeated octaves, and even the dotted figure that follows is restrained. That restraint goes through the central movement, which the German scholar Hermann Abert noted, had 'indescribable inwardness of concept in the slow movement'.

🎧 K493, K478
Emanuel Ax, Isaac Stern, Jaime Laredo, Yo-Yo Ma
Sony SK 66841
🎧 K493 with chamber version of K414
Alfred Brendel, Alban Berg Quartet
EMI 5 56962–2
🎧 K478, K493 Clifford Curzon, Amadeus Quartet
Decca 425 960–2

Piano Trio No. 2 in G K496
Piano Trio No. 3 in B flat K502*
Piano Trio No. 4 in E K542
Piano Trio No. 5 in C K548
Piano Trio No. 6 in G K564

There's an interesting transition from the baroque trio sonata – two equal instruments over a basso continuo keyboard instrument which provides the harmonies – to the classical piano trio in which a treble and bass instrument duet with a keyboard. Though the piano trio started as essentially a keyboard sonata with doubling from violin and cello, it quickly became emancipated to a stage where the three instruments had equal freedom, and then to a new stage, identified by some scholars, in which the pianist's two hands, in the treble and bass register, contribute their own independent material, making a quasi-quartet texture. When Mozart wrote out his piano trios, he interestingly always placed the violin above the piano part, and the cello beneath it, so they were written closest to the treble and bass texture of the piano. (A modern edition would put violin and cello together, above the piano part.)

The five here fall into two groups: K496 in G was completed (with much use of red and black ink) on 8 July 1786, and the B flat on 18 November 1786. The other three come together from 1788. All are popular in style, with few complications. K496 in G major ends with a set of variations; the B flat has a lovely running finale, with clever returns to the rondo theme; the E major is almost wistful in tone, its central movement credited with 'Schubertian serenity'; while the C major is a majestic work. The final G major trio is less interesting, and the keyboard part (though certainly by Mozart) was written out by another hand.

🎧 *Complete Piano Trios* Trio Fontenay
Teldec Ultima 8573 87794–2

Violin sonatas

Mozart wrote music for violin and keyboard (initially 'for keyboard with violin accompaniment') for much of his creative life. His development in this field, as so often, is complemented by developments in the form and the social circumstances for which the music was written. In the beginning the pieces were aimed at domestic players, which is presumably why Leopold wanted to publish these works first, rather than ensemble pieces. Later, as they became more complex, Mozart wrote them for, and played them with, his pupils, giving rise to famous accounts of his improvising the piano parts because he had not had time to write them down.

Sonata in C K6
Sonata in D K7
Sonata in B flat K8
Sonata in G K9

Mozart's first four sonatas were published in Paris in 1764 as Opp. 1 and 2. Leopold wrote of 'the furore they will make in the world when people read on the title page that they have been composed by a seven-year old child'; as in other cases it seems that Leopold had a hand in their composition, perhaps editing them for publication from Wolfgang's original ideas. With their cheerful arpeggio basses and minimal contributions for the violin, they are not really remarkable, but it is interesting how even so early Mozart makes the violin contribute to the texture: a little echo in K6, an imitation in K8. It is unusual to find the second minuet of K8 in B flat minor; all these sonatas end with a pair of minuets. (The next sonatas to be published, as Mozart's Op. 3, were K10–15: with their optional cello parts they fall between violin sonatas and early piano trios.)

🎧 *Complete Violin Sonatas and various pieces* Poulet, Verlet, van Keulen, Brautigam etc.
Philips Complete Mozart Edition Vol. 15 422 515–2 (7 CDs)

🎧 *Violin Sonatas Vol. 1* Rachel Podger, Gary Cooper
Channel Classics CCS SA 21804

Sonata in E flat K26
Sonata in G K27
Sonata in C K28
Sonata in D K29
Sonata in F K30
Sonata in B flat K31

The six sonatas K26–31 were published in The Hague in 1766 as Mozart's Op. 4. Already in K26 in E flat, the violin imitates the keyboard entry, though it then confines itself to brittle repeated notes (composers sometimes asked that in such accompanied sonatas the violin should play with a mute so as not to distract from the piano!). The final movement of this sonata is a witty Rondeau in which the violin enters as if it were a tutti section. A more interesting sharing of material occurs in the first movement of K28 in C, where shooting scales answer each other; in the second movement the violin is given an equal share of thematic material. There is a little more imitative work in K29 in D, though in K30 most of the attention will be on the keyboard's hand-crossing. The energy of K31 in B flat is typical; this sonata is concluded by a movement in a form which will become familiar, the theme and variations – not that the violin has much to add to the situation. (The next set of sonatas, listed as K55–60, are definitely spurious.)

🎧 *Sonatas K26, K29, K31* Frederic Fernandez, Pierre Hantai
Opus 111 OPS10–013

Sonata in G K301
Sonata in E flat K302
Sonata in C K303
Sonata in E minor K304**

Sonata in A K305
Sonata in D K306
Sonata in C K296
Sonata in B flat K378

The next authenticated set of violin sonatas, K301–6, comes from a decade later, published in Paris in 1778, again as Op. 1. The earlier ones in the set were written in Mannheim in early 1778, and another three were added in the summer. At once there is a clear emancipation of the violin from its accompanying role. It announces the open, singing melody of K301, and has a tune of its own in the middle of the final Allegro. The vigorous opening of the E flat sonata is familiar from Mozart's symphonic style at the time; in the finale the violin oddly doubles the keyboard right hand an octave below. The C major sonata has a slow introduction which recurs in mid-movement, and this is full of ingenious modulations. But the gem of this set is K304 in E minor – serious, suppressed, intense, like the E minor of Haydn's piano sonata or 'Trauer' Symphony. (For those who value the biographical connection, this sonata was written within a month of the death of Mozart's mother.) The great moment in the first movement is the recapitulation, where the violin sings the theme unaccompanied but the piano comes crashing in with a totally unexpected chord. The spirit of the concluding E minor minuet is almost baroque, but with a healing trio in E major, sounding like Schubert in its contrast of major and minor modes.

After this the remainder of the set sounds lightweight, though the A major has an elaborate set of variations and the D minor an interesting piano cadenza. From the same year is a chirpy little C major sonata intended for the daughter of Mozart's landlord in Mannheim, Therese Serrarius, and a B flat sonata K378, published in Vienna in 1781 but perhaps written earlier.

Sonata in G K379
Sonata in F K376
Sonata in F K377***
Sonata in E flat K380
Sonata in B flat K454**
Sonata in E flat K481
Sonata in A K526***
Sonata in F K547

> Today (for I am writing at 11 o'clock at night) we had a
> concert, where three of my compositions were performed
> – new ones, of course . . . a sonata with violin accompani-
> ment for myself, which I composed myself between eleven
> and twelve (but in order to be able to finish it, I only
> wrote out the accompaniment for Brunetti [leader of the
> Salzburg court orchestra] and retained my own part in my
> head) . . .

So wrote Mozart to his father Leopold about the G major
sonata K379, and even taking into consideration a certain
amount of bragging, this was a remarkable feat. The form of
this sonata is unusual and seems to have been taken as a
model by Beethoven in his violin sonatas. The next two
sonatas are both in F, but this repetition of keys would not
have been suitable in a published set of pieces, so Mozart
inserted the earlier sonata in C between the two. Actually
they are very strongly contrasted, and the second of them,
K377, is one of his happiest inspirations: under the theme in
the piano comes a chugging array of triplets for violin, then
transformed into arpeggios for the piano as the violin takes
off with the theme. The theme and variations in D minor is
full of turns and suspensions (the last variation is a direct echo
of the D minor string quartet K421), and finally there is a
minuet.

The E flat Sonata has an impressive opening with solid
chords and a wandering line for the piano: the profusion of
the themes that follow is almost too great. But the majestic
B flat sonata K454 is altogether more integrated. It was

written for Regina Strinasacchi, who, as Mozart wrote, had 'a great deal of taste and feeling in her playing. I am at this moment composing a sonata for her, which we are going to play together on Thursday at her concert at the theatre.' Once again it seems Mozart couldn't quite get round to writing down his own part, and performed it from blank pages. It is a symphonic-scale sonata with a slow introduction and majestic Allegro, a singing Andante, and a full-scale concert-like Rondo: it sounds very orchestral. The last of the set is in E flat, and is dated Vienna 12 December 1785; the finest movement is the central Adagio in A flat which slides unnervingly between keys.

The A major Sonata K526 was written during work on *Don Giovanni*. There is a triple-time opening movement and an Andante over bare piano octaves; the dashing finale is in the *moto perpetuo* tradition, but Mozart surely never wrote a more subtle movement of this kind, with lovely counterpoint in the piano part – the surprises here can actually, like some of Haydn's, make an audience laugh. The final, inconsequential sonata in F K547 (reverting to the idea of 'a little piano sonata for beginners, with violin') was written in July 1788; there are also a couple of sets of variations K359 and K360, as well as fascinating fragmentary sonatas.

𝇫 *Complete Violin Sonatas* Szymon Goldberg, Radu Lupu
Decca 448 526–2 (4 CDs)
𝇫 *Complete Violin Sonatas* Itzhak Perlman, Daniel Barenboim
EMI 463 749 (4 CDs)

Keyboard music

Piano sonatas

Mozart's earliest piano works should be seen against the background of the infant prodigy's tours, and the influence of his father Leopold. He wrote keyboard music from an early age, and his sister's music notebook includes many such pieces written down by Leopold and others. We can never be sure how altered or edited these versions are, but the 'London sketchbook' from their tour to England probably includes examples of raw sketches that Leopold did not touch. There are some further early pieces, including four early sonatas whose initial themes were listed in the Breitkopf and Härtel manuscript catalogue of Mozart's work, but they have disappeared.

To a large extent Mozart's genius at the piano was for improvisation: we read of him at home playing from nine o'clock in the evening and having to be put to bed at midnight. All of his early tours included major moments of improvisation, and we know that when he felt the audience was appreciating his skills, he could continue for hours. Of an occasion in Prague, we read that 'at the end of the concert, when Mozart extemporised alone for more than half an hour at the fortepiano, raising our delight to the highest degree, our enchantment dissolved into loud, overwhelming applause'.

So perhaps it was only later, with the opportunity for publication, that some of these pieces were codified and written down in detail. Others were written for teaching and instruction purposes. Although every pianist plays and loves them, it is difficult to feel that the piano sonatas represent the full wealth of Mozart's skill. The marvellous isolated piano pieces, such as the C minor Fantasia, A minor Rondo and B minor Adagio, are quite another matter: they surely are the codified outcome of some of those magical moments of improvisation.

Piano Sonata No. 1 in C K279
Piano Sonata No. 2 in F K280
Piano Sonata No. 3 in B flat K281
Piano Sonata No. 4 in E flat K282
Piano Sonata No. 5 in G K283
Piano Sonata No. 6 in D K284

It is possible that when he wrote K279–84 in Munich, early in 1775, Mozart had already seen Haydn's 1773 set of piano sonatas. The music has a virtuoso display announced in the opening flourishes of the first three, and indeed several of the first movements sound like orchestral reductions. The last in D captures the symphonic mood of J. C. Bach's sonata in the same key; there is a Rondeau en Polonaise and a theme and variations, just the sort of public *divertissement* Mozart learnt from the younger Bach. The F major is a witty and characteristic work, and the E flat's opening Adagio achieves real eloquence, while its rondo finale has strong reminders of Haydn.

♩ *Complete Piano Sonatas* Mitsuko Uchida
Philips Complete Mozart Edition Vol. 17 422 517–22 (5 CDs)

Piano Sonata No. 7 in C K309
Piano Sonata No. 9 in D K311
Piano Sonata No. 8 in A minor K310****

These three sonatas were published together in Paris as Op. 4 in 1782, and the first two were written in Mannheim towards the end of 1777; but there is a complete contrast between the pleasant music of K309 (written for Rosa Cannabich, daughter of the Mannheim composer) and K311 (the final rondo of the D major again sounding distinctly Haydnesque in places) on the one hand, and the titanic A minor sonata K310, for which nothing prepares us. Its composition has been linked to the death of Mozart's mother in Paris in 1778, but a completely different type of influence may have been Mozart's new-found enthusiasm for the pianos of Stein, about which he wrote enthusiastically in October 1777. Once heard played on an early piano, the opening of the A minor sonata may be difficult to accept on a modern instrument. The strident chordal accompaniment sounds fatally weakened if played down as an accompaniment, and the superb coda figure striding over three and a half octaves in the bass lines is tremendous when delineated by the changes of register in the early piano. In the development, chains of suspensions over angry bass burblings, and phrases with leaping octaves and turns, lead back to the main theme. This sequence is uncannily paralleled in the Andante cantabile, whose noble first section does not lead one to expect the dissonant trills and harmonies of the second section. The *moto perpetuo* finale is one of Mozart's fiercest: none of the good humour of the F major Violin Sonata here, but rather a headlong rush to despair (with an ethereal A major section in the middle). This music seems to reach far beyond the immediate circumstances of Mozart's life.

🎧 *Complete Piano Sonatas* Maria João Pires
DG 439 760–2 (6 CDs)
🎧 *Piano Sonatas K310, K533/494 etc.* Richard Goode
Nonesuch 7559–79831–2

Piano Sonata No. 10 in C K330*
Piano Sonata No. 11 in A K331*
Piano Sonata No. 12 in F K332**
Piano Sonata No. 13 in B flat K333***

The next group of sonatas has now been dated by Alan Tyson's watermark studies to Munich or Vienna 1781–3, but they were published in Vienna in 1784. The C major K330 and the A major K331 sound as if they were designed to be popular. Notable is the Andante cantabile of K330, which establishes itself in F but then slips into an expressive A flat major. There are four final bars in the first edition but not in the autograph, a wonderful Mozartian second thought (hopefully really his!), bringing the A flat material back in F to round off the movement wistfully. This and the A major have been thought to be teaching material: the famous variations of the A major and the 'Rondo alla turca' have ensured its place in piano lessons ever since, but it is not honestly among the more interesting sonatas.

The second pair have more to offer, showing Mozart's free-flowing idea of structure. The first movement of K332 is a deliciously contrasted succession of varied material: a flowing rising theme, a contrasted dotted-rhythm figure, a new leaping theme in D minor and then an innocent theme in C major which takes off into a brooding chord sequence whose sudden fortes and pianos knock the triple-time rhythm briefly back into duple time. Students of sonata form would have difficulty disentangling all this: the development introduces yet more new material and a repetition of the chord sequences, this time leading towards the home key. The B flat sonata K333 shows the style of J. C. Bach raised to its highest level. The accompaniment is unobtrusive, there is little contrast between themes, but the succession of melodies is perfectly organised; a slight intensification in the development (a leap of an octave and a fifth onto a syncopated accent) is enough to point home the climax of the movement. The slow movement in E flat has a remarkable twist at the start of the second section: a chromatic dissonance sends the music into D flat and thence to F minor, reducing it to no more than a pulsating bass line on F and a wandering treble line before it finds its way home to the comfort of A flat. This movement, orchestrated in serenade style, could easily be written for clarinets or basset horns and bassoons. The finale sounds like a full-scale concerto finale with its solo–tutti contrasts and a magnificent cadenza 'in tempo'. This sonata shows Mozart's extrovert style at its very best.

🎧 *K330, K331, K533/494* Murray Perahia
Sony SK 48233
🎧 *K332, K333* Malcolm Bilson
Nonesuch
🎧 *K332, K333, K457, Adagio K540* Alfred Brendel
Philips 468 048–2

Piano Sonata No. 14 in C minor K457***
Piano Sonata No. 18 in F K533*/K494*
Piano Sonata No. 15 in C K545
Piano Sonata No. 16 in B flat K570*
Piano Sonata No. 17 in D K576*

The Sonata K457 was first published with the C minor Fantasia (see below). The first Molto allegro movement is based on the double question-and-answer structure also heard, for example, in the 'Jupiter' Symphony, but with the added power of the minor mode. The Adagio (with an unusual slow indication) becomes more and more elaborate as it progresses, almost breaking the music down in a welter of decoration, as Beethoven was to do in his Op. 111 sonata. The finale makes use of a frequent Mozartian device, the suspension across the bar-line, to add to the impetuosity and urgency of the music. The F major Sonata includes a revision of the Rondo K494 as its finale: another bold development section, in the Andante, takes the movement's opening theme, puts it in the bass line, and then weaves a chromatic web around it. The F major rondo finale includes a warm A flat major section in string quartet style and a glorious final return that builds from the piano's low C with entries piled on top of each other till they reach the F four and a half octaves higher! The theme is finally heard *sotto voce* entirely in the piano's bass (another effect that needs the clarity of the early piano in this register).

The famous C major Sonata 'for beginners' needs little introduction, except to say that for all its regularity it does not conform to accepted ideas of sonata form and recapitulates its subject in the 'wrong' key, F instead of G (a procedure not at all uncommon in real eighteenth-century sonatas). There is no breath of danger in the remaining two movements. The remaining two sonatas do not add a great deal, though the first movement of the B flat has an arresting start to the development (the closing cadence of the exposition repeated in an unexpected key) and the Adagio is another wind serenade in E flat with a C minor interlude (like the

Piano Concerto K491). The D major has a hunting-style first movement and a boundlessly extrovert rondo finale with Haydnesque writing for the upper part of the keyboard alone.

𝆕 *Piano Sonatas K330, K331, K570, Rondo in A minor*
Alfred Brendel
Philips 462 903-2
𝆕 *'The Vienna Years': Sonatas, Fantasias, Rondos*
Jos van Immerseel
Sony Vivarte S2K 62979

Piano variations

Mozart wrote numerous sets of variations for solo keyboard, mostly based on operatic arias of the moment. Among the composers honoured (or developed) in this way are Salieri (K180), Grétry (K352), Paisiello (K398), Gluck (K455) and Sarti (K460), whose *I due litiganti* is also referred to in the finale of *Don Giovanni*. Mozart also used some instrumental tunes by J. C. Fischer (K179 – popular in Munich, according to Leopold) and the cellist J.-P. Duport (K573). They look like examples of the improvisations with which he dazzled audiences at his concerts, possibly watered down for publication. The best-known are those on 'Ah vous dirai-je maman' (K265, published Vienna 1785, thought to be associated with Paris when his mother was dying). The last set, K613, clearly connected with the origins of *Die Zauberflöte*, in published March/April 1791, vary a song by one of Schikaneder's circle: 'Ein Weib ist das herrlichste Ding'. But none is as moving as the piano-duo Variations K501 (see below).

𝆕 *Variations for Piano etc.* Ingrid Haebler, Mitsuko Uchida (piano), Ton Koopman (harpsichord)
Philips Complete Mozart Edition Vol. 18 422 518-2 (5 CDs)

Miscellaneous piano pieces

Andante in C K1a
Allegro in C K1b
Allegro in F K1c
Minuet in F K1d
Minuets in G and C K1
Minuet in F K2
Allegro in B flat K3
Minuet in F K4
Minuet in F K5

Mozart's earliest compositions were entered in Leopold's hand in the music notebook of Nannerl (see chronology for 1760–62), so it's impossible to say to what extent he edited or refined them. The notebook, whose surviving pages were analysed by Alan Tyson, was eventually split up and the pages distributed around the world. The most famous page, containing the pair of minuets K1, is in Salzburg and not dated, but some of the others have very precise datings: K1c is 11 December 1761, K1d is 16 December 1761, then from 1762 the next pieces are from January, 4 March, 11 May, and 5 July, showing the progress of the young composer. The clearest influences on his style are the pieces he was studying by his father and Wagenseil.

Prelude and Fugue in C K394
Suite in C K399
Fantasia in C minor K396 (completed Stadler)
Fantasia in D minor K397**
***Marche funèbre de sigr maestro Contrapuncto* in C minor K453a**
Fantasia in C minor K475***
Rondo in A minor K511****
Adagio in B minor K540****
Minuet in D K355**
Gigue in G K574**

In these isolated movements are some of Mozart's finest pieces for piano: performers and teachers alike would be well advised to seek them out in preference to some of the blander sonatas. Several, like the C major Prelude and Fugue, show Mozart struggling with the baroque idiom that Baron van Swieten's musical gatherings brought back to his attention. The fugue here is very foursquare, as is that in the overture of the baroque-style Suite K399. But the Courante of the Suite is beautiful, almost as if Mozart had heard Scarlatti's sonatas.

The Fantasia in D minor is actually incomplete but is probably the most frequently performed of all Mozart's fragments after the Requiem and C minor Mass. It has an improvisatory opening in D minor, leading to an Adagio, then through a cadenza-like Presto back to the Adagio, and then a song-like Allegretto. An editor has provided a sensible enough flourish to finish this section, but it would have been more likely that this was the middle section of the piece, and that the opening D minor material would have returned to conclude the Fantasia. (Mitsuko Uchida has written such an ending.) The big-boned C minor Fantasia K396 was probably intended for violin and piano; Mozart never finished it and the development was added by Stadler. The little Funeral March of Maestro Counterpoint could be a perfectly serious C minor March if it didn't have a jokey title: what was this joke aimed at? The much better known Fantasia in C minor K475 was published together with the C major Sonata K457, but stands very well on its own: its brooding unison opening and more lyrical succeeding section leads to an absolutely titanic sequential section which one can imagine bursting from Mozart as he improvised. The opening then returns with added power. This fantasia interestingly follows C. P. E. Bach's instructions as to how to improvise, but creates a quite different musical effect.

The A minor Rondo is entirely unique in Mozart's output and is one of the most personal utterances of the Classical period. From a gently pulsing melody, marked crescendo (the markings throughout are exceptionally detailed and precise),

Mozart weaves a constantly evolving line which changes at its every appearance. The contrasting material, in F major, is broad and serene, rising through the whole piano keyboard in its development (and touching top E) before subsiding through an unearthly chromatic sequence back to the theme. There is a moment of piercing sunlight in the A major episode, but then the A minor theme returns, more intense than ever, developed with falling sevenths and expressive turns, before collapsing to a two-part counterpoint and then a wisp of a fragment which cannot struggle beyond repeating its first bar. The manuscript is dated 11 March 1787: those who want to read Mozart's biography into every piece have a hard time of it accounting for this extraordinary masterpiece.

The Adagio in B minor is dated a year later, 19 March 1788: its passionate, anguished progress is crowned by a masterstroke as its conclusion – after all the pain of B minor, the final chromatic coda slips as if by magic into B major. Performers can take very different approaches to this conclusion: is it a moment of balm and serenity, or still ineffably sad? The effect can be very different depending on the tuning system used, for B major in unequal temperament is not a very comfortable key. In this piece Mozart comes closest to re-interpreting the legacy of C. P. E. Bach, whose fantasias provide the model for this disjointed, pause-ridden work.

Among the many other fascinating single-movement pieces is the Minuet in D (K355) previously thought to be 1789–90 but now assigned to 1786, very experimental in the clashing unprepared dissonances of its second section, and in its gorgeous reharmonisation of the theme when it returns. Stadler added an irritating trio which it is easy to ignore. The Gigue in G of 16 May 1789 (when Mozart visited Leipzig and reportedly looked at J. S. Bach's motets) is so chromatic that it becomes almost atonal before finding its tonal feet again.

♫ *K511, K475, K616, K485, Sonatas K545, K570*
András Schiff (on Mozart's piano)
Salzburg Mozarteum ISM 91/3

254 MOZART: THE MUSIC

🎧 *K410, K540 etc.* Alfred Brendel
Philips 446 921
🎧 *K399, K574, K511, K408 etc.* Richard Goode
Nonesuch 7559–79831–2

Piano duets

?Sonata in C K19d
Sonata in D K381
Sonata in B flat K358
Sonata in D for two pianos K448***
Sonata in F K497****
Variations on an original theme in G K501***
Sonata in C major K521*
Fugue in C minor for two pianos K426
Larghetto and Allegro in E flat for two pianos**(ed. Levin)

'In London, little Wolfgang wrote his first piece for four hands. No one had ever written a four-hand sonata before.' Leopold Mozart was credited in Nissen's biography with writing that sentence on 9 July 1765, but it may be a later addition. Wolfgang and his sister did perform regularly together at one keyboard on tour, and this was something of a prime attraction in their visit, for whether there were any real piano-duet sonatas from before this date, the Mozarts made a feature of the genre. (The famous painting of the Mozart family from around 1780 by Della Croce recaptures this, with brother and sister at the same keyboard with hands crossed.) The *London Daily Advertiser* announced 'to all Lovers of Sciences' that 'the great Prodigy that Europe or that even Human Nature has to boast of, is, without contradiction, the little German Boy Wolfgang Mozart . . . the two children will play also together with four hands upon the same harpsichord, and put up on it a handkerchief, without seeing the Keys.' In this context, piano duets were linked with the circus elements of the tour, but they quickly developed a more serious musical purpose.

Doubt has been cast on the earliest piano-duet sonata which survives, K19d; whoever really wrote it, this is the kind of piece the brother and sister team might have played, and it sounds more like a reduced symphony than an enlarged sonata. Perhaps this is because it was made for public display, not for the private entertainment which we now associate with piano-duet playing. The textures are as simple as a Mannheim symphony, with the bright exchanges between *primo* and *secondo* sounding like cheerful horns and trumpets. That is true of the authentic works here as well: they are written as an essay in communicating to an audience, not just a meditation for two performers. It appears that K381 and K358 were also written before other duet works: the young J. C. Bach certainly wrote duets, and C. P. E. Bach also wrote four small duets for two keyboards as well as his singular concerto for harpsichord and fortepiano.

The D major Sonata for two pianos is a unique work written to complement the two-piano concerto, for a concert on 23 November 1781 when Mozart partnered Josepha Auernhammer, who was described as talented but extremely plain. The concert was an important one, for in the audience were Countess Thun, Baron van Swieten and Karl Abraham Wetzlar, Baron von Plankenstern – the latter two of great significance for Mozart, as sources of financial help and commissions. To match the occasion Mozart created a work of perfect poise and balance. It has no great unexpected depths, but as Alfred Einstein wrote:

> The art with which the two parts are made completely equal, the play of the dialogue, the delicacy and refinement of the figuration, the feeling for sonority in the combination and exploration of the different registers of the two instruments – all these things exhibit such mastery that this apparently superficial and entertaining work is at the same time one of the most profound and mature of Mozart's compositions.

With the F major Sonata K497 we are on completely different ground: a work of the greatest seriousness worthy to rank with any of Mozart's mature symphonies and concertos, which caught the attention of the great analyst and composer Donald Tovey: 'a superb piece of chamber music in no way inferior to the great string quartets and quintets of its period'. As he wrote, it is a piece that shows itself by nature to be a four-hand duet 'and nothing else in the world'; he also pointed out an anticipation of Sarastro's priests in the running bass lines of the development. The opening slow introduction has a vast scope, as if raising the curtain on a new world, and the first movement's themes are splendidly contrasted and developed. The slow movement contrasts a singing first subject with a hectic second subject. Its four-part imitation is angular and intricate: Tovey said that 'four Chinese dragons might achieve its august poise and agility'. The rondo finale ranges far and wide, though it is based on a light triple-time theme; there is much use of powerful ascending scales across the two pianists in the development.

The G major Variations K501 are finer than any of the sets of variations for piano solo, with a theme that lends itself to exchanges between the treble and tenor of the keyboard. There is a beautiful minor-mode variation, but the triumph is the understated conclusion, with the theme echoing between the pianists and then evaporating. The C major Sonata is a robust and extrovert work, but less substantial than the F major. The baroque-style C minor Fugue for two pianos survives mainly in its later arrangement for strings alongside the Adagio in C minor K546. Finally, there is a Larghetto and Allegro for two pianos which is incomplete and not listed in Köchel; it has been completed in sparklingly idiomatic style by Robert Levin.

🎧 *K503 etc.* András Schiff, George Malcolm
Salzburg Mozarteum ISM91/2
🎧 *K448, Larghetto and Allegro compl. Levin, etc.*
Robert Levin, Malcolm Frager
Salzburg Mozarteum ISM90/1

🎧 *K448 etc.* Murray Perahia, Radu Lupu
Sony SK 39511
🎧 *K488*, *K501*, *K521*, *K381* Martha Argerich, Alexandre
Rabinovitch
Teldec 91378

Organ and mechanical organ pieces

Church Sonata No. 1 in E flat K67
Church Sonata No. 2 in B flat K68
Church Sonata No. 3 in D K69
Church Sonata No. 4 in D K144
Church Sonata No. 5 in F K145
Church Sonata No. 6 in B flat K212
Church Sonata in G K241
Church Sonata No. 9 in F K244
Church Sonata No. 10 in D K245
Church Sonata in C K263
Church Sonata No. 11 in G K274
Church Sonata No. 12 in C K278
Church Sonata No. 14 in C K329
Church Sonata No. 13 in C K328
Church Sonata No. 7 in F K224
Church Sonata No. 8 in A K225
Church Sonata No. 15 in C K336*

'A Mass, with the whole Kyrie, the Gloria, the Credo, the
Epistle Sonata, the Offertory or Motet, the Sanctus and the
Agnus, must be last no more than three-quarters of an hour,'
wrote Mozart to his mentor Padre Martini in Bologna, clearly
somewhat frustrated. This was the strict regime imposed by
Archbishop Colloredo in Salzburg after 1769. The aspect of
this list that has least relation to present-day practice is the
Epistle Sonata, which took the place of the traditional Gradual
sung between the reading of the Epistle and Gospel (as the
Offertory motet took the place of the Mass proper sung at that

point). These Epistle Sonatas are single-movement works lasting three or four minutes each, featuring the organ with
strings. The style develops from the innocuous in K67–9 (written in Salzburg in 1772) to the fully fledged in K336 (March
1780), which sounds more like an organ concerto. Some are
miniature symphonies, like K69 in D or K144 in D. Often
there are touches of imitative writing, usually at the start of the
second half of the movement. Trumpets are introduced in
K263 of December 1776, and that piece is probably related to
the two C major masses of that time. K278 in C, from March
or April 1777, adds oboes and timpani to the trumpets and
would not disgrace the opening movement of a mature symphony. But the organ here has only a continuo role. K329 in C,
perhaps of March 1779, is equally dramatic and powerful, and
here the organ emerges into its own, duetting with strings and
the pair of oboes. After the smaller K328, there is the finest of
the set, K336, which could easily be a keyboard concerto
movement with its own place for a cadenza. It was probably
intended for use with Mozart's last Salzburg mass, K337.

◯ *Epistle Sonatas*
Ian Watson / The King's Consort / Robert King
Hyperion CDA66377

**Adagio and Allegro in F minor for mechanical organ
 K594****
Fantasia in F minor for mechanical organ K608****
Andante in F for mechanical organ K616*

Three fine pieces about which Mozart complained bitterly. In
1791 a mausoleum was opened in Vienna in memory of
Field-Marshal Baron von Loudon; it featured a mechanical
organ for which Mozart was commissioned to write some
'Funeral Musique' by Count Joseph Deym von Stržitež. The
music was repeated each hour, and the place was 'splendidly
illuminated till ten o'clock at night'. Mozart found the task of
writing the music irksome, as he wrote to Constanze:

So I firmly resolved to write the adagio for the clockmaker and then to put a few ducats in my dear little wife's
hands; I have been at it, too – but it is loathsome work, I
have been so unhappy that I cannot complete it – I work
on it every day – but always lay it aside for a time because
it bores me – and of course if it was not being done for
such an important reason I would surely abandon it
entirely – well if it were a big clock and thing sounded like
an organ, it would be nice; but instead the organ has only
little pipes that sound too childish to me.

The tone of special pleading in Mozart's letter is unmistake-
able, but clearly the money was an incentive.

The Adagio and Allegro contrasts a flowing movement in
the minor with a martial Allegro. The Fantasia, which is now
well known in arrangements for organ solo or piano duet, is
surely one of his finest contrapuntal compositions. An introduction powered by turns leads to a fugue which is concluded with the flourishes of the introduction; a flowing Andante
in A flat with a supple accompaniment (one can imagine that
Mozart baulked at that being played mechanically) has a
cadenza-like finish. It leads back to the first section, but when
we arrive at the fugue, this is now splendidly decorated with a
new, fast-moving counter-subject. The fugal entries pile up
in a final exhilarating stretto, creating a wonderful sense of
excitement.

The Andante in F is actually found on a barrel organ which
belonged to Haydn's clockmaker. But it is not in fact linked to
von Deym's contraption, and was described by Mozart as 'for
a cylinder in a small organ'. It can be played as an effective
solo keyboard piece, and shares the simple textures of *Die
Zauberflöte*.

☊ *Organ Sonatas and Solos* Daniel Chorzempa (organ) /
Deutsche Bachsolisten / Helmut Winschermann
Philips *Complete Mozart Edition* Vol. 21 422 521–2 (2 CDs)
☊ *Organ solos, K616* Leo Van Doeselaar
Globe 6041

Church and choral music

Among a large number of masses and liturgical music that Mozart wrote, there are a few superb pieces, and several examples that ought to be better known. Did Mozart write church music out of obligation or out of enthusiasm? Or were the two motives inextricably mixed? Clearly most of these pieces were written because Mozart had to write them, though that does not mean he put less effort into them. H. C. Robbins Landon, as so often, gives Mozart the benefit of the doubt and has suggested that the church music Mozart composed enabled him to reach a much wider audience than did his court music:

> It was composed for and performed in the huge Salzburg Cathedral, which was attended by men and women from every walk of life. Copies . . . were made by local scribes and circulated widely . . . he seems to have been concerned . . . to write genuinely popular church music, masses and litanies that would uplift men's hearts; in this he was eminently successful.

That does not quite square with the evidence that when Michael Haydn was appointed to succeed Mozart as court organist in 1782, he was given 'the additional stipulation that he show more diligence, and compose more often for our cathedral and chamber music, and in such cases, himself direct in the cathedral on every occasion'.

Masses

Missa brevis in G K49
Missa solemnis in C minor, 'Waisenhausmesse' K139
Missa brevis in D minor K65
Mass in C, 'Dominicus Mass' K66

This is a group of early Salzburg masses, including a small Missa brevis from autumn 1768. The large-scale 'Waisenhausmesse', for the dedication of the Orphanage Church in Vienna on 7 December 1768, was such a large undertaking that scholars used to doubt that Mozart could have composed this mass at that age. But an account of the occasion says that the mass was 'completely newly composed for this ceremony by Wolfgang Mozart who is well known because of his special talents and is the twelve-year-old son of Leopold Mozart', and also that it 'was performed with the greatest accuracy' in the presence of Maria Theresa. Perhaps Leopold, an experienced church-music composer, helped with some aspects of this imposing but faintly tedious composition.

Then there is another typically small Missa brevis for Salzburg, dated 5 February 1769, written to open the forty-hour vigil, with the text of the Credo sung simultaneously by four voices. The more ambitious 'Dominicus Mass' for St Peter's Abbey on 15 October 1769 was composed for the son of the Mozart family friends, the Hagenauers: Cajetan had been ordained and was celebrating his first mass. This is a festive work in cantata form, clearly a more extended affair because it was not performed in the cathedral. (Some of the Masses attributed to Mozart in Köchel, including K115 and K116, are now thought to have been written or copied by his father Leopold, while doubt still surrounds the Missa brevis K140, which is in the *Neue Mozart Ausgabe* though most believe it to be spurious.)

𝆓 *Early Masses* soloists / Cologne Chamber Orchestra / Collegium Carthusianum / Peter Neumann
Virgin 5 61769–2 (5 CDs)
𝆓 *K66 and Vespers K321* soloists / Schoenberg Choir / Concentus Musicus Wien / Nikolaus Harnoncourt
Teldec 2292 46469–2

Mass in C, 'In honorem Ssmae Trinitatis' K167
Missa brevis in F K192

Missa brevis in D K194
Mass in C, 'Spatzenmesse' K220
Missa longa in C K262

Mozart would have encountered Italian liturgical music during his journeys there; combined with the new liturgical restrictions in Salzburg, this created a new mood in his church music. In this group of masses, K167 has four trumpets and so is clearly intended for a festive and solemn occasion. K192 includes in its Credo the famous tag theme from the finale of the 'Jupiter' Symphony, not so much as a quotation but more as a use of a traditional theme. The 'Trinity Mass', from June 1773, is extrovert and instrumental in concept; there is much chordal declamation alongside the traditional fugue for 'Et vitam venturi saeculi'. K192 of 24 June 1774 is a compact mass for liturgical requirements, based on a symphonic style but with a winding Agnus Dei in D minor that anticipates later liturgical music in this important key.

The Missa brevis K194 of 8 August 1774 is a bright and cheerful work, with very rapid-fire declamation of the text, but adding an elaborate choral 'Dona nobis pacem'. K220 dates from the early months of 1775 or 1776 and includes a Credo written in Munich around the time of *La finta giardiniera*; it takes its nickname from a chirping birdlike figure in the Sanctus. The Missa longa K262 is just that: it has 824 bars, and was written in Salzburg in April 1775, but it is doubtful whether it could have been performed in the cathedral because of its extended final fugues in the Gloria and Credo. It is not obvious that the length brings benefits: there is a really quite stolid Adagio at 'Et exspecto resurrectionem mortuorum', and then a C major fugue at 'Et vitam venturi saeculi' which looks forward to the later and greater C minor Mass.

🎧 *Three Salzburg Masses etc.: K192, K275, K220* soloists / Winchester College Choir / Amadi Orchestra / Julian Smith Proudsound CD128

Mass in C, 'Credo' K257
Missa brevis in C, 'Spaur' K258
Missa brevis in C, 'Organ solo' K259
Missa brevis in B flat K275
Mass in C, 'Coronation' K317*
Missa Solemnis in C K337

The first group of three Masses, all in C major, conform to Salzburg practice by including trumpets in D, with the organ sounding at the usual ecclesiastical high pitch (some added woodwind parts have been found for these Masses, and they are written in D, which we must presume matched the church instruments in C). The 'Credo' Mass written in Salzburg in November 1776 uses the same 'Jupiter' Symphony tag as K192, but gets its nickname probably from the constant repetition of that single word. The so-called 'Spaur' Mass or 'Piccolominimesse', from Salzburg in December 1775 (though the date was later oddly altered), is another Missa brevis. The 'Organ solo' has a solo part for that instrument which links it with the tradition of the Epistle Sonatas discussed above. The Mass in B flat written for 21 December 1777 in St Peter's Abbey is once again for a smaller ensemble without trumpets.

The 'Coronation' Mass was always the most popular of Mozart's settings during his lifetime, and it was usually assumed from its nickname that it was composed for the annual coronation of the Virgin in the church of St Maria am Plain, a pilgrimage church above Salzburg. But H. C. Robbins Landon has suggested that it was intended for Salzburg Cathedral, to mark the Easter celebrations of 1779; it is certainly significant that the mass follows the Salzburg practice of adding trombones to double the alto, tenor and bass voices, and also omits violas from the strings. The nickname probably originates from the fact that Salieri conducted it at festivities for the coronations of Leopold II in 1791 and Francis I in 1792 after Mozart's death. There are echoes here of Mozart's operatic world, notably in the soprano's

Agnus Dei, a clear ancestor of the Countess's 'Porgi amor' from *Figaro*. But the whole nature of the music here is revealingly different: the individual psychological penetration of Mozart's operatic character is replaced by a universalised emotion, which draws worshippers into its healing, spiritual peace.

🎧 *Coronation Mass and Requiem* soloists / Leipzig Radio Choir / Dresden Staatskapelle / Peter Schreier
Philips 464 720–2

Mass in C minor K427****

The finest of all Mozart's masses before the Requiem survives only as a fragment, and the story of its composition is very uncertain. We know from Mozart's typically self-justificatory letter to his father of 4 January 1783 that he had begun a mass to honour Constanze. But the language is such as to argue special pleading – as usual when Mozart has something to avoid, he starts by saying he can only write a short letter, in this case because he has to change his clothes for a later engagement:

> It is quite true about my moral obligation and indeed I let the word flow from my pen on purpose. I made the promise in my heart of hearts and hoped to be able to keep it. When I made it, my wife was still single; yet as I was absolutely determined to marry her soon after her recovery, it was easy for me to make it. The score of half a mass which is still lying here waiting to be finished, is the best proof that I really made the promise.

We cannot be sure whether Mozart ever intended to finish the mass (see chronology, 1783). But following the birth of their son Raimund Leopold on 17 June 1783, the couple made the long-delayed journey from Vienna to Salzburg, arriving on 29 July, and bringing the score of the mass with them. On 19 August Raimund died in Vienna. In October, we learn from Nannerl Mozart's diary, the incomplete mass was rehearsed on 23 October and performed on Sunday 26 October, with Constanze Mozart as one of the soprano soloists. No one can say whether the missing parts were supplied from other masses, or whether the incomplete Credo was included in the performance. But a set of parts survived, bequeathed by Nannerl, from which an Augsburg choirmaster, Pater Matthaus Fischer, assembled a score in 1808: this contains only those sections that Mozart completed.

One of the most exciting Mozartian events of 2005 was the first performance of a new completion of the Mass in C minor by the American Mozart scholar and performer Robert Levin, commissioned by Carnegie Hall in New York, which offered a chance to encounter a certainly mythical, but remarkably convincing, vision of what the work might have been. Levin drew on several incomplete sketches from around the time of Mozart's work on the C minor Mass (some of which are printed at the back of the *Neue Mozart Ausgabe* edition of the piece), including one with the text 'Dona nobis pacem', found at the end of the draft of his unfinished opera *L'oca del Cairo*. These Levin worked up with great virtuosity and knowledge of Mozartian style, and added to them two arias, one for the 'Et in spiritum sanctum' and the other for the Agnus Dei. For these he went to the cantata *Davidde penitente* K469, which Mozart reworked from the material of the C minor Mass for later use in Vienna. The fact that Mozart took the music of the incomplete work and reused it in the cantata seems strong evidence that he was declaring his intention (at least to himself) not to finish the mass. He rarely reused material so blatantly in this way (though for a previous generation, that of Bach and Handel, it would have been far more natural).

The movements by Mozart in the usually performed torso begin with the Kyrie, a dark and brooding C minor movement which gives way to a radiant central section in E flat for solo soprano, 'Christe eleison', lifting the material for the choral section that follows from the minor into the major, before subsiding again to C minor at the close. The Gloria, in blazing C major, has a lively solo aria, 'Laudamus te', sung by Constanze (for which Mozart wrote her out some exercises, a solfeggio), a chromatic chorus, 'Gratias agimus', a duet, 'Domine Deus', for two equally sensual sopranos matching each other with their high notes, a massive Handelian double-choir chorus, 'Qui tollis', and then a 'Quoniam' for trio which starts in spare imitative style in E minor but becomes increasingly lyrical and operatic. The choral outburst 'Jesu Christe' leads to a fugue on 'Cum sancto spiritu' which is on a rather stolid subject and counter-subject, but Mozart makes it inexpressibly exciting by ratcheting up the tension and providing a virtuosic running bass under the theme and then repeating a soprano tag hypnotically as the bass line rises inexorably – a great, and totally Mozartian (rather than baroque) moment.

The incomplete Credo is usually performed as an opening chorus, and then the exquisite 'Et incarnatus', which is preserved in enough detail to be performed. It is one of the most wonderfully florid yet concentrated arias Mozart ever wrote, and it is phenomenally difficult to perform. I wonder if Mozart began to write it for Constanze, but then found she couldn't sing it?

Levin then adds a dark D minor chorus, 'Crucifixus', a bounding 'Et resurrexit', the aria 'Et in spiritum sanctum' for tenor, 'Et unam sanctam', and an 'Et vitam venturi' fugue. The Sanctus and Hosanna are restored to double-choir texture, the Agnus Dei added, and the final 'Dona nobis pacem' emerges as a jovial, unbuttoned, almost Haydnesque plea for peace.

🎧 *Mass in C minor K427* McNair, Montague, Rolfe Johnson, Hauptmann / Monteverdi Choir / English Baroque Soloists / John Eliot Gardiner
Philips 420 210–2
🎧 *Mass in C minor K427*
Auger, von Stade, Lopardo, Hauptmann / Bavarian Radio SO and Chorus / Leonard Bernstein
DG 431 791

🎧 *Mass in C minor K427* Oelze, Larmore, Weir, Kooy /
Collegium Vocale Gent / Orchestre des Champs-Elysees /
Philippe Herreweghe
HM80 1393

Requiem in D minor K626****

Sometimes powerfully mythical stories turn out to be true.
Who would have predicted that the evidence would one day
turn up to support the oft-told tale of the dark messenger
who commissioned the Mozart Requiem? But it happened in
the 1960s, when a document emerged written by the teacher
and choirmaster Anton Herzog which told the story of how
Count Franz von Walsegg-Stuppach habitually commissioned music to be performed under his own name, and
arranged for a requiem to be commissioned from Mozart in
honour of his recently dead wife. The reason for the secrecy,
however, was evidently bizarre rather than sinister: the Count
was in the habit of performing works at his residence and
rather assuming that those present might conclude that they
were by him. So has arisen one of the most powerful stories
surrounding the history of any piece of music, for the composition of Mozart's Requiem is surrounded by myth and
fantasy to a greater degree than almost any other single
work in musical history. Much that is fictional in the story of
the Requiem may be discarded ('I was writing the requiem
for myself'), but a surprising amount of the story of its
commissioning has been confirmed. Hence the saga of the
composer's early death, with the music still incomplete, and
the problems connected with its subsequent completion have
ensured it a unique and complex history.

The commission for the Requiem arrived in July 1791,
from a representative of Walsegg-Stuppach, who proposed to
pass it off as his own at a private performance. Mozart was
busy with his operas, and it is unlikely that any substantial
progress was made on the piece before he left for Prague and

the final stages of *Tito*. The bulk of the work was done in the last three months of his life, and nothing in the autograph score was written down before his return from Prague and the completion of *Die Zauberflöte* in September 1791. There are affecting stories of Mozart's wife Constanze removing the score from him because he became too sick to work on it, but the facts of the matter are far from clear. We can certainly dismiss the imaginative picture presented in the film – though not the far more serious original play – of Shaffer's *Amadeus*: that Salieri was actually Mozart's accomplice in writing down the Requiem, for all the world like Eric Fenby taking dictation from Delius.

What is certain is that the work as it has come down to us is not only in Mozart's handwriting. After his death, for instance, his pupil Franz Xaver Süssmayr wrote Mozart's signature on the first page, dating the work 1792: a weird and naive act, since no one could have been unaware that Mozart was dead by then, unless this was Constanze's only way of claiming that the commission had been completed and hence earning the promised final fee. Certainly Constanze Mozart depended on the Requiem to a disturbing extent in securing her future, and she has been accused of much dissimulation in the accounts she gave of its origins over the succeeding decades.

Mozart's score of the initial 'Requiem aeternam' movement is complete, but already in the Kyrie there are other hands involved in the instrumental parts. Then from the 'Dies irae' Mozart's outline of the score remains, but the completion of the material in the autograph score was made by his pupil Joseph Eybler, who was with him in his last illness. It is at least possible that Mozart oversaw this part of the work, but it is more likely that the filling-in took place after his death, when Constanze gave Eybler the Requiem score in a desperate attempt to have it finished quickly.

Eybler, not surprisingly, felt himself unequal to the task. When he came to Mozart's incomplete 'Lacrimosa', of which only eight bars were written, he attempted to add a couple of bars of melody but then gave up the struggle. Süssmayr was less worried, and on Constanze's request continued his completion to the end of that movement and the end of the work – with what use of Mozart's own sketches we shall probably never know. Mozart himself had gone forward over that section to write in his score the two movements of the Offertory, 'Domine deus' and 'Hostias' – vocal parts only, with just some tiny clues for the orchestra. Possibly the very last thing he wrote in his score – or were these words too written by someone else? – was the instruction 'Quam olim da capo' at the end of the 'Hostias' movement, indicating a repeat of the fugue to those words. (When the autograph score of the Requiem was on display at the Brussels World Fair of 1958, this tiny bit of the score was torn off. Does someone, somewhere, have some of Mozart's last words? Or was the thief a victim of Mozart myth?)

Süssmayr's completion of the full work is the traditional form in which the Requiem has come down to us, and it has at least as much authority as the first published version of the Clarinet Concerto, or the anonymous published arrangement of the 'Coronation' Concerto, neither of which survive in a finished form by Mozart himself. Süssmayr may well have had sketches on which to base the Sanctus, Benedictus and Agnus Dei: most likely some choral parts were written in outline, while he supplied the orchestration. Other scholars may perfectly reasonably want to present solutions to the Requiem riddle that are more purely Mozartian, or which attempt to correct Süssmayr's deficiencies. Franz Beyer's version of 1971, Richard Maunder's more radical but less musical completion recorded in 1983, including a version of the Amen fugue at the end of the 'Dies irae', and other accounts of the score by Duncan Druce and Robert Levin have given varied interpretations of what remains, and have struggled with the challenge of working it into a coherent whole.

But the inadequacies of Süssmayr's version, such as they are, present in a moving and graphic form what has been described by Christoph Wolff as the struggle of the Mozart circle of friends, after his death, to cope with an overwhelming legacy which they could not fully comprehend or come to terms with. Süssmayr's 'Mozart Requiem' takes us directly into the realm of what we, his successors, have made of Mozart; it begins the future of 'Mozart'.

As one can see from the many different editions and versions in the recordings below, many people have made many things of Mozart's Requiem. But after all the complexities and complications of the story, the music of the Requiem speaks with a power that is acknowledged by Roger Fiske in his essay in the Penguin symposium *Choral Music*:

> The mixed authorship gives the work an uncomfortable feel, and there is not enough of it in Mozart's hand to justify the number of performances it receives. And yet as I write this sentence I remember the very first bars for orchestra alone, some of the most moving bars in all music . . .

♩ *Requiem (ed. Süssmayr)*, *Kyrie K341* Bonney, von Otter, Blochwitz, White / Monteverdi Choir / English Baroque Soloists / John Eliot Gardiner
Philips 420 197–2

♩ *Requiem (ed. Süssmayr)*, *Britten in conversation* Harper, Hodgson, Pears, Shirley-Quirk / Aldeburgh Festival Chorus / English Chamber Orchestra / Benjamin Britten
BBC Legends 4119–2

♩ *Requiem (ed. Druce)*, *Ave verum corpus etc.* Argenta, Robbin, Ainsley, Miles / Schütz Choir / Roger Norrington
Virgin 5 61520–2

♩ *Requiem (ed. Robbins Landon)* Ulewicz, Holzl, Hering, Van der Kamp / Tafelmusik / Bruno Weil
Sony SK 60764

♩ *Requiem (ed. Beyer)*, *Exsultate jubilate*, *Litany K195*, *'Coronation' Mass* Cotrubas, Watts, Tear, Shirley-Quirk / Academy of St Martin-in-the-Fields / Neville Marriner
Decca 443 009–2 (2 CDs)

🎧 *Requiem, Kyrie K341* Rubens, Markert, Bostridge, Muller-
Bachmann / Collegium Vocale Gent / Orchestre des
Champs-Elysées / Philippe Herreweghe
Harmonia Mundi 901393
🎧 *Complete Masses* soloists / various orchestras / Kegel,
Davis, Gardiner, Schreier, Harrer
Philips Complete Mozart Edition Vol. 19 422 519–2 (9 CDs)

Other sacred works

God is our refuge K20

At the end of their stay in London in 1765 the Mozarts visited the British Museum in its first home in Montagu House,
where the present Museum now stands. Nannerl noted 'the
library, the antiquities, birds of all kinds, fishes, insects, fruits
. . . a rattlesnake'. They presented the library with Mozart's
recently published Op. 1 and 2 sonatas, an engraving of the
famous Carmontelle watercolour of the family, and this
motet, his only piece entirely to English words. Leopold had
evidently helped Wolfgang to compose it and write it out,
and the music perhaps owes something to a setting of the
same text by Battishill, whom Mozart may have met while in
England. The Museum replied with thanks on 19 July 1765,
and the motet has graced many of their postcards since; most
recently it has been reproduced on a souvenir mug, though it
is rare to hear it performed.

Kyrie K33
Veni sancte Spiritus **K47**
Benedictus sit Deus **K117**
Te deum laudamus **K141**
Ergo interest **K143**
Miserere K85
Quaerite primum regnum Dei **K86**

Regina coeli K108
Inter nateos mulierum K72
Regina coeli K127*
Sub tuum praesidium K198
Misericordias Domini K222**
Venite populi K260**
Alma Dei creatoris K277
Sancta Maria, mater Dei K273

This is a selection of the smaller liturgical pieces that Mozart wrote as part of his duties, largely as court organist in Salzburg – though we know that this was never a post he relished or was thought by his superiors to have put enough effort into. K33 is a good example of a joint Leopold–Wolfgang project: the father writes out the first three pages, but from about bar 18 Wolfgang takes over himself. K47 is a large-scale work associated with the consecration of the Vienna Orphanage in the autumn of 1768, for which Mozart wrote a huge mass. K85 was written in collaboration with his Bologna teacher Padre Martini in mid-1770. Particularly attractive are the *Regina coeli* settings: K108 is quite elaborate and extended; K127 was written for the wife of fellow composer Michael Haydn, and contains plenty of coloratura. K117 is the 'grand offertorium' referred to by Leopold in his correspondence.

The setting of *Misericordias Domini* K222 as an Offertory produces a strikingly powerful piece in D minor which anticipates some of the Requiem, especially in the strongly contrasted phrases that will recur in 'Confutatis maledictis' and 'voce me cum pietatis'. *Venite populi* K260 is a strong double-choir motet from 1776, which Brahms admired and conducted; it looks forward to the double-choir writing in the C minor Mass from the following decade. (*Scande coeli limina* K34 and *Regina coeli* K276, though both in the *Neue Mozart Ausgabe*, lack any authentic sources, while the two settings of *Tantum ergo* K142 and K197 are by J. Zach, and the Offertory K177 is by Leopold Mozart.)

Exsultate jubilate K165**

On 17 January 1773 Mozart wrote from Milan: 'I am about to write a motet for the *primo uomo*, which is to be produced at the Theatine Church tomorrow.' This was a motet for the castrato Rauzzini, and has become one of Mozart's most eternally popular works. There are two bubbling and extrovert F major Allegros around a central recitative and aria. The final Alleluia is one of Mozart's most famous tunes, and has been featured the world over, even at an English royal wedding: the composer would doubtless be astounded.

🎧 *Exsultate jubilate K165* Cecilia Bartoli /
Vienna Chamber Orchestra / Georg Fischer
Decca 443 452–2
🎧 *Exsultate jubilate K165* Emma Kirkby /
Academy of Ancient Music / Christopher Hogwood
Decca Oiseau-Lyre 411 832
🎧 *Exsultate jubilate K165*
Felicity Lott / London Mozart Players / Jane Glover
ASV PLT8514

Litaniae Lauretanae in B flat K109
Litaniae de venerabili altaris sacramento in B flat K125
Litaniae Lauretanae BVM in D K195
Litaniae de venerabili altaris sacramento in E flat K243
Dixit and Magnificat in C K193
Vesperae de Dominica in C K321
Vesperae solennes de Confessore in C K339*
Kyrie in D minor K341**
Ave verum corpus **K618*****

Mozart's settings of Vespers and Litanies were an important part of his job as a church musician in Salzburg. The first Vespers sets only one psalm and the Magnificat, but the two later sets have all the psalms of the Roman liturgy and the Magnificat. The most famous individual movement has become 'Laudate Dominum' from K339, often sung on its own. The Litanies originated from the repeated invocations to the Blessed Virgin and the Saints which formed part of the Holy Week liturgy, and were sung at afternoon services on feast days; the texts also include the Kyrie and Agnus Dei of the Mass Ordinary; many Salzburg church musicians had set them, including Mozart's father Leopold. The Litany of Loreto K109 is a five-movement work, but the Litany of the Blessed Sacrament K125 has nine movements (and is based on a setting by Leopold) while the later Litany K243 has ten movements, full of oft-repeated invocations to the Saints and the Virgin, which must have been a challenge to Mozart.

Nobody is able to agree on the origins of the splendid Kyrie in D minor K341, which sounds like a cross between *Idomeneo* and the Requiem. Was it intended to be part of a mass? Is it a fragment which was completed by someone else? In any case, it touches a vein of *opera seria* as well as one of lavish sonority; it is an isolated gem.

Finally, the touching miniature *Ave verum corpus*, written for Mozart's friend Anton Stoll, who conducted the choir in Baden where Mozart's wife Constanze took the waters in his last months. For the feast of Corpus Christi in July 1791 he wrote this perfect, tiny motet which has become perhaps his most famous single piece of church music. It blends the simplicity of his late style with a contained chromaticism; it does not sound at all sickly, though it undoubtedly is the source of many subsequent pieces that do.

♫ *Litanies, Vespers* soloists / Leipzig Radio Choir and Orchestra / Herbert Kegel, and London Symphony Orchestra / Colin Davis
Philips Complete Mozart Edition Vol. 20 422 520 (5 CDs)
♫ *Ave verum corpus K618, Requiem*
Les Arts Florissants / William Christie
Erato 0630 10697–2

Cantatas and oratorios

Die Schuldigkeit des ersten Gebots (Part I) K35
Grabmusik K42
La betulia liberata K118*

The first pair of pieces, both written in 1767, are two of
Mozart's earliest publicly performed works, showing
Leopold's desire to have his son advance in composition as
soon as they returned from their exhausting European tour.
Die Schuldigkeit was written as a contribution to an allegorical
drama for Salzburg, known as a 'sacred Singspiel'. Adlgasser
and Michael Haydn wrote the other two parts, but their
music has not survived. The young Wolfgang's contribution
was carefully preserved by Leopold, who had participated in
the writing, certainly by copying all the recitative text into the
score, improving some features of the arias and adding
dynamics. Perhaps Leopold's degree of collaboration in his
son's music became well known and the object of suspicion,
for the story associated with the *Grabmusik* K42 is that the
Archbishop, not crediting that such masterly compositions
were really those of a child, shut Wolfgang up for a week, during which he was not permitted to see anyone and was left
only with music paper and the words of an oratorio. During
this short time Wolfgang composed 'a very capital oratorio,
which was most highly approved of on being performed'.

The *Grabmusik* is a dramatised Passion oratorio, written
for performance on Good Friday: a dialogue between the
soul and an angel. The work was not forgotten because a few
years later it was revived and a new final recitative and chorus
added.

The origin of *La betulia liberata* in the Mozarts' first Italian
journey is unclear; it may have been commissioned for Padua
when they arrived there in March 1771, but it was not finished
until after the Mozarts returned to Salzburg; where and when
is was performed is not certain. The libretto, by Metastasio,
had been avoided even by Hasse, who set many of the great

Italian poet's texts. It tells the story from the apocrypha of the saintly widow Judith, who just as the city of Bethulia was about to fall in siege to the Assyrians, went to their leader Holofernes. She offered herself to him, and then cut off his head. The oratorio is essentially static in that the central scenes are only related from afar, and not depicted. But this suits the 'mind's eye' drama of the oratorio style, which Handel had used in his unstaged dramatic oratorios. The city of Bethulia is under siege, the chorus sing of their despair, but Ozia the prince says he will never surrender, though his advisors urge him to, and he obtains a stay of five days. Judith, emerging from her four-year hiding since the death of her husband, exhorts the Israelites to fight. She asks permission to leave the city with her maid: 'I go forth unarmed and unafraid.' The chorus sing in puzzled praise: 'She promised nothing, yet gives us all hope.' In Part II, Achlor, who has been thrown out of Holofernes' camp for excessive praise of the Israelites' bravery, engages in a discussion with Ozia about the existence of the one true God. As final peril threatens the city, Judith returns, telling the tale of her entry into the Assyrian camp, her encounter with the tyrant, and her beheading of him. She has returned bringing Holofernes' severed head with her. Achlor takes this opportunity to convert to Christianity. The Assyrians, despairing after the murder of Holofernes, flee, and the Bethulians are left to thank God for their deliverance.

The oratorio shows Mozart grappling with the problems of imbuing a biblical narrative with dramatic force. In several movements, Gluck appears to be his model: the opening sequence seems to echo the overture to Gluck's *Alceste*, with its use of the D minor tonality that was to become so important to Mozart. The use of the chorus, too, especially in the finale, is strikingly Gluckian. (Here Mozart uses a Gregorian psalm-tone melody that was to recur at the very end of his life at the 'Te decet' in his Requiem, also in D minor.) There are no ensembles: only the choruses interrupt the sequence of arias which power the piece.

🎧 *Oratorios, Cantatas, Masonic Music*
soloists / various orchestras / Leopold Hager, Neville
Marriner, Peter Schreier
Philips Complete Mozart Edition Vol. 22 422 522–2 (6 CDs)

Davidde penitente K469*

Mozart very rarely recycled his music. Invention did not
seem to come slowly to him, so perhaps he had no need to
rework old ideas: the evidence of his many abandoned beginnings of works and fragmentary pieces is that he had too
many ideas, not too few. So it is perhaps surprising to find
him reworking an entire incomplete composition here.
Mozart was anxious to become a member of the Vienna
Tonkünstler-Sozietät, a benevolent society for musicians, but
he never got round to sending in his birth certificate. Had he
done so, and become a member, Constanze would have
received a pension on his death. In January 1785 the society
asked him for a new piece for their Lenten benefit concert.
He did not feel inclined (or persuaded by the fee) to write a
new piece, but did offer a reworking of the incomplete fragments of his Mass in C minor (which may have been rendered
irrelevant by liturgical change and Josephinian reforms).
Maybe Mozart saw this music as one of his incomplete fragments which could be useful in a new form, and he reworked
it for this Latin text which has sometimes, without any foundation, been attributed to Lorenzo Da Ponte. He reworked
the text for the Kyrie and Gloria, omitted the Credo numbers, and added two new arias, one for the tenor Johann
Adamberger, and one for the soprano Caterina Cavalieri,
which he clearly took seriously as new works, because he
entered them in his thematic catalogue. Nevertheless, it looks
as if it was done in haste, because the word-setting is quite
clumsy in places. The premiere performances on 13 and 15
March 1785 were dismally attended. But Mozart may have
seen this as the most appropriate completion of his C minor

Mass fragments, and it arguably remained so until the Mozartian scholar Robert Levin decided to readapt the arias for a new completion of the C minor Mass in 2005.

🎧 *Davidde penitente K469* Marshall, Vermillion, Blochwitz / Stuttgart RSO and Choir / Neville Marriner
Philips 422 522–2

Dir Seele des Weltalls **K429**
Die Maurerfreude **K471**
Zerfliesset heut **K483**
Ihr unsre neuen Leiter **K484**
Die ihr des unermesslichen Weltalls **K619**
Laut verkünde unsre Freude **K623**

Freemasonry was an important feature of Viennese life, and although it had been repressed at various times under Maria Theresa, Joseph II found the enlightened ideas of Masons an important support in carrying out his social reforms. Mozart joined the Masonic lodge 'Zur Wohltätigkeit' (Beneficence) in December 1784, but it was at the more important lodge 'Zur wahren Eintracht' (True Concord) that he was admitted on 7 January 1785. In 1786 various lodges were amalgamated to form the lodge 'Zur gekrönten Hoffnung', (New Crowned Hope). Mozart wrote several specifically Masonic pieces – from which one can also judge that several others, notably *Die Zauberflöte*, use Masonic symbolism. K429 is an incomplete cantata in the Masonic key of E flat which Stadler completed. *Die Maurerfreude* was written for a ceremony which both Wolfgang and his father Leopold (who was admitted while visiting Mozart in Vienna) attended on 24 April 1785. Mozart's friend Adamberger was the soloist.

Then there are two songs K483 and K484, related to the opening of the new lodge in 1786, for tenor soloists and male chorus, and a solo cantata from the summer of Mozart's last year, *Die ihr des unermesslichen Weltalls*, whose sequence of brief numbers echoes the pared-down style of his late music.

The cantata *Laut verkunde unsre Freude* is the very last work Mozart entered in his own thematic catalogue (for him, the Requiem was never finished). He completed it on 15 November, conducted it at a Masonic ceremony three days later, and died on 5 December.

🎧 *Masonic Music* Krenn, Krause / Edinburgh Festival Chorus / London Symphony Orchestra / István Kertész Decca 425 722–2

Arrangements of works by Handel

Acis and Galatea K566**
Messiah K572**
Alexander's Feast K591*
Ode for St Cecilia's Day K592*

One of the most fascinating (to us, if not necessarily to him) tasks that Mozart undertook in the late 1780s was the reorchestration of works by Handel. These were undertaken for Baron van Swieten, to perform at his explorations of baroque music in Vienna. The first was *Acis and Galatea*, made in November 1788; *Messiah* followed in March 1789, with *Alexander's Feast* and finally the Ode for St Cecilia's Day in July 1790. (They were preceded by a performance of C. P. E. Bach's *Resurrection Oratorio* which Mozart conducted in February 1788, but he did not rescore that work, only adding instruments to one aria, 'Ich folge dir'.)

Christoph Wolff has shown how thoroughly, in preparing the *Messiah* arrangement, van Swieten and his associates prepared the material for Mozart, writing out blank staves for him to add instrumental parts. It is clear he was given instructions on what was required (a practice van Swieten followed when preparing *The Creation* and *The Seasons* for Haydn). What is difficult to assess is how much creative endeavour Mozart actually put into these arrangements. They are full of significant touches, bringing Handel's music up to date and matching it with the practices of the time, for instance adding instrumental scoring where the baroque would simply have used continuo instruments, harmonising passages which Handel left in unison ('The people that walked in darkness'), and making clear what happens at various cadential points which in the original scores would have been left to the performers ('I know that my Redeemer liveth'). They are wonderful testaments to the desire of Mozart's time to let these masterpieces speak again. Whether these updated scorings are still relevant to us is a matter for debate: the sounds of clarinets in *Messiah* have of course become familiar to generations through later rescorings of the piece by Prout (who adopted some of Mozart's scoring), Thomas Beecham, Eugene Goossens and others. Mozart's versions can certainly be of help in translating Handel's oratorios into larger concert halls than those in which they were originally performed (although ironically Mozart's arrangements appear to have been originally performed in a tiny space in Vienna). In any case, these arrangements are a vital part of Mozart's legacy, and he took them seriously because he entered them in his thematic catalogue.

♫ *Acis und Galatea arr. Mozart* soloists / English Concert / Trevor Pinnock
DG 447 700
♫ *Ode for St Cecilia's Day, Acis und Galatea arr. Mozart* soloists / Das Neue Orchester / Christoph Spering
Opus 111 OPS 45–9109/10 (2 CDs)
♫ *Messiah arr. Mozart* soloists / Huddersfield Choral Society / Royal Philharmonic Orchestra / Charles Mackerras
ASV RPO 001R (2 CDs)

Operas

Opera was the art-form to which Mozart aspired above all. It was the genre which enabled him to express most fully the range of emotions he experienced, to explore in the greatest depths the human relationships which (it is surely not unreasonable to guess) he found it quite difficult to sustain in everyday life, and to realise them in complex, extraordinarily subtle music. As a performer he could and did turn the piano concerto into his own personal opera, but he still longed to write the drama of characters that interacted, based on text and on musical structure, in a way that previous eighteenth-century composers had achieved only within a strictly limited framework. Far from entering into the business of composing opera thoughtlessly or without challenging tradition, as Wagner suggested, the evidence is that Mozart gave a huge amount of thought and planning to the shape, direction and content of his mature operas. And Mozart's genius, as we now recognise, was to capture in his music the ambiguity of life's relationships. Other great composers have expressed the extremes of life: affirmation, despair, sensual pleasure, bleak emptiness, but only in Mozart can all these emotions co-exist within the space of a short phrase, in a few bars of *Figaro* or an ensemble from *Così*. This is surely one element of Mozart's art which binds him most surely to our time.

At the start of the twenty-first century, Mozart's mature operas are all classics, never out of the repertory. But it was not always so. The Italian operas took a while to establish themselves, especially as *Così fan tutte* was frowned upon in the nineteenth century. But the German operas fared better: *Die Entführung* was an almost immediate international success, and *Die Zauberflöte*, at the very end of his life in 1791, provided a sudden triumph for the composer. As a result of this, it is sometimes said that had he lived he would have turned the corner financially and history might have turned out differently. That may be wishful thinking (it is not clear what share of the profits he would have been entitled to under his arrangement with the wily librettist and manager Schikaneder), but it is certainly true that soon after his death his last operas were performed around Europe. *La clemenza di Tito*, which contemporaries found tedious at its first performance, and is the most recent of the mature operas to have been accepted into the modern canon of the Mozart repertory, became the focus for the classicising of Mozart in the late eighteenth century, the focus of his transformation from a working composer into the subject of noble myth and pristine purity.

Mozart, perhaps especially in opera, was a tireless worker, planning and revising and reworking his material for different performing situations, working within the conventions of his time, but always stretching and challenging them to achieve new heights. He was above all receptive to performing circumstances because that was the tradition he had grown up in. Reinhard Strohm has shown definitively how in the earlier eighteenth-century world of *opera seria*, it was the performance and not the work that was primary. Singers came first, composers adapted their writing to whoever was available to sing, and that took precedence over any grand scheme for 'the work itself', which as a concept scarcely existed:

> What was clearly fixed and predetermined about any production in those days had so little to do with the score and so much to do with the presentation of the drama by a single, individual singer that a revival of an *opera seria* today should really concentrate less on what Handel or Hasse wrote than on what Senesino or Farinelli did with the chief role . . . it might not matter that some of his arias were by Harnoncourt and not by Handel. In fact they could even be by Penderecki; a conclusion that is only apparently absurd, since the claims of history in the matter of musical performance always collapse in cases where the performer has to become the creator.

Daniel Heartz (whose superb sequence of essays – *Mozart's Operas*, with Thomas Baumann – is the most stimulating current guide to the richness of the innovations in the later operas) has shown how the conventions of Mozart's great operas grew out of those of his contemporaries. By developing the mixture of the two genres previously separate as *opera seria* and *opera buffa*, Mozart and his librettists eventually created an operatic form which could range across the bounds of society, bringing together (in *Don Giovanni*) a *seria* character, Anna, a *buffa* character, Zerlina, and a mixed, serious/comic character, Elvira. Hence the revolutionary character of *Le nozze di Figaro* is not the overtly political one of Beaumarchais's play; however hard you strive to find in Mozart an anti-establishment rebel, the evidence is that he was never interested in politics except if it affected his everyday life. No, the true revolution of *Figaro* is that musically, the coming together of master and servant, countess and maid, soldier and gardener – relationships Mozart understood very well – is more subtly delineated than ever before in music.

As has been repeatedly emphasised here, Mozart did sketch and work out his music in detail. Even for *Die Zauberflöte*, that rushed masterpiece of his final year, there are sketches for part of the Act I finale, Tamino's dialogue with the speaker, a snatch of the Act II finale, and even a discarded plan for an overture to the opera. And, tricky contrapuntal combinations were carefully planned in advance: in *Così* the canonic moment in the Act II finale; in *Zauberflöte* the chorale of the Armed Men. Witness too the extensive series of letters to his father Leopold about the composition of *Idomeneo*, and the evidence of the autograph scores for the first two acts of that work, where Mozart is continually modifying and polishing his thoughts in order to increase the continuity and cogency of the drama. He spent a lot of time searching for good libretti, searching for plays, not finding much that met his high standards. He had a keen instinct for what he wanted and needed, and one of the high points of his operatic progress was to have found a librettist in Lorenzo Da Ponte with whom he could work productively (what would we give for an eye-witness of their collaboration on *Figaro*, *Giovanni* or *Così* in the same way that we have Mozart's evidence about *Entführung* and *Idomeneo*!). And yet by the end of his life, Mozart was not hampered in *Zauberflöte* by a libretto that was far less than perfect: he simply turned it to his musical ends, and made it his own.

Scholarly work on Mozart's operas has advanced rapidly in recent years, moving from analysis of their internal structures and musical content (which has reached new subtlety in the studies by James Webster) to a greater concern with social context, the processes of production, and a valuable exploration of the surrounding genres of opera which identify how much Mozart owed to those around him and hence highlight his individuality. Dexter Edge has written about Mozart's copyists; and a valuable conference on the *opera buffa* in Vienna during the 1780s has made clear the context in which he operated, examining how Mozart might have engaged with contemporary fashions, conventions of musical entertainment, new scientific developments, and politics.

With this has perhaps come a decline in the emphasis on the traditional analysis of the tonal organisation of these scores, which so interested Hans Keller, H. C. Robbins Landon and a generation of scholars. In an important article on Mozart in *The New Grove Opera*, Julian Rushton rightly draws attention to the landmarks of Mozart's operatic development, commenting that the leap forward of *Figaro* is remarkable: 'Mozart's own genius is needed to account for the radical nature of the transition from the uncompromisingly extended musical developments of *Die Entführung*; from now on, the symbiotic harmony between music and drama is complete.' But then Rushton is dismissive of the fact that operas begin and end in the same key ('to relate other keys to this tonic proposes a scheme too vast to be grasped'). Yet to most of us innocent listeners, simple sonata-form arguments are not 'grasped' in that simplistic sense; they exist as a subconscious background which is perceived as an organising force; hence the continuing importance of key structures within Mozart's operas and especially their finales, which are discussed here.

We know from an account that Salieri gave of opera composition that the setting of the keys for each number was a critical first step. Another surprising claim in *The New Grove Opera* is that by writing in keys that relate to each other tonally, Mozart had to abandon the expressive character of different keys which has so often been noted here in his symphonies and concertos: 'The claims of affective key structures and tonal architecture are virtually irreconcilable.' Surely that is just the sort of challenge Mozart loved, so that within the schemes of his operas, the expressive A major of the Ferrando/Fiordiligi seduction scene in *Così*, or the popular G major of the *Figaro* contredanse in the Act II finale, or the blazing C major of 'Viva la libertà' in *Don Giovanni* fit perfectly within a key scheme that unifies the work as a whole.

Whatever one's misgivings about Rushton's arguments about key and structure, (and one can not quite agree with *The New Grove Opera* that Mozart 'is the first operatic composer whose work as a whole has never needed to be revived', which is true only of a very few works) it is certainly the case that Mozart's operatic output 'is likely to remain the touchstone of operatic achievement'.

Apollo et Hyacinthus K38

At the end of November 1766 the Mozart family returned to Salzburg from the long tour during which Wolfgang first found fame as a child prodigy. Less than nine months later they left again, this time for Vienna, but in the mean time Leopold made the most of the fame which Wolfgang's activities had attracted. He was in constant contact with the University, for the chapel boys who sang under Leopold also attended the university school, where they were educated, in much the same manner as Leopold had been during his childhood in Augsburg. So it was doubtless through his agency that Wolfgang was commissioned to produce the music for a Latin drama to be performed around a Latin play, *Clementia Croesi*. It was the third year of the school, called (after the Jesuit manner) 'Syntax', who performed the entertainment, to a text by their teacher Rufinus Widl. Two twelve-year-old boys took the parts of Apollo and Hyacinth, and the performance was followed by the young Mozart alone: 'in the evening he gave us excellent proof of his musical skills on the keyboard.' The music does not seem to have been performed again, although one duet was rescued by Mozart in his symphony K64. Leopold entered it in his catalogue of his son's compositions, and it seems to have been Mozart's sister Nannerl (she was presumably at the performance) who gave it its present title.

Mozart's music tells the story of Apollo and Hyacinth, and the jealous south wind Zephyr, who blows Apollo's discus so that it kills Hyacinth. In its original version the story has distinctly homoerotic overtones, but the libretto for Mozart's piece makes Hyacinth's sister Melia the cause of rivalry, thus avoiding problems. Mozart's music, even if his father helped, shows real poise and beauty for an eleven-year-old. Some of the arias are static, but others have original ideas, and most remarkable are a couple of recitatives accompanied by hesitant, jabbing chords and vigorous staccato passages. The loveliest moment is a serene passage for strings and horns as Hyacinth dies and flowers grow from his grave.

Mozart's first operatic essay was forgotten for over a century. But it was revived in Rostock in 1922 and Munich in 1932, and a puppet version became popular in Salzburg. It has received some concert performances in the UK, notably at the Fortune Theatre London on the 199th anniversary of Mozart's birth, and in the Mozart Now bicentenary series on the South Bank in 1991.

🎧 Tolz Boys Choir / Nice Baroque Ensemble / Gerhard Schmidt-Gaden
Pavane ADW 7236/7 (2 CDs)

La finta semplice K51

Following the success of their European tour, Leopold was anxious to make the most of his son's gifts and so took him to Vienna in September 1767 with the idea of persuading the Emperor to commission an opera from him, possibly for the wedding celebrations of Archduchess Maria Caroline and King Ferdinand of Naples. The children did not arrive until 10 January 1768 because a smallpox epidemic confined them in Olmutz.

How interested the Emperor actually was is not clear, but the impresario Giuseppe Afliggio, who ran the court theatres, provided a hundred ducats and the resources of the theatres. Wolfgang went to work on a version of a play by Carlo Goldoni – a vitally important playwright whose development of libretti mixing serious and comic characters led the way for Mozart's achievements in his later operas. However, it seems that then all hell broke loose, with the forces of conservatism in Vienna (even including Gluck, whom Leopold thought he had squared off) conspiring against Mozart. Leopold reported:

> Envy has broken forth on every side . . . the singers were incited and the orchestra stirred up against us, everything was done to prevent the performances of this opera from going ahead . . . in the mean time it was put about by certain persons that the music was not worth a rap, while others were saying that the music did not fit the words of the meter, since the boy did not understand the Italian language well enough.

The evidence that Mozart completely rewrote two arias for the singers and altered another suggests that the last criticism might not have been completely inaccurate. Nonetheless, Leopold was furious and complained directly to the Emperor. But there was nothing to be done and so they returned to Salzburg, where it is probable that a performance (for which Mozart made some revisions) took place in 1769.

Mozart borrowed his symphony K45 to use as the overture, making the end of the second movement lead into the drama – ironically, a rather Gluckian effect.

The story, set in Cremona, revolves around the ups and downs of two brothers, Polidoro and Cassandro, and their romantic intrigues. The heroine, Rosina, who in the end manages to fix it so that everyone marries the right person, is a Susanna from *Figaro* in the making – and she has two outstanding arias, one a set-piece in a garden like Susanna's Act IV aria. As Erik Smith has commented, 'half the arias are old clichés about the pros and cons of marriage, not calculated to bring out the best in a twelve-year-old composer.' But the music shows the strong influence of Italian composers whose operas Mozart would have encountered; you begin to sense, in the bustling nature of the finales, the taut dramatic structures that Mozart would create in the years ahead.

Mozart's early work has not been often revived, though there were some new versions in the 1920s in Vienna and Prague. The Salzburg Mozart week in January 1956 brought it to the Salzburg Landestheater, and it then came to the main Salzburg Festival in 1960. Among other revivals was a lively one in Venice during 2005.

♫ Hendricks, Lorenz, Murray, Lind, Blochwitz, Schmidt / C. P. E. Bach Chamber Orchestra / Peter Schreier
Philips Complete Mozart Edition Vol. 28 422 528–2 (2 CDs)

Bastien und Bastienne K50*

This was the most popular of Mozart's early operas, and has proved the most practical for present-day use, perhaps because it is in the form of a one-act Singspiel or German opera with dialogue (like *Entführung* and *Zauberflöte*) rather than a full-scale *opera seria*. The piece was written in 1768, but mystery surrounds the statement of Mozart's biographer Nissen (Constanze Mozart's second husband) that it was intended for the garden theatre of the Vienna physician

Anton Mesmer (whose experiments in magnetism Mozart was to parody hilariously in *Così fan tutte*). The open-air theatre had not been completed in 1768, so perhaps the work was given at his home, or a later performance took place outdoors. The score was certainly written in Vienna, and does not require much in the way of resources – three singers, a mute chorus and small orchestra.

It was revived around the Mozart celebrations of 1891 and found favour in German translation in many German opera houses in the succeeding decades. After a Covent Garden presentation – surprisingly early, in 1907 – it disappeared until broadcast in an English version by Eric Blom in March 1933. It reached the Salzburg Festival in 1969.

The opera is based on a parody of Rousseau's famous pastoral *Le devin du village*, which had a great impact in France during the mid-eighteenth century. Its Arcadian shepherds were transformed by the Comédie Italienne into French peasants who sing and dance to their own rustic airs. This piece, *Les amours de Bastien and Bastienne*, had been performed in Vienna and later translated into German. A final link in this complex chain is that Johann Andreas Schachtner, the Salzburg court trumpeter, wrote some recitatives to replace the spoken dialogue. (This may have been undertaken for a later Salzburg performance which turned the piece into more of an opera and less of a Singspiel.)

The simple plot concerns the machinations of the magician Colas to reconcile the unfaithful Bastien to Bastienne, who still loves him. She is advised by Colas to pretend to have lost interest in Bastien. The situation becomes worse before it gets better, but eventually they are reunited with a little help from Colas's magic. The best music is light and pastoral in tone, with some high-flown magic-music for Colas, and one scene which really looks forward to Mozart's dramatic act finales: the two lovers fighting, reconciling and then celebrating in one splendid sequence (as Mozart was to achieve with two couples simultaneously in the Act II finale in *Entführung*).

🎧 Gruberova, Cole, Polgar / Liszt Chamber Orchestra /
Raymond Leppard
Sony SK 45 855
🎧 Soloists of the Wiener Sängerknaben, Wiener
Symphoniker/ Uwe Christian Harrer
Philips 422 527–2

Mitridate, re di Ponto K87*

This was Mozart's first great operatic success and a major step
forward in the career of the fourteen-year-old composer.
Leopold had again seen an opportunity for advancement, and
the setback in Vienna over *La finta semplice* had made him
even more determined. 'Why should I stay put in Salzburg,
sighing and hoping vainly for a stroke of luck, seeing
Wolfgang grow up . . . why should my son take his first step
in vain, thanks to the Vienna opera, and not even attempt to
pursue the path so clearly indicated for him?' So Leopold
obtained an introduction to Italy from the most famous opera
composer of the day, Johann Adolf Hasse, and set out on 13
December 1769: the Archbishop of Salzburg even contributed to the trip. There were still show-off concerts and
advertised tricks, but a new seriousness entered their presentation of the young genius. They met the English historian
Charles Burney, who was impressed: 'there is no musical
excellence I do not expect from his extraordinary quickness
and talents.' In March, Mozart wrote some arias for Count
Firmian (nephew of the former Archbishop of Salzburg,
which must have also provided an introduction); this was
influential in acquiring him the opera commission from
Milan that Leopold had so strongly wished for.

On 17 October 1770 the Mozarts reached Milan, which
then as now housed one of the leading theatres in Italy.
Wolfgang had already been writing recitatives for the opera,
but only now, with the singers arriving, could he really get to
work on the arias. The frantic, comic activities reported in

the family correspondence give a vivid insight into the workings of an eighteenth-century opera house. Mozart wrote and rewrote for the singers, including rewriting the opening tenor aria three times, and he directed the initial performances from the keyboard himself. By December, Leopold could finally report home: 'God be praised . . . the first performance of the opera took place on the 26th and won general applause . . . after almost all the arias there was extraordinary applause and cries of "*Evviva il Maestro! Evviva il Maestrino!*"'

One would not have immediately singled out *Mitridate* for present-day revival among Mozart's early operas, as it was completely forgotten in the eighteenth and nineteenth centuries, and E. J. Dent's pioneering book about the operas of 1913 gave it no space at all. But it was revived at the Salzburg Festival 1971 and then at the Mozart week in 1977, when it was recorded. The first modern performances in the UK took place as recently as 1979 in London (in concert) and 1989 in Wexford (on stage). But it took wing in two effective stagings, by Jean-Pierre Ponnelle for Zurich in 1985, and then by Graham Vick at the Royal Opera House in 1991.

The libretto is by the Italian poet Vittorio Cigna-Santi, and had been set to music three years earlier by Gasparini for performance in Turin. It is derived from Racine's play *Mithridate*, written in 1673, and tells the story of one of the opponents of the Romans, who ruled Pontus in Asia Minor during the first century BC. He attempted to gain other territories, successfully adding the area around the Bosphorus as far as the Crimea, but was then repulsed in the Mithridatian wars by Sully and Pompey. The action of the opera takes place in the last days of Mitridate's life, around Nympheaum. Arbate, the governor, and Sifare, Mitridate's son, hear that he has been killed, but this turns out to be untrue. Mitridate returns and tells Farnace that he is to marry the Parathion princess Ismene. Farnace plots against the king, but Arbate tells him of Farnace's baseness. In the second act Mitridate repulses Ismene, and entrusts Aspasia to Sifare's care. But when she reveals her love for Sifare, he is overcome by his conflict of loyalty to his father and his love for her. Aspasia says she will commit suicide and – in the magnificent final duet of Act II – Sifare implores her to let him die with her. The third act opens with Mitridate embattled, deaf to all pleas. The Romans land and he departs to fight. Mitridate is fatally wounded, but forgives his two sons; Sifare is united to Aspasia, while Farnace manages once again to love Ismene.

The music of *Mitridate* is in fine conventional style, but bears fewer of the hallmarks of Mozart's style even than earlier pieces. The Mozart biographer Alfred Einstein thought Leopold ought to have advised his son to keep his hands off the piece, since it was beyond his abilities. The demands of the singers for extrovert virtuoso material were unrelenting, there is only one (excellent) duet and a final ensemble: all the rest is made up of da capo arias, and there were few opportunities for Mozart to display the inwardness for which his style was to become noted. Still, one can see him grappling with the structural and expressive problems of the texts he set, highlighting words and phrases that are important to the dramatic structure. Near the start is Aspasia's impressive G minor aria 'Nel sen mi palpita'; a couple of minor-mode arias, one with horn obbligato, are powerful, and the accompanied recitative for Aspasia 'Pallid' ombre' is outstanding. However, he clearly learnt a lot in the process. Mozart was never invited to compose for the new Teatro alla Scala that opened (after fire destroyed the previous building) in 1778.

🎧 Bartoli, Dessay, Sabbatini, Asawa /
Les Talens Lyriques / Christoph Rousset
Decca 460 772-2 (3 CDs)

Ascanio in Alba K111

Following the success of *Mitridate*, Mozart was commissioned to write a *festa teatrale* for the wedding celebrations of Archduke Ferdinand and Princess Maria Beatrice Ricciarda of Modena. Hasse was to write an opera, and Mozart the *serenata*. He started work in August 1771, and seems also to have added a ballet between the acts; ballet was an integral part of the celebrations. Leopold told his wife the commission 'will not only fill you with amazement, but will bring our son imperishable honour'. The serenade was a success, and Leopold tactlessly claimed that it 'had beaten the opera by so much that I cannot describe it'. Hasse was apparently more generous, and said: 'this boy will mean that we are all forgotten.' As a result the young prince Ferdinand wanted to take Mozart into his service, but Maria Theresa warned him against the importuning nature of the Mozart family.

The libretto was by Abbate Giuseppe Parini, orator of the University of Milan, and hymns the married couple as well as paying tribute to the prince's mother, the Empress. Venere (symbolising Maria Theresa) wishes her son to marry Silvia, but first he must prove his steadfastness in love, which of course he does. The son Ascanio and Fauno were both played by brilliant castrati, as is evident from their demonstrative music. Otherwise there is little here that pushes forward the young Mozart's dramatic style, though the composer is said to have regarded the piece as attractive and special. The specialness is perhaps the influence of the French style, with its associated grandeur. It was revived in the 1958 Mozart week in Salzburg, and came to the Salzburg Festival in 1976. Has it ever been staged in Britain?

♫ Chance, Windsor, Feldman, Milner, Mannion / Budapest Concerto Armonico / Jacques Grimbert
Naxos 8.660040–2 (2 CDs)

Il sogno di Scipione K126

This little piece, in an overture and twelve numbers, was originally intended for the fiftieth anniversary of the Archbishop of Salzburg's ordination on 10 January 1772. But he died less than a month before that landmark, and the work was transferred to the celebrations of his successor on 29

April 1772. The new Archbishop was Colloredo, who was going to be far less sympathetic to Mozart's activities than his artistically inclined predecessor. There is no record that it actually was performed in 1772. The libretto is by Metastasio: the Roman general Scipione, captor of Carthage, has to make a choice between the goddesses Costanza and Fortuna as his protector. He is taken to heaven to seek advice, receives messages in aria form from Publio and Emilio, and finally decides to stick with constancy rather than luck. Fortuna is predictably furious.

The key structure of this piece is more sophisticated than before: Fortuna has some effective coloratura in C, while Costanza answers in gentle A major with equally virtuosic music (are the two sisters of *Così* already in view here?) Publio sings in B flat, and then in C, Emilio in G. Costanza gets increasingly perturbed, Publio's verdict is delivered in B flat and then Fortuna bursts out in a D major accompanied recitative which plunges through E flat before returning to D. The 'Licenza', or final aria of praise for the present, leads to a four-part chorus to round off the proceedings. The piece has very rarely been revived, though it did reach the Salzburg Mozart week in 1979.

♀ Schreier, Popp, Gruberova, Ahnsjo, Moser, Mathis /
Mozarteum Orchestra / Leopold Hager
Philips Complete Mozart Edition Vol. 31 422 531–2 (2 CDs)
♀ soloists / Freiburg Baroque Orchestra / Gottfried von der Goltz
Naïve E8813

Lucio Silla K135**

This is the most exciting and musically stimulating of Mozart's earliest operas, and shows Mozart making huge strides in manipulating his operatic resources. The commission came as a direct result of the success of *Mitridate*, for the 1772–3 carnival season, and marked a major step forward for the sixteen-year-old composer. The libretto was written by Giovanni de Gamerra, but was submitted to Metastasio as court poet, who made some suggested emendations after Mozart had started to compose the recitatives. (A version of the same libretto was subsequently set by Johann Christian Bach in Mannheim.) It represents traditional *opera seria* at the height of its development, and shows Mozart pushing forward to create the most human and involving drama possible within this strict framework. To a large extent this is expressed in the accompanied recitatives, which have an exceptional richness in this work. Mozart waited for the arrival of his singers before writing the arias, and there was particular interest in Anna de Amicis as the prima donna Giunia. 'With passages so novel and amazingly difficult . . . her singing quite astounds me,' wrote Leopold. Wolfgang wrote to his sister Nannerl in mid-composition that he still had fourteen pieces to write: 'my mind is full of ideas for my opera, and I am in danger of writing you a whole aria instead of words.'

Leopold's account of the premiere is vivid: 'Just imagine, the whole theatre was so full by half past five that no one could get in. The singers on the first evening were in such a state of nerves at having to perform in front of such an imposing audience.' The inexperienced tenor exaggerated his outbursts and caused mirth, upsetting Anna de Amicis, who was further disconcerted by the fact that as soon as the castrato came on stage the archduchess applauded: 'This was a castrato's trick, for he had had the archduchess informed beforehand that he would not be able to sing for fright, to ensure that the court gave him encouragement and support.' The piece was a success and was given twenty-six performances in all; but it did not lead to the post Leopold had wished for for his son, and the Mozarts returned home at the beginning of March disappointed.

The plot concerns the dictator Lucio Silla, who has banished the senator Cecilio, but Cecilio has returned to hear from Cinna that his bride Giunia has been taken by Silla to his palace. Silla asks his sister Celia to persuade Giunia to look on him more positively, and Celia advises him to try kindness, against the advice of Aufidio, who recommends force. Giunia refuses the advances, and looks forward to death so she can be reunited with Cecilio. Silla is furious. Cecilio conceals himself in a cemetery (in a pre-echo of *Don Giovanni*) where Giunia comes to lament his fate. They meet and celebrate their love.

In Act II Aufidio tries to tell Silla to take Giunia as his bride by force. Celia tells him that his efforts to win her over have been in vain, so he decides to proceed, and tells Celia he will give her to Lucio Cinna. Cinna suggests that Giunia accept the marriage proposal, then kill Silla; she refuses, so Cinna thinks of killing Silla himself. Silla confronts Giunia publicly at the Capitol, but she still rebuffs him. Cecilio enters with drawn sword and is put in chains. In the final trio of the act, the two lovers find comfort in the thought of dying together, but Silla is isolated, recognising their love. In Act III, Cecilio is visited in prison by Cinna. Giunia is tormented by her thoughts but is ready to die. Matters come to a head at the Capitol, where the senators and the populace have gathered. Silla is comprehensively outnumbered by those who support Cecilio, so he announces that he will abdicate and live as a simple citizen. Finally, he is acclaimed by all.

The music of *Lucio Silla* is still dominated by the da capo aria and the coloratura of the *opera seria*, but the characterisation is far more advanced than before, and the depth of feeling is paramount. The music for the heroine Giunia is the grandest and heaviest, while the lighter role of Celia has music more in the *buffa* tradition. The two castrato roles are also clearly contrasted (Cinna was sung by a woman at the first performance). Cinna is more extrovert and dashing, while Cecilio is nobility personified, with great dignity. As an example of Mozart's subtlety in this opera, we could point to just one sequence of movements from Act II: an Adagio for Cecilio, 'Ah se a morir', with eloquent oboes and horns, leading to a middle section in C minor and then back to the

Adagio. Giunia and Celia then enter, and Celia has the ravishing aria 'Quando sugl'arsi campi', in a relaxed and chirrupy A major with coloratura staccato high notes looking forward to the Queen of the Night. From that we plunge immediately into Giunia's accompanied recitative in D minor which works its way through a variety of dramatic moods before coming to 'Parto, m'affretto', a wild aria in C major. The chorus comes in F and the act ends with the anguished Terzetto in B flat, with Silla singing against the lovers and the crowd. This magnificent sequence shows Mozart fully in command of large-scale structure.

Opinions of *Lucio Silla* have varied widely. Einstein's opinion – 'as a whole it is a highly unfortunate and uneven piece of work' – has set the tone, and even the enlightened E. J. Dent wrote of it simply as 'an episode in the development of a great man'. In recent years the trend has been revised and Gottfried Kraus wrote of it as 'one of the greatest examples of Mozart's operatic genius. Despite its conventional libretto and contemporary circumstances one must without reservation admit it is a masterpiece.' Its modern reputation stems from the recording and performances in the 1975 Salzburg Mozart week, which led Jean-Pierre Ponnelle (Zurich Opera, 1981) and Patrice Chéreau (La Scala, 1984), no less, to stage it. A superb recording by Harnoncourt (1989) has advanced the claims of the piece, and he revived it in the Vienna Festival of 2005. It has had concert performances but never a professional staging in the UK; an Amsterdam production was premiered in December 2004, and one in Santa Fe in 2005.

🎧 Schreier, Gruberova, Bartoli, Upshaw, Kenny / Concentus Musicus Wien / Nikolaus Harnoncourt
Teldec 2292–44928–2 (3 CDs)
🎧 soloists / Salzburg Mozarteum Orchestra and Choir / Leopold Hager
Philips 422 532 (3 CDs)

La finta giardiniera K196**

It was another two years before Mozart received his next opera commission, for an *opera buffa* at the carnival in Munich during January 1775; its first performance was shortly before his nineteenth birthday. He had hoped it would be staged in December, but there were the usual delays (as Leopold tactfully put it, 'so that the singers can lean their parts properly, and once they have the music in their heads, act with greatest confidence, so that the opera is not ruined in consequence'). It was not until 13 January that the successful premiere took place. It used to be thought that the libretto was by Calzabigi, revised by Marco Coltellini, but it is now credited to Giuseppe Petrosellini, and is the same libretto that was set by Anfossi in Rome a couple of years earlier. It is described by Daniel Heartz as 'a clumsy offspring' of the hugely influential Goldoni libretto *La buona figliuola*, written in Parma in 1756. In Piccinni's famous setting of this libretto the characters keep themselves apart and the serious singers do not participate, for example, in the act finales which are dominated by the *buffa* characters. It was Mozart's skill (and a reflection of the temper of the times) that these boundaries of class and musical style were increasingly broken down in his operas.

The opera had a second life in the form of a Singspiel, in German with dialogue, and that was prepared with Mozart's help for Augsburg in 1779–80. It was performed in that version more often than in the original, and was revived in Frankfurt and Mainz in 1789. The German version was probably made by Johann Andreas Schachtner or the bass Franz Joseph Stierle, and Mozart copied it into his score. (The Philips Complete Mozart Edition gave the two versions equal status.) For many years the first act of the autograph (including the recitatives in Italian) was lost, and so the Italian version was unperformable, but a Moravian copy including all the recitatives turned up in time for the opera to re-establish itself, following its publication in the *Neue Mozart Ausgabe* in

1978. There were stagings in Salzburg and Aix-en-Provence, but the production that really put this opera on the map was that by the Hermanns conducted by Silvain Cambreling in Brussels in 1986, an evocative staging designed in a grove of trees that were full of natural noises. It is being staged for the Mozart anniversary of 2006 at the Royal Opera House, Covent Garden.

The opera combines serious and comic elements in a way that foreshadows the greatest achievements of the later operas. Here are three-dimensional figures who do not simply sing in pre-ordained patterns, but relate to each other and develop their personalities in the course of the opera. The plot revolves around the Podesta (mayor or governor) of Lagonero, who has taken on a new garden assistant, Sandrina. She is actually a disguised Marchesa, fleeing the attacks of her lover Count Belfiore, with her servant Roberto. But the Podesta's niece, Arminda, says she is actually going to wed Belfiore, causing total confusion. Sandrina denies she is the Marchesa, until Belfiore is threatened with punishment for causing the Marchesa's death. However, she then denies again being the Marchesa and Belfiore is doubly confused. Sandrina is miserable and hopes to take refuge in a cave, but as everyone gathers in the dark by the cave, the situation becomes increasingly confused. Sandrina and the Count both lose their reason and believe themselves to have become mythical creatures. In the short third act, as was traditional in this genre, harmony is restored and the couples' relationships are restored, except for the Podesta, who wisely stays single, doubtless on the lookout for another Sandrina.

The editors of the *Neue Mozart Ausgabe* have taken the heading on the libretto, *dramma giocoso*, in preference to the traditional description of *opera buffa*, and it is clear they were right to do so, for this is the first of Mozart's unique series of achievements in this genre. This libretto, with its confusions and mixings of the classes, lends itself perfectly to Mozart's aims. Indeed in one character, Sandrina, he found a perfect mix of a *seria* personality, the real Marchesa, with a *buffa* style, her assumed character as a gardener. The serious lovers are Arminda and Ramiro, both sopranos, and Ramiro has the most extended coloratura passages in the opera. Daniel Heartz notes that 'Arminda establishes her credentials as a seria character with a very long aria in G minor, allegro agitato, at the start of Act II. Yet they take part in the finales and in this respect are less set apart than earlier *parti serie*.'

This is a fully achieved piece, but it also points forward to Mozart's later operatic style. As Gottfried Kraus has remarked:

> All the characters familiar to us from the great Mozart operas appear here in embryonic form: Sandrina, the woman in love, sorely tried by fate, who despite her rebuff and the pain arising from it accepts hardship for the sake of her love – she is in the line of Mozart's feminine figures extending from Bastienne via Constanze to Pamina. Her foil is Serpetta, the simple peasant girl, half Zerlina and half Despina, for whom love is a game.

The flexibility with which Mozart brings these varied characters to life is remarkable, and the act finales in particular are models of the complexity he would later bring to perfection in *Figaro*. The arias are now no longer da capos, but in sonata form. In the end, does Mozart's genius overcome the weaknesses of the libretto? Modern productions have suggested that it does.

🎧 Gruberova, Margiono, Bacelli, Upshaw, Moser, Heilmann, Scharinger / Concentus Musicus Wien / Nikolaus Harnoncourt
Teldec DAW 9031 72309–2 (3 CDs)

Il re pastore K208*

This modest opera, also called a *serenata* in some sources, was written for the visit to Salzburg of the youngest son of Maria Theresa, Archduke Maximilian Franz; for the same occasion the more obscure composer Domenico Fischietti also provided an opera. The text had been written by Metastasio in 1751 and set to music several times before Mozart's day, notably by Giuseppe Bonno, who was later to become Kapellmeister in Vienna (and much later to have a bit part in the film *Amadeus*). Mozart's writing is now extremely resourceful in terms of making the shape of each aria different, and it is clear too that the libretto by Metastasio has been modified, in order to provide the extra flexibility that Mozart needed. This work was probably undertaken by Varesco, who had been appointed to the Salzburg court and was to provide the libretto for *Idomeneo*. Prominent in the score is the use of the solo violin, notably in the aria 'L'amero saro costante', and there is a direct echo of the G major Violin Concerto K216 in the aria 'Aer tranquillo e di sereni'; it is no coincidence that this dates from the rather short period when Mozart was engaged with writing solo violin music for the Salzburg court.

Il re pastore comes near the end of Mozart's operatic apprenticeship, and he evidently gave the piece a good deal of care; the circumstances of the first performance at the Archbishop's Palace on 23 April 1775 are not known, and it may even have been a concert performance; but we do know that Mozart returned to the work in 1778 to extract music to be sung by Aloysia Weber in Mannheim, and again in Vienna in 1784. He was frustrated by not being able to develop his operatic skills in Salzburg, and longed for an opportunity to write opera in Vienna.

The plot of *Il re pastore* might well have appealed to Mozart because, as in *La finta giardiniera*, it contains mistaken identity and mixed classes. The shepherd Aminta is actually the rightful heir to the Kingdom of Sidon. Alexander the Great, Alessandro, has liberated the kingdom from its tyrant ruler, but Aminta does not want to rule in his place. He prefers to stay a shepherd and enjoy the love of Elisa. Similarly the tyrant's daughter Tamiri is disguised as a shepherdess, who loves Alessandro's friend Aegenore.

There is difficult conflict between love and duty, but eventually Alessandro realises that lovers cannot be parted and brings the two couples together. Aminta accepts the throne as long as he can keep Elisa. Alessandro wishes them well and is praised by the people: 'Good fortune for the country with a Shepherd King!'

Il re pastore was not published until 1879 in the old Mozart Edition, and it was translated into English in 1917. The *Neue Mozart Ausgabe* edition appeared in 1985, and it has since been staged for the Salzburg Mozart week.

🎧 Hadley, Blasi, McNair, Vermillion, Ahnsjo / Academy of St Martin-in-the-Fields / Neville Marriner
Philips Complete Mozart Edition Vol. 35 422 535–2
🎧 soloists / Concentus Musicus Wien / Nikolaus Harnoncourt
Teldec 4509 98419–2

Thamos, King of Egypt K345**

Mozart was a great theatregoer, and loved his visits to the theatrical troupes which visited Salzburg and then Vienna. This powerful set of incidental music seems to have its roots in a request from the playwright Baron von Gebler for Mozart to contribute music to a performance of his new play in Vienna in April 1774: the opportunity to write for Vienna was something Mozart strongly desired, and so he poured considerable effort and skill into his music even though he was not in control of the drama. Mozart was not yet a Freemason, but he was intrigued by the symbolism which Gerber worked into his play, and indeed there are significant anticipations of *Die Zauberflöte* in this music, and a bold symbolic use of trombones in the orchestra.

Only parts of the music were written for those 1774 performances; orchestral numbers were added for a later performance in January 1776, when the play came to Salzburg. And then in 1779 the play was revived by his friend Johann

Heinrich Bohm, adding a new choral finale with a text by Schachtner. Together this made an impressive collection of music of which Mozart was proud. As he wrote to his father in 1783: 'I am extremely sorry that I shall not be able to use the music of *Thamos*, but this piece, which failed to please here, is now among the rejected works which are no longer performed. For the sake of the music alone it might possibly be given again, but this is not likely. Certainly it is a pity!' However, some of the music was recycled by Bohm into incidental music for a play called *Lanassa*, and Mozart actually heard the music in this form when he was in Frankfurt in 1790. So his effort was not wasted, and the music has become prized among Mozart connoisseurs for its dark and veiled power.

🎧 Alastair Miles / Monteverdi Choir / English Baroque Soloists / John Eliot Gardiner
DG Archiv 437 556–2

Zaide K344*

This is a rare example of a piece which Mozart appears to have begun to write without the definite promise of a commission, but maybe in the hope of one. It was started in 1779–80; without the stimulus of a performance, it remained unfinished. But its fifteen numbers contain some glorious music and many performers have been drawn to it. *Zaide* was one of the earlier Mozart pieces to be revived in the nineteenth century in Germany and Austria, and it has also inspired contemporary composers: Luciano Berio surrounded Mozart's music with sounds of his own in *Before, During and After Zaide*. The text was based on the libretto *Das Serail* by Franz Josef Sebastiani, set as a Singspiel by Karl Joseph Weiss in 1779; the Mozarts seem to have acquired this libretto, seen an opportunity, and asked their family friend Johann Andreas Schachtner to fashion it into a German Singspiel. (Schachtner's original libretto has been lost, and the piece

was first called simply *Zaide* by André, who published it in
1803.) Mozart used this opportunity to experiment with new-
style melodrama, in which spoken text was announced over
music. He had admired the melodramas of Benda, becoming
interested in Mannheim during 1778, and saw *Medea*, of
which he thought very highly: 'You know, of course, that
there is no singing in it, only recitation, to which the music is
like a sort of obbligato accompaniment to a recitative. Now
and then words are spoken as the music goes on, and this produces the finest effect . . . I think that most operatic recitatives
should be treated in this way, and only sung occasionally.'
Mozart began a melodrama of his own, called *Semiramis*,
which is referred to in his letters but has completely disappeared.

The music of *Zaide* combines a new complexity allied to
simplicity of melody which matches the style of the Singspiel
and recurs in *Entführung* and *Zauberflöte*. Among the most
felicitous moments is an ensemble which hymns the rising of
the sun: announcing the theme, the orchestra implies that the
music starts in triple-time, in 9/8; but when the soprano
enters it is clear that it is a lilting 6/8 siciliano rhythm. Does
Beethoven's *Fidelio* also lurk in the wings here? Mozart seems
to have realised that the chances of performing the new
Singspiel were slight, particularly when in December 1780
the theatres closed in mourning for the death of Maria
Theresa on 29 November. Perhaps more importantly, greater
ambitions had overcome him: Mozart was by then in Munich
working on a new commission, and *Idomeneo* took over his
creative life.

The plot is straightforward. Two slaves from Europe are
living in the harem of the sultan Soliman: Zaide, whom
Soliman loves, and the nobleman Gomatz, who falls in love
with Zaide. Gomatz and Zaide declare their love for each
other and plan to escape with the help of Allazim, Soliman's
chief guard. They are foiled, and all three condemned to
death. It is revealed that Allazim once saved Soliman's life,
but this has little effect. However, Soliman shows himself to

be a wise ruler, and listens to their pleas for compassion. The lovers are given their freedom.

🎧 Dawson, Blochwitz, Lippert, Bär / Academy of Ancient Music / Paul Goodwin
Harmonia Mundi HM90 7205

Idomeneo, re di Creta K366****

At this point in his operatic history, Mozart's first fully mature masterpiece appears: a work of such richness and power that it exerts an almost frightening grip on the imagination, containing some of his greatest music in any genre. In the libretto we are still dealing with the distant past – the island of Crete after the Trojan War – and so we are still some way away from the Mozartian reform of opera which was to bring the lives of everyday people into the operatic theatre. But the characters here are flesh and blood, and their dilemmas of love, power and sacrifice are clear dilemmas. 'The audience must believe it is real,' Mozart wrote of the oracle. So do we of the whole opera. For this ancient but powerful story Mozart created some of his most sensuous and deeply felt music, which has only begun to be fully appreciated in modern times.

The commission from Munich came from Count Joseph Anton Seeau, perhaps at the prompting of Mozart's Mannheim friend Christian Cannabich and the singer Anton Raaff, who was to be the first Idomeneo even though he was of advancing years. The Elector Karl Theodor of Bavaria, in whose gift the commission lay, had previously been in Mannheim, and had moved to Munich in January 1778, ensuring that his famous orchestra moved too. The story of the work's preparation from Mozart's arrival in Munich on 5 November 1780 until his father arrived on 26 January 1781 is told in the family correspondence; this is an invaluable document of an artistic process in action, and shows how detailed were the specifications to which the composer had to work. It seems likely that the subject of the opera was not in Mozart's hands, but that he was able to influence the choice of librettist: it was to be Gianbattistsa Varesco of Salzburg, with a German version again being made by Schachtner. The cast had been agreed, and various changes were made to the libretto which altered Mozart's work. Because he knew several of the singers, including Elisabeth Wendling (who was to sing Elettra) as well as Raaff, he may well have written their first numbers in Salzburg, and he could also have written recitatives and choruses in advance.

Composition and rehearsal proceeded apace alongside each other, and on 10 January the decision was taken to delay the first night by a week from 22 to 29 January. As Leopold and Nannerl set out from Salzburg, the trail of correspondence ceases, and they arrive in time for the dress rehearsal on 27 January. There were only three performances: reading the whole correspondence makes one realise what an extraordinary amount of work went into an artistic experience that was glimpsed by so few. The many changes and alterations serve also to reinforce the notion that Mozart was essentially writing for performers and for a performance: there was no sense at all of a work being conceived apart from its actual performance circumstances, and the piece was continually adapted to meet the needs of those taking part.

The ballet was a crucial part of *Idomeneo*, and because the score was to be played by his much-admired colleagues from the Mannheim orchestra, Mozart seems to have poured a wealth of accomplishment into the ballet numbers at the close of the opera. Though the ballet numbers are frequently omitted in present-day revivals, they provide a culminating shape and purpose to the score, and the final chaconne is, at around fifteen minutes, Mozart's longest continuous orchestral composition (and one of his most thrilling), taking the French baroque tradition of the chaconne and elevating it to an exciting demonstration of the Mannheim crescendo in all its vigour.

Mozart loved the work – there is a famous story of him bursting into tears while singing the famous Quartet with friends – and hoped to revive it, but only a single revival by amateur performers in the Auerperg Palace in Vienna on 13 March 1786 kept it from obscurity. (Yet again Mozart made several revisions for this single performance: 'Spiergarti non poss'io' K489 was added, as well as the aria 'Non temer, amato bene' K490.) If *Idomeneo* has a fault, it is the constant intensity of the musical argument, every number lavishly elaborated, without the relief of simplicity. This should perhaps justly have been the opera of which Joseph II said 'too many notes'.

The plot of *Idomeneo* revolves around the vow that Idomeneo makes, in gratitude for surviving a shipwreck, to sacrifice the first person he sees. As he lands in Crete, the first sight tragically turns out to be his son Idamante. The overture in D major launches the opera with colossal power, with a swirling seascape that calms down over chromatic wind lines and thundering accents in the strings before expiring completely. Ilia, who has been brought captive to Crete after the fall of Troy, laments her fate in a touching G minor aria and Idamante declares his love for her in an elaborate large-scale B flat aria. The Chorus arrives in bright G major, freed by Idamante, but Arbace brings dreadful news that Idomeneo has perished in the shipwreck. Elettra is already furious at this point in the opera with Idamante's hold over Ilia. The scene changes to a stormy beach where the sailors lament their fate in a chromatic C minor, but Neptune calms the waves, and Idomeneo appears, decisively turning the music towards an E flat major cadence. He reverts to C minor to recall his unhappy vow, and the inevitable encounter with his son provokes one of Mozart's finest accompanied recitative dramas. Idamante is more puzzled than distraught (the aria is again long and elaborate, this time in F major). The people arrive in a dance divertissement (with a long choral chaconne that balances the danced Chaconne at the very end of the opera) celebrating the safe return of their king.

The second act finds Idomeneo planning with Arbace to send his son into exile. But the love of Idamante (expressed in a B flat aria with soaring violin solo) and Ilia (a muted B flat aria with beautiful independent obbligati for flute, oboe, bassoon and horn) is too great. The orchestra – in a highly original Mozartian idea – echoes the aria, but darkly, in the minor, as Idomeneo becomes increasingly furious. His outburst 'Fuor del mar' was written first with extensive coloratura and then in a much simpler form for the aged Raaff. But the virtuosic version is generally preferred by tenors. Elettra is not unhappy at the prospect of exile with Idamante and sings, in a mock-restrained G major, 'Idol mio'. From the distance, the sound of a march advances (Mozart was to do this again in *Figaro*), and the chorus arrives to hymn the calm sea in an exquisite siciliano, 'Placido e il mar', over which Elettra soars. In a trio she, Idamante and Idomeneo bid farewell, but Neptune is displeased, whips up a storm and the chorus is petrified. Once again Idomeneo twists the music into his own key, D major, and confronts the god. But the tempest continues and the chorus escapes from the scene over shooting D minor scales that recall the overture.

Act III finds Ilia in the king's garden, singing gently to the breezes. Ilia and Idamante admit their love for each other in a duet (this was the number replaced for the Vienna performance by 'Spiegarti non poss'io'), but they then realise they must part, and the great Quartet 'Andro ramingo e solo' begins. This is a magnificent E flat scene, which unfolds over a quiet, hesitant chord sequence that returns to finish the scene, while in the middle it rises to heights of powerful emotion as the characters' conflicts emerge. Here the plunging modulations (into C flat at one point) and chromatic yearning of the lines express both the common agony of the participants and their individual emotions. This was a masterpiece Mozart never surpassed.

Arbace urges Idomeneo not to delay carrying out his vow and as the chorus assembles, Idomeneo reveals that it is his own son he must sacrifice. 'O voto tremendo' is chanted over rising triplets in gloomy C major, and then an ethereal contrapuntal march in F (with beautiful inner parts) leads to

Idomeneo's prayer and the arrival of the victim. In music of the utmost tenderness Idamante accepts his fate. Ilia pleads to be killed instead, and Neptune relents. The oracle speaks, in music which evidently caused Mozart much trouble because he wrote several versions. Idamante is spared: he and Ilia will reign in Crete. Idomeneo in yet another rich E flat accompanied recitative declares how happy he is, and the chorus takes over, leading to the ballet music which concludes the proceedings with majestic excitement. Mozart's music spirals from one invention to the next: at one moment, a dark D minor Gluckian ballet, then a sequence of sparkling wind chords and a solo oboe line. A Largo introduces a French overture for a solo dancer with great solemnity, from which the music gradually builds a grand crescendo over several minutes, piling suspension on suspension, until an ululating pair of oboes in thirds push the music onwards to its tremendous conclusion.

Richard Strauss admired the music and edited a version of *Idomeneo* first performed in 1931 which had several different productions during that decade. Georg Solti conducted it as early as 1951 at the Salzburg Festival, the same year Glyndebourne triumphantly brought it to the repertory in the UK under Fritz Busch, in a cut version that John Pritchard subsequently conducted. Caspar Neher designed a famous production which Karl Böhm conducted and recorded, but the most influential of modern times was Jean-Pierre Ponnelle's in Cologne, Zurich and Salzburg, especially with Harnoncourt in Zurich in 1980 and at the Metropolitan Opera in New York with Pavarotti in 1982. Johannes Schaaf directed it in Vienna and London, and there were subsequent Glyndebourne stagings by Trevor Nunn and Peter Sellars (with Simon Rattle conducting, 2003).

🎧 Hollweg, Schmidt, Yakar, Palmer, Equiluz, Tear, Estes / Mozart Orchestra and Choir of the Zurich Opera House / Nikolaus Harnoncourt
Teldec 8.35547 (3 CDs)

🎧 Rolfe Johnson, McNair, von Otter, Martinpelto /
English Baroque Soloists / John Eliot Gardiner
DG Archiv 431 674–2 (3 CDs)
🎧 Pavarotti, Gruberova, Baltsa, Popp, Nucci /
Vienna Philharmonic and Opera Chorus / John Pritchard
Decca 411 805–2 (3 CDs)

Die Entführung aus dem Serail K384***

One of Mozart's constant aims was to write a German opera
for a Viennese audience. Following his break with the
Archbishop of Salzburg and his move to Vienna, he was given
the opportunity to write an opera for the Burgtheater, where
a German opera company had been established. The playwright Gottleib Stephanie befriended Mozart in Vienna, and
promised him a new libretto on the Turkish subject that he
had tackled in *Zaide*. The libretto was delivered in July 1781,
and Mozart hoped to perform the work to coincide with the
visit of the Russian Grand Duke in the autumn of 1781. But
that visit kept being put off and it was not until 16 July 1782
that the work was staged: the premiere appears to have been
a success and the repeated performances of the piece made it
one of Mozart's more remunerative operatic efforts.

The plot is a simple one, centred on the attempts of
Belmonte and his servant Pedrillo to rescue Belmonte's
beloved Constanze from the clutches of the Pasha Selim and
his grotesque servant Osmin. This latter role, specially created for the bass Johann (Karl) Ludwig Fischer, dominated
Mozart's thoughts as he wrote the piece, and he created for
him a quite new vocal character, a *basso buffo*.

From the start, Mozart used the fashionable Turkish
effects of the moment to enhance the music: cymbals and
drums and a relentless triangle decorate the overture in C
major, which has the ingenious idea of creating as a central
section the aria with which the opera will start. Immediately
the total difference of idiom between this Singspiel and the

opera seria of *Idomeneo* is noticeable: there is far less decoration, and crisp, well-shaped melodies are the order of the day, though coloratura is still required of the main characters. Belmonte encounters Osmin, and their first duet is already a racy *buffa* number. Osmin has two arias in a row, the second with piccolo and more Turkish percussion. Belmonte realises that Constanze is alive and sings of his happiness in a sweet A major aria that rises to heights of passionate elaboration. The Janissaries enter with the Pasha: their C major Turkish chorus is surprisingly cheerful, doubtless to set off Constanze's tragic B flat lament over a piercing oboe (resembling the great B flat wind serenade) which takes her up to a top D on several occasions, very carefully written for the skills of Salieri's mistress, Caterina Cavalieri. The Pasha decides to employ Belmonte as an architect, and Osmin, Pedrillo and Belmonte finish the act with a ludicrously comic trio, 'Marsch, marsch, marsch'.

The second act begins with Constanze's maid Blonde in a poised aria whose coloratura shoots one note past her mistress's to top E. She is an English girl, and so will not give way to Osmin, though they argue violently in a duet which is notable for the fusing of two wholly independent vocal characters. Constanze is still cast down, and her intense lament this time is in G minor, 'Traurigkeit', pointing forward to Pamina's aria in the same key. Provoked by the Pasha's advances, she then storms without respite into 'Marten aller Arten' in C major, a huge aria to sing after the previous number, which is possibly one reason why Mozart provided it with a vast introduction, a whole *sinfonia concertante* for flute, oboe, violin and cello. This is the most extraordinary outburst, one of the longest-sustained arias Mozart wrote (319 bars long), fantastically demanding and impressive. (It is used in *Amadeus*, to show, without any evidence, that Mozart and Cavalieri must have had an affair, rousing Salieri's ire.) The final angry C major scales come to a sudden rest on top A flat for the word 'Tod' (death), before rushing to their close.

Light relief is provided by cheerful arias for Blonde and Pedrillo, and then the predictable drunken duet for Pedrillo with Osmin. Finally Belmonte manages to see Constanze, recognises her and sings a long aria which we may suppose was written for Mozart's friend Johann Adamberger. It would have been far more effective to keep the moment of recognition for the beginning of the act-finale, and in fact, Mozart seems to write this moment into the music, with Constanze's sudden rapturous cry 'Ach Belmonte', off the beat when we least expect it. This final quartet is a masterpiece of an ensemble: the whole story of the relationship of two couples is encapsulated here. First there is careless rapture, in D major, then there is doubt, in G minor; from E flat a fierce quarrel takes the music into E major, whence the healing balm of reconciliation takes place in a few easeful bars of A major. From there rapture returns, thrillingly so in the final climax of D major. This extrovert scene is the inverse of the introverted *Idomeneo* quartet, but both are supreme examples of Mozart's skill at delineating and bringing together different characters.

As usual in this genre, the final act is short. The two men take ladders to try and rescue the girls, Belmonte singing a lyrical aria and Pedrillo a little ballad interrupted by dialogue. But Osmin discovers them, and sings another rampaging D major aria, descending to a bottom D (the vocal range of this opera must be as great as any), 'O wie will ich triumphieren'. Belmonte and Constanze express their love for each other before they die. Belmonte reveals himself to the Pasha as the son of his oldest enemy, but the Pasha does not wish to behave in the same way as Belmonte's father did towards him, and so relents. The happy pair are set free. In a final number entitled 'Vaudeville', the Singspiel nature of the opera reaches its apotheosis in a wonderful little strophic number for all the soloists in turn, with a moralistic chorus. Even here Osmin manages to disrupt the proceedings with a flurry of Turkish fury, and it takes a while for the characters to pull back to the vaudeville conclusion. The Janissaries pay their C major respects in a final noisy conclusion.

Entführung is far more flawed dramatically than other operas whose poor libretti have been blamed for the failure of the music. The planning is lax, the sequence of arias must be challenging to sing, and it is surprising that Mozart did not exert more control over the sequence of events. Yet it has held the stage triumphantly because of the sheer exuberance of the music and the clarity of the plot. It proved easily adaptable to the massive neo-classical stagings which were popular in Munich and Berlin during the nineteenth century, and equally suitable for the rococo fantasies that were favoured at the start of the twentieth century. Modern productions have veered from the decorative (Covent Garden, designed by Timothy O'Brien in 1987) to the politically obtrusive (Johannes Schaaf in Salzburg, 1987 and oft-revived); it is a work that can take a myriad of interpretations, perverse or peculiar.

♫ Organasova, Sieden, Olsen, Peper, Hauptman /
English Baroque Soloists / John Eliot Gardiner
DG 435 857–2 (2 CDs)
♫ Schäfer, Petibon, Bostridge, Paton, Ewing /
Les Arts Florissants / William Christie
Erato 3984–25490–2 (2 CDs)
♫ Gruberova, Battle, Winbergh, Zednik, Talvela /
Vienna Philharmonic Orchestra / Georg Solti
Decca 417 402–2 (2 CDs)

L'oca del Cairo K422

Mozart was very serious about this Italian opera, which he told his father in December 1782 had been ordered by Count Franz Xaver Wolf von Orsini-Rosenberg – the unassuming name of the court theatre intendant in Vienna. 'I've looked though a hundred libretti, probably more,' he told Leopold. He was hopeful that Lorenzo Da Ponte might provide something, but he was very busy and also 'If he's in league with Salieri, I'll never get anything out of him as long as I live.' So he turned instead to Varesco, who had written *Idomeneo*, and even though they had quarrelled over that text, Mozart asked him to provide something comic. A revealing statement comes in another letter to his father: 'The music after all is the most important thing about an opera; and so if it is to find favour he will have to alter things and recast them as much and as often as I wish.' So there, the primacy of the composer asserted once and for all, and also Mozart's telling confidence in his own abilities. He apparently completed some of the score by December 1783 but then broke off and nothing more got done.

Alan Tyson believed that the paper he was writing on for the Act I finale was not used before early 1784, so perhaps that was the last movement to be finished. The next we hear is that he was complaining to Varesco in February 1784 that he should not write too fast because the quality was suffering. Perhaps this was Mozart's way of delaying him, but nothing more is heard of the project.

The music that survives is quite substantial: three arias, two duets, a quartet and a long and dramatic finale; the ensembles are particularly enjoyable. (On the back of one piece of manuscript is a sketch for a 'Dona nobis pacem', related to the Mass in C minor.) Various modern versions have been made, some including music from the contemporary unfinished project *Lo sposo deluso*; the composer Stephen Oliver made a successful version for the Batignano Opera Festival in Italy. Erik Smith, who has also edited the numbers for performance, comments that it offered Mozart few opportunities, but says: 'what could he do? At least he learned to avoid hopeless libretti.'

🎧 (*with Lo sposo deluso*) Fischer-Dieskau, Wiens, Schreier / C. P. E. Bach Chamber Orchestra / Peter Schreier
Philips Complete Mozart Edition Vol. 39 422 539–2

Lo sposo deluso K430

The second abandoned project of the early 1780s had a more promising plot, adapted from Cimarosa's famous opera *Le donne rivali* of 1780. It's unclear where Mozart got his libretto, but it was probably not, as sometimes thought, from Lorenzo Da Ponte. He imagined a cast for the piece including Nancy Storace and other singers who would appear in *Figaro*, and Cavalieri (the first Constanze), and wrote accordingly. But there is nothing about this project in his letters, and whether the cast he imagined had any basis in reality remains a mystery. Only an overture, quartet, two arias and a trio were completed, doubtless because Mozart had no occasion for performance. Constanze Mozart sang the part of Eugenia in later performances of the trio, and isolated numbers have been revived. Erik Smith orchestrated the numbers effectively for the Philips Complete Mozart Edition, and in the 1950s it was made into a show combined with music from *L'oca del Cairo* and performed in an arrangement by John Coombs as *The Deluded Bridegroom*. Alan Tyson thought that two of the arias must come from Vienna in 1784, so that was probably the latest Mozart worked on the score.

🎧 (*with L'oca del Cairo*) Grant, Palmer, Rolfe Johnson, Tear, Cotrubas / London Symphony Orchestra / Colin Davis Philips Complete Mozart Edition Vol. 39 422 539–2

Der Schauspieldirektor K486**

This effervescent collection of incidental music was created for one half of an entertainment in Vienna at the Orangery of Schönbrunn on 7 February 1786, in honour of the Governor-Generals from the Netherlands and local aristocracy. The major work in the programme was an opera by Salieri, *Prima la musica poi le parole*, performed on a stage at one end of the hall; Mozart's more skittish collection of pieces were inserts in a play called *The Impresario* performed at the other; he received 50 gulden, Salieri 100. Still, the opportunity to poke fun at operatic convention clearly amused him, and the two prima donnas in the performance were Caterina Cavalieri and his former love Aloysia Lange as Mme Silberklang and Mme Herz. The rather tedious play concerns the rivalry of two sopranos and the machinations of a theatrical impresario: it would be impossible to revive this text, but Mozart puts the whole matter into his music far more concisely. The two women vie for supremacy in a pair of arias and a hilariously elaborate trio, where the sort of coloratura Mozart had frequently written in his serious operas is jokingly extended into the upper stratosphere. The libretto sets literal musical instructions: 'Adagio, Allegro, allegrissimo, pian'pianissimo . . .' Both singers have to reach top notes far beyond anything sensible: top D, E flat, and then F, where they sound like a pair of Queens of the Night. In the final moralistic Singspiel number, calm and harmony is restored, except that Silberklang forgets, and races off again in another absurd coloratura phrase. The overture is a splendid piece of work that has remained popular on its own; many attempts have been made to make the whole piece suitable for modern performance, but to little avail. Mozart needed to be his own dramatist, and was just about to become so.

🎧 *(with selection of concert arias)* Gruberova, Te Kanawa, Heilmann, Jungwirth / Vienna Philharmonic / John Pritchard
Decca 430 207–2
🎧 *(with Thamos, King of Egypt)* Nador, Laki, Hampson / Concertgebouw Orchestra / Nikolaus Harnoncourt
Teldec 4509 95979–2

Le nozze di Figaro K492****

We know far too little about the genesis of one of the world's most popular operas. Its revolutionary nature is now acknowledged, but it is far from being clear how it came into being as the harbinger of a new kind of opera, and also far from clear how much Mozart himself contributed to its creation. What we think we know of the story of *Figaro*'s origin is mainly the creation of Lorenzo Da Ponte, in his lively but self-serving memoirs written very much later. Da Ponte tends to simplify for dramatic effect, as no doubt any good librettist should. For example, he wrote that 'The emperor had shortly before forbidden the company of the German theatre to perform this comedy, which he said was written too liberally for a proper audience.' What Joseph had actually ordered was that 'the censor will either reject it altogether or have such changes made in it that will allow him to take responsibility for its performance and the impression it makes on the public' – not quite the same thing.

In effect, the changes required were those that Da Ponte's libretto made, for it reduced the inflammatory elements of Beaumarchais's play to the background, and the characters (determined as ever by the singers on hand) created the personal drama. Leopold provides a few clues when he writes to Wolfgang's sister Nannerl that 'in order to keep the morning free for composing he is now taking all his pupils in the afternoon. I know the piece; it is a very tiresome play and the translation from the French will have to be altered very freely if it is to be effective as an opera.' Probably the opera was meant to be staged during the carnival season at the start of 1786, but many problems intervened, with the usual cabals against it; extended rehearsals finally postponed it from 28 April to 1 May. The payment Mozart received did not solve his financial problems, and it was around this time that he conceived the idea of going to Italy, perhaps with his pupils Thomas Attwood and his colleagues Nancy and Stephen Storace, intending to leave his two children with his father – a most unwelcome prospect to Leopold.

The opera was well received in Vienna but there were significant forces there, at court and elsewhere, who did not want Mozart to succeed. It was in Prague, where it was performed at the end of 1786 and 1787, that *Figaro* became a real popular success. Perhaps there, audiences with fewer pretensions could see that this opera, almost for the first time, was actually about them.

The overture in D, starting very quietly ('already too loud!' said one famous conductor as he brought his baton down for the opening notes) plunges us into the middle of feverish action, though its music is not at all related to what follows. (Mozart planned a slow contrasting middle section in the minor, but in the end went with one continuous bustle of fast music.) As the curtain rises, valet and maid, Figaro and Susanna, are measuring out their new quarters which they will use once they are married. Their room is placed between those of the Count and the Countess, and in a second duet (B flat following G major) Figaro and Susanna imagine the demands of the pair: that of the Count on Susanna being especially problematic. Figaro's famous 'Se vuol ballare', taking the accents of the courtly minuet and making it his own, is a menacing threat to his lord and master. Enter, with a great deal of pomp, Doctor Bartolo and Marcellina. In a magnificently overblown D major aria (surely a parody of some of Mozart's earlier *opera seria* efforts), Bartolo seeks vengeance for Marcellina by forcing Figaro to marry her. In an A major duet, Susanna and Marcellina exchange elaborate but insulting greetings (did Mozart ever write a wittier duet, surely based on close observation of real life?).

Then Cherubino the page enters, bursting with youthful ardour. His first impulsive E flat aria, 'Non so più', panting with sighs and broken at the end with fitful pauses, fits so seamlessly into the action that it rarely gains applause – the end is marked 'attacca subito Recitativo'– but it is one aria for which Mozart wrote out his own version with keyboard accompaniment. The Count now imposes himself on the proceedings, and Cherubino hides – unfortunately in a place too similar to that where the Count previously discovered him in Barbarina's lodgings. When Basilio approaches the Count too hides, but then emerges to tell the story of Cherubino's discovery. In doing so he again reveals Cherubino, much to Basilio's glee. The skill with which this

dramatic action is folded into a B flat trio is quite beyond anything in Mozart's *buffa* operas so far, especially as the recapitulation of the trio then provides a perfect dramatic irony
for Basilio's sarcasm. The chorus come at Figaro's invitation
to greet the Count; they praise him for being about to give up
the *droit de seigneur* that threatens Susanna. The Count, like
any true manager, postpones the decision, gets out of the
awkward situation, and sends the chorus away. He proposes
to send Cherubino to join a regiment, and in the first-act
finale Figaro conjures up the life that the young boy will miss
and the one that he will join: 'Non più andrai' is famous for
its cheery contredanse melody, but its distant harbingers of
war in the wind and brass chords are truly disturbing, and the
curtain is brought down with a suddenly flaring fanfare.

At the start of Act II we are introduced to the missing person in this drama, the young Countess, who in a brief aria
yearns for the love of yesteryear; 'Porgi amor' is a beautiful
but totally economical aria in E flat, as befits her station and
her vulnerability. Figaro arrives to outline the plan: to test the
Count, Susanna will arrange to meet him in the garden, and
the Countess will pretend to have an assignation as well. The
trick depends on Cherubino's involvement, and his degree of
attractiveness to the Countess (depending on the production,
this can vary all the way from casual interest to sexual passion)
is a key element in what follows. First Cherubino sings his
perfect set-piece aria 'Voi che sapete', which he has brought
with him: has a more poised and beautiful aria ever been written, as ordered and contained as his first aria was impulsive
and disorganised? Next, Cherubino has to be dressed up as a
girl, and this Susanna proceeds to do in a G major aria which
is pure action: 'Venite inginocchiatevi'. (Interestingly, when
the more static Adriana Ferrarese del Bene took over this part
in the 1789 Vienna revival, she insisted on a new aria which
didn't involve so much acting. Mozart said, 'it would be a success if she is capable of singing it in an artless manner, which
I very much doubt.') Just when Cherubino is not at his most
presentable, the Count demands entry. The Countess locks

Cherubino in the closet, but the Count is suspicious. The Countess declares Susanna is in there, and the Count tells her to come out. This trio in C major introduces a symphonic dimension to the score, with the call and answer of the opening bars echoing many early orchestral movements. As the tension builds, Count and Countess exchange threats in A flat while Susanna comments, hidden on the sidelines. The music rises to a top C: Susanna or the Countess seem to have taken this top line in different versions. The Count takes the Countess away with him and locks the door. Susanna emerges and lets Cherubino out of the closet; he jumps to safety through the window in another deft and breathless duet, which on some occasions was replaced by a recitative, probably because it was so difficult to keep together. (The different pairing of female voices in duet, first Susanna and Marcellina, then Susanna and Cherubino, then Susanna and the Countess, is a striking feature of the score.) Susanna dashes into the closet and locks it.

As the Count and Countess return to the room to unlock the closet, all seems unchanged. So the Countess, not realising what has happened in her absence, decides to confess to the Count that it actually is Cherubino in there, and the Count erupts. The second-act finale which then unfolds is generally credited to be one of the greatest dramatic scenes in all opera, all the more powerful for its understatement, superb pacing, and inexorable musical logic. First in E flat, the Count and Countess trade warnings and recrimination; then as the closet door opens and Susanna steps innocently out, an elegant little B flat Minuet ensues (usually taken far too slowly), leading to total amazement for all, with hazy triplets over a tonic pedal. Now as the music becomes more hectic in B flat, it is the Count's turn to apologise, even using the Countess's name, Rosina, which we never hear elsewhere. A glorious moment of reconciliation is achieved, only to be disrupted by the arrival of Figaro with another G major dance; the Count delays matters by testing him with the anonymous letter, but over one of the most expressive of tonic pedals the protagonists beg forgiveness, while the Count waits impatiently for Marcellina to arrive. Once again things are disrupted, now by the arrival of the gardener Antonio (once again, Mozart's development of the triplet motifs in this section is symphonic in scope). He complains that his plants have been damaged by someone jumping from a window. Figaro claims to have injured his leg in the fall, and the music shifts to a tense staccato 6/8 as the ramifications of this are played out, with the Count testing Figaro yet again: what were the documents he dropped? The ladies identify it as Cherubino's commission and tell him just in time. Another pause; another disruption: Bartolo, Basilio and Marcellina arrive to trap Figaro, and the music returns to E flat for a tumultuous final section which superbly pits the just-arrived trio plus the Count against Figaro, the Countess and Susanna, with the latter in the lead – Susanna and the Countess rise in upward scales of thirds. In the final bars a Prestissimo (the fastest of all Mozart tempi, used very rarely) erupts in fury as the sparks fly between the two groups.

The third act begins with the Count puzzling over the ease with which he seems to have attracted Susanna. Their formal A minor duet perfectly matches words to music, Susanna's 'yes' changing to 'no' at the crucial moment. Susanna boasts of her success a little too loudly to Figaro, and the Count is left to bemoan his fate in a recitative and aria in D major that uses noble-style scales and suspensions to conjure up his strong but damaged spirit. Marcellina's bid for Figaro is somewhat disrupted by the discovery that she is his long-lost mother. This discovery gives rise to much sentimental rejoicing in the sextet 'Riconosci in questo amplesso', which Mozart declared one of his favourite pieces. Its combination of detailed thematic planning, straightforward humour, and expressive lyricism make it one of the cleverest and most attractive ensembles in any of his operas. The only person who is not impressed is Susanna, who sees Figaro embracing Marcellina, and slaps him; but all is quickly explained, and they unite in their resolve to trick the Count.

The Countess, alone again, hopes that constancy may bring the Count back to her; 'Dove sono' is a full-scale though again quite reserved aria in C, with prominent oboe but (compared, say, with *Idomeneo*) no elaboration at all. The expression is concentrated into a relatively narrow line, only expanding in the coda from C major arpeggios up to a heartbreaking A, A flat, G and thence to the close. (When the opera was revived in Vienna in 1789 and Caterina Cavalieri sang the Countess, Mozart provided a more elaborate but emotionally emptier version of this aria.) Susanna arrives, practical as ever. They write the letter to the Count in another 'action' piece, a delicious duet in B flat. In come the villagers with flowers: Cherubino is still among them, but is discovered by Antonio. The wedding march approaches from afar in triumphant C major, and a duet announces a wedding dance: an A minor fandango of great elegance, over which Count reads his letter and pricks his finger on a pin.

The fourth act, set in the garden, finds Barbarina searching for her pin, in a little F minor siciliano. Marcellina complains about the treatment of women, in an aria which is too often cut (the postlude alone would make it worthwhile); and Basilio sings how useful it is to be an ass (in an aria which is more dispensable). Figaro becomes exercised about his fate in his pungent E flat aria with horns, 'Aprite un po' quegl'occhi'. He hides, and Susanna enters, singing of the joys of love in an aria in F which brings the wind instruments into prominence but, once again, not over-elaborately, just in perfect balance (the echo here is of the central movement of the Piano Concerto K459). Everyone has taken their positions and the fun can begin: the finale of the opera starts in the home key of D major. Cherubino runs in looking for Susanna, but there is total confusion in the garden as the Count gets kissed, Figaro gets slapped and then has to watch as the Count sings to the Countess, thinking it is Susanna. A placid moonlit interval in the serenade key of E flat lasts but a moment before chaos returns, and Figaro, recognising Susanna, teases her by pretending to address the Countess –

a scene of comic musical exaggeration rather than parody. The Count summons everyone: he will reveal this gross betrayal by his wife and servant. The music turns from G major, as the Countess appears, into a mysterious, confused G minor. The Count realises the game is up, and begs for pardon in an open, almost sacral G major. The Countess offers her pardon, the chorus add their assent. There is an agonising moment as the music almost stops with uncertainty as to what will happen next – can we believe the reconciliation? – but the chorus know what they have to do: joyous celebration erupts, the pain that has been revealed is swept under the carpet, and life is back to normal.

Mozart must surely have learnt from *Figaro* that less is more. He curbed his ability to do anything, so much in evidence in *Idomeneo* and *Entführung*, and concentrated on those gestures that were actually meaningful to singers and audience, with triumphant success.

Since its Prague premiere, *Figaro* has been so popular that its productions chart the history of the operatic stage. The opera has taken on the nature of every generation that has staged it: the neo-classical sternness of early German designs and then the grandeur of the later century, turned into increasingly rococo innocence in the twentieth century. Everything from Wagnerian abstractness to contemporary high-life has been foisted on the opera, right up to Peter Sellars's staging in the Trump Tower, New York. The best *Figaro* story has to be Jonathan Miller's: he says he was told about a production in Germany where the characters all wore jeans turned the wrong way out, because the producer's concept was that the opera is about 'how do you say it in English, the seamy side of life'.

🎧 Gens, Ciofi, Kirschlager, Regazzo, Keenlyside, McLaughlin / Concerto Köln / René Jacobs
Harmonia Mundi 901818.20 (3 CDs)
🎧 Salomaa, Bonney, Hagegard, Auger, Nafee, Jones, Feller, Gimenez / Drottingholm Court Theatre / Arnold Ostman
Decca Oiseau-Lyre 421 333–2 (3 CDs)

🎧 Te Kanawa, Popp, Von Stade, Ramey, Allen, Moll, Tear /
London Philharmonic Orchestra / Georg Solti
Decca 410 150–2 (3 CDs)
🎧 Schwarzkopf, Moffo, Taddei, Cossotto, Waechter /
Philharmonia / Carlo Maria Giulini
EMI CDM 7 63409 2 (highlights)
🎧 Jurinac, Sciutti, Stevens, Sinclair, Cuenod, Bruscantini,
Calabrese, Wallace / Glyndebourne Festival Chorus and
Orchestra / Vittorio Gui
EMI CZS 5 73845–2 (2 CDs)

Don Giovanni K527****

Correctly called *Il dissoluto punito, ossia Il Don Giovanni*
(though it is fruitless to argue against the habits of opera
houses around the world), this second collaboration with Da
Ponte was first mounted in Prague, where *Figaro* had been
such a success. It was commissioned to celebrate the marriage
of Archduchess Maria Theresa, the Emperor's niece, to
Prince Clemens of Saxony, who later became Emperor Franz
II. Even given the last-minute nature of these arrangements,
it seems extraordinary that the Mozarts arrived in Prague
only a fortnight before the planned premiere, on 4 October
1787, with much music still to write. Because Mozart knew
most of the principal singers from Vienna, he was able to start
the score before leaving, but was still far from completing it.
The premiere was eventually postponed and replaced with a
revival of *Figaro*; *Don Giovanni* was eventually heard on 29
October (the overture having been hastily written, according
to differing reports, on the night before or the penultimate
day before the performance). It was a huge success – 'nothing
to equal it has ever been heard in Prague' – and this led to a
production in Vienna on 7 May 1788 for which Mozart wrote
new music for different singers, including a new Elvira scene
for the demanding Caterina Cavalieri.

Da Ponte claimed that he suggested the subject to Mozart,

but who can tell? Bondini, who ran the company in Prague, is also said to have put forward the idea: it was a popular subject, and a little piece by Gazzaniga to a libretto by Bertati, which was put on in Venice in January 1787, is very close to Da Ponte's treatment. Many books and learned articles have been written on the background to the Don Juan story and its influence on this opera, but (as with his awareness of Beaumarchais's revolutionary background) one must question how aware Mozart was of the wider philosophical issues raised by the Don Juan legend, and how simply taken he was by the opportunity for an elemental opera with a rattling good story, which he could fill with music of astonishing power. The revolution here is not political but one of operatic form: the development of the characters towards the fully fledged *dramma giocoso* style that encompassed all human ranks has now been fulfilled – they are definitively mixed here, in the story of the libertine whose conquests know no social barriers.

The opening of the overture, with its pounding D minor summons and winding chromatic lines, echoes what we cannot know but surely sense will be the climax of the opera. That gives way to an energetic D major which captures the restlessness of Don Giovanni's life, but which comes to rest quietly in C, leading to the F major of the opening scene. (The overture was later provided with a concert ending.) No opera plunges us so suddenly into the middle of events: Leporello is complaining while waiting for his master to emerge from an assignation at the Commendatore's house, 'Notte a giorno faticar'; he is disturbed by Giovanni and Anna, bursting from the house together as she accuses him. Her father the Commendatore appears to defend her honour; he challenges Giovanni, there is a breathless pause, and in a duel of shooting scales in the orchestra, Giovanni wounds the Commendatore. Over tense C minor triplets in a marvellous *sotto voce* trio, the Commendatore expires and Giovanni and Leporello escape. Anna returns with Ottavio to find her father dead. After an impassioned recitative, she makes Ottavio swear vengeance in a D minor duet, 'Fuggi, crudele, fuggi', and the tumultuous opening scene (a mini-opera in itself) is over. In the street Leporello and Giovanni now encounter another abandoned lover, Elvira; she tries to sing a lovelorn aria, 'Ah chi mi dice mai', but is interrupted by the pair. Giovanni finally recognises her as a woman he has deserted, and disappears. Leporello explains the situation to her in the famous 'catalogue aria', 'Madamina', in which the opening of the recent C major string quintet reappears in D; the second half of the aria has Leporello parodying the courtly minuet to show Giovanni's amorous treachery.

Giovanni has turned his attention to the peasant wedding of Zerlina and Masetto (which the chorus are celebrating in a conventional skipping gigue-like G major), and in particular to the bride. Masetto is disposed of, and huffs off sarcastically, 'Ho capito!' Don Giovanni seduces the only temporarily reluctant Zerlina in a supremely subtle duet of quasi-pastoral innocence in A major, 'La ci darem la mano', in which her uncertainty and his clarity of purpose are both wonderfully combined. However, as they leave they are confronted by Elvira, who denounces him in a D major mock-baroque aria, 'Ah fuggi il traditor'. When Anna and Ottavio arrive she warns them against Giovanni in another great ensemble, the quartet 'Non ti fidar, o misera', but Giovanni puts her complaints down to madness. Anna has, however, recognised Giovanni as her attacker, and the orchestra screams out in pain as she recalls to Ottavio in some self-justificatory detail the horrors of the night, ending with a turbulent aria, 'Or sai chi l'onore'. At this point, for the Vienna performance, Mozart put in a simple eloquent aria for Ottavio, 'Dalla sua pace', which is usually sung today.

Don Giovanni looks forward to his licentious party in a manic G major aria, 'Fin ch'han dal vino' – which is the nearest in the opera he is allowed to come to revealing his true character. Zerlina and Masetto are reconciled in her sensual F major aria 'Batti, batti' (which echoes some of Mozart's jokes in his letters to his absent wife), with running cello lines in the second section. But as the finale begins in C major, trouble looms as Giovanni returns. He goes into the party with Zerlina and Masetto, but Anna, Elvira and Ottavio arrive as a masked trio in a sinister D minor section. As a minuet begins distantly to sound, Giovanni and Leporello invite the trio in and they take a solemn vow of vengeance dominated by Anna's rising scales. Inside, the dances begin in earnest in E flat, Giovanni proclaims the victory of 'La libertà' in martial C major, and then one of Mozart's most original ideas ensues. Three orchestras onstage play different dances combined in one texture: a triple-time minuet, a contredanse and a German dance for the peasants – a brilliantly symbolic musical concept to represent both the mixing of the classes and the sowing of confusion. Giovanni pulls Zerlina away behind the scenes, but she cries out and the righteous trio moves to rescue her. Giovanni comes back in with Leporello, whom he blames in decisive F major for the whole incident. The trio unmask themselves and denounce Giovanni as the villain. In increasingly frenetic exchanges, confusion reigns in C major as the curtain falls. Somehow, Giovanni escapes.

The second act starts with Leporello complaining again, 'Eh via buffone'. Giovanni persuades Leporello to pretend to be him and to seduce Elvira, who has appeared on her balcony in another aria, this time in balmy A major, in which they join: 'Ah taci, ingiusto core'. Giovanni, in Leporello's costume, is more interested in her maid, and serenades her in a formal canzonetta with mandolin accompaniment (Mozart wrote a couple of other examples of this type of song), 'Deh vieni alla finestra'. But he is interrupted again, this time by Masetto searching for Giovanni. Masetto is pointed this way and that in Giovanni's 'Meta di voi qua vadano', but then Giovanni beats him up and leaves him to be nursed by Zerlina in another sensual aria, 'Vedrai carino', in C major (with beautiful inner part-writing). Now Elvira comes back with Leporello, still disguised as Giovanni, and is confronted by Anna, Ottavio and Zerlina and Masetto, in a sextet (which may originally have been planned as an act finale). Charles

Rosen has written magnificently about this ensemble, one of Mozart's greatest, which begins in E flat but 'then with a soft drum-roll the music luminously moves to the remote key of D' as Ottavio sings. Indeed the whole build-up of this ensemble of perplexity is perfect: as Leporello reveals himself everyone is amazed and the music judders uncertainly; they all lament the 'mille turbidi pensieri', the thousand thoughts that crowd into their minds. As Abert says, 'the music with which they express their sorrow in the second half of this sextet touches on the profoundest human sentiments, and rises above even the highest theatrical level to the most radiant summit of art.' In the following *buffo* G major aria Leporello finally manages to escape; Ottavio is left to praise Anna, 'Il mio tesoro', in a virtuosic aria. A duet for Leporello and Zerlina, usually omitted, was inserted here for Vienna, and then Elvira's big set-piece 'Mi tradi', inserted for Cavalieri to sing in Vienna; it is a fixture for most Elviras of our day (for both her other arias have been interrupted) but in fact its grandeur is slightly out of her vocal character.

Giovanni and Leporello meet in a cemetery dominated by the statue of the Commendatore. Challenged by Giovanni, it speaks and in the tones of an oracle invites Giovanni to supper. In an ensemble which heightens the tension, sliding down through modulatory keys which seem to reflect fear in the pit of his stomach, Giovanni accepts. Now Anna has a big scene, and Ottavio's offer to marry her at once enables her to show proper reverence for her father, in an aria ('Non mi dir, bel idol mio') which Berlioz and others felt went just too far in the search for coloratura, though in the light of our knowledge of Mozart's early operas we can see it is here comparatively restrained and dramatically effective. After that F major scene we are back to the cheerful serenade key of D major for the finale where, as if to parallel the multiple dances of the Act I finale, stage wind band plays extracts from popular operas of the moment, including *Figaro*. Elvira bursts in, Giovanni finally rejects her but as she leaves we hear her scream, like Zerlina in Act I but for a different reason – the

Commendatore has arrived. We recognise his terrifying music from the overture. This is now superbly developed over a confrontation scene which has no equal in opera, at once exciting, powerful, and elementally chilling. The Commendatore confronts Giovanni, grasps his hand and drags him down to hell. The music, which has been battering our senses in D minor, suddenly veers into D major – as Abert, following Heuss, described it: 'an incomparable effect, not in the sense of a happy resolution, but as an expression of cold pitiless majesty'. The last scene greatly offended Romantic sensibilities with its bathetic return to normality, and was usually omitted (it may even have been omitted in some performances in Mozart's lifetime, possibly even in Vienna in 1788, but the evidence is doubtful). But the scene is surely vital, for it shows everyone coming to terms with Giovanni's disappearance, Ottavio and Anna pledging their love, and then everyone pointing to the moral in a Presto D major ensemble of quicksilver confidence: 'Questo il fin'; 'that's how wrongdoers end'. At the end the music whisks itself away in two unaccompanied violin lines, which the wind colour chromatically to draw the curtain down over the unimaginable scene. Which is the greater reality: the once-in-a-lifetime epic trauma we have witnessed, or the domestic world that endures from day to day?

The power that *Don Giovanni* unleashes is almost too great; if it is an uneven work then it is imperfect only in the way that *King Lear* is imperfect, from an excess of feeling. As Abert summarised it, in spite of the finale, 'the point of the opera is not to proclaim a universal moral, but to depict the decisive battle between two tremendous forces. We sense the ultimate connection between even the most restless, passion-ridden human existence and the whole universe.' Like *Figaro*, *Giovanni* has held the stage from its premiere through to the present; it has fitted the nineteenth century's wish for a Romantic, powerful Mozart and the twentieth century's for a politicised, critical Mozart. Rudolph Angermüller chronicles just a few recent production ideas for the climax of the opera:

in the 1978 Darmstadt production, there were projected pictures of all the women who drove Giovanni to distraction; in Heidelberg in 1978 and Stuttgart in 1984 the hero died of heart failure; in Bonn in 1983 Masetto entered, disguised as the Commendatore; the 1969 Amsterdam production saw the Don as the henchman of American imperialism; while Kassel in 1981 set the piece inside a huge stylised human brain. But in some productions the hero has survived: in Ludwisgburg in 1977, for example, 'he handed out the music for the final sextet'. To which we might add the Harlem-based, drug-pushing, McDonald's-gorging Giovanni of the Peter Sellars staging of the Da Ponte trilogy. Truly Don Giovanni is a man for all interpretative seasons.

🎧 Brownlee, Souez, Helletsgruber, Baccaloni, Franklin, Mildmay, Henderson / Glyndebourne Festival Orchestra / Fritz Busch
EMI CHS 7 61030 2 (3 CDs)
🎧 Schmidt, Miles, Halgrimson, Dawson, Ainsley, Yurisich, Argenta, Finley / London Classical Players / Roger Norrington
EMI 7 54859 2 (3 CDs)
🎧 Keenlyside, Salminen, Remigio, Heilmann, Terfel, Isokowski, D'Arcangelo, Pace / Chamber Orchestra of Europe / Claudio Abbado
DG457 601–2 (3 CDs)
🎧 Waechter, Sutherland, Schwarzkopf, Sciutti, Alva, Taddei / Philharmonia / Carlo Maria Giulini
EMI CDS 5 56232–2 (3 CDs)

Così fan tutte K588****

Mozart was gratified by the success of *Don Giovanni* in Prague, and on his return to Vienna he gained an appointment as the Emperor's court composer in 1787 following the death of Gluck. But this did not earn him enough to live on, and though it gave him a certain status, it did not really enable him to do what he wanted to do: go on writing opera. *Figaro* was successfully revived in the summer of 1789 at the Vienna Burgtheater, and perhaps this brought him into favour again with the Emperor. But it is not quite clear how and when the commission for *Così fan tutte* came about, and Da Ponte gives little illumination in his memoirs. The score was written under difficult conditions in late 1789 (the Mozarts' fifth child, Anna Maria, was born and died in one day on 17 November), and the premiere took place on 26 January 1790, with the composer directing. But we know little about the process of composition; Alan Tyson did some detective work on the score, showing that the ensembles were written before the arias, and demonstrating the pressure that Mozart was under to shorten and simplify his score after the premiere. But this is above all an ensemble opera, in which the arias seem to be secondary to the interaction of the group of six singers whose fluctuating relationships make the story so vivid. The story is a relatively simple one, and Da Ponte seems to have borrowed one or two details from the Spanish playwright Tirso de Molina, especially from *El amor medico*, which Molière turned into *L'amour medecin*. But one senses Mozart's hand in the parody of Mesmer's magnetism, since he had been a friend from Salzburg days. Clearly there was also more than a little resonance for Mozart in the story of two sisters who were tricked into exchanging lovers: earlier in the 1780s he had fallen in love with Aloysia Weber, and eventually he married her younger sister Constanze, so he certainly knew one version of one side of the story.

The opera begins with a cloudless overture, its call-and-response opening (more directly than usual a male–female duality?) leading through the five chords that Alfonso will sing to the words 'Così fan tutte' to a bubbling prelude of hectic activity. In a Naples café two officers, Ferrando and Guglielmo, are boasting to the cynical Don Alfonso about the fidelity of their fiancées, Dorabella and Fiordiligi (trio, 'La mia Dorabella'). Alfonso bets them a hundred zecchini that their lovers will be no more faithful than any other women.

The officers accept the bet and agree to follow Alfonso's orders for the day. Another trio ('Una bella serenata') opens with a wonderfully turned phrase for Ferrando (Mozart's rhapsodic shaping of melody achieves its height in this opera). The two sisters, Fiordiligi and Dorabella, are in their garden contemplating pictures of their beloved in a gracious but perhaps bored A major. Alfonso comes in with the news that the two men must go to war that very day. They enter and the over-emotional quartet 'Sento oh Dio' combines their feelings with a touch of parody. The distant march of the chorus is heard, and a quintet ('Di scrivermi ogni giorno', in F major) increases the tension as the girls ask them to write every day: in sobbing single notes over a magical orchestral accompaniment the four lovers part, but Alfonso can scarcely conceal his guffaws at the bottom of the texture. As so often in this opera, we are not sure how much of this is to be taken seriously (Stravinsky copied this quintet closely in *The Rake's Progress*), but as the men leave, Alfonso joins the two girls in a trio of utter seriousness and unearthly beauty, the E major 'Soave sia il vento' with undulating thirds in the muted strings and a chromatic chord at the climax that twists the heart.

Meanwhile the girls' maid, Despina, is complaining about her lot, but Dorabella sweeps her aside with her exaggerated E flat aria of despair, 'Smanie implacabili', with its swirling quaver triplets, like a seasick heart. Despina tries to persuade the girls that love is casual in 'In uomini, in soldati', but fails to convince them. Alfonso introduces two Albanian visitors (Ferrando and Guglielmo in disguise), with yet another rich ensemble in C major, 'Alla bella Despinetta' (which could be an act-finale). The girls are furious at being doorstepped in this way. There is a dramatic recitative (including a moment of C minor passion where some productions make the girls start to look at the other's partner) and Fiordiligi erupts in her famous aria 'Come scoglio' (whose nature as a static display-piece aria has been attributed by Daniel Heartz to the inability of the original singer, Adriana Ferrarese, to act). This magnificent set-piece aria in B flat teeters on the edge of caricature, but Mozart just holds back from making her ridiculous. Guglielmo offers a rather weak aria, 'Non siate ritrosi', which Mozart later replaced with 'Rivolgete a lui'. The men think they have won the battle, and laugh with Alfonso in 'E voi ridete', but he will not admit defeat. Ferrando's much more attractive 'Un aura amorosa', a sustained melody in serenade style, seems complacent in this context. Alfonso and Despina plot their next move. In the first act-finale – one of the most outstandingly complex yet effective sequences Mozart ever wrote – the deadly game reaches its climax. Starting and finishing in the key of D, but moving through sections in G, B flat, E flat, G and B flat again and thence back to D, Mozart takes us on a journey from the bliss of the opening; through the appearance of the Albanians, who have taken poison; through the farce of Despina's appearance disguised as a doctor with her magnet which cures all illnesses; to the final resurrection of the lovers, who beg for a kiss and are rebuffed. All this is achieved musically with the subtle use of tiny fragments and motifs that advance the musical argument, building to a huge climax in the final section: if staged not too coyly, this can be one of the funniest of all operatic scenes.

Act II begins with the sisters sitting around, and Despina trying to persuade them to give the Albanians a chance. She sings in G major, in 6/8, 'Una donna a quindici anni': any woman of fifteen should 'give ear to a hundred men at once, give hope to all, know how to conceal the truth'. Her amoral stance begins to have an effect and the sisters decide which one to take: 'Prenderò quel brunettino', in B flat, in music which sets apart Dorabella's flighty character from Fiordiligi's more serene lines. In a garden by the seashore the Albanians bring on the full apparatus of a serenade with chorus in E flat to influence the situation. Alfonso and Despina urge the men to get on with it in a crisp D major quartet, but they are tongue-tied and reduced to discussing the weather and the plants. Dorabella weakens first, and in the duet 'Il core vi dono' – deliberately simple in texture and substance, compared with the later Ferrando/Fiordiligi scene – she exchanges lockets with Guglielmo. Ferrando remains true to his convictions in 'Ah lo veggio' (though this long aria is often omitted). Fiordiligi admits her feelings in another set-piece aria, 'Per pietà', in E major with two horns – this time it is poignant and entirely serious, and the music points forward to Beethoven's Leonora. Ferrando feels vindicated by her, but then Guglielmo gloats about his success with Dorabella and reflects on all women: 'Donne mie, la fate a tanti'. Ferrando gives vent to his anger in the C minor 'Tradito, schernito', but Alfonso uses the opportunity to press the message home and forces him to make a final attempt on Fiordiligi.

Dorabella adds to the pressure on Fiordiligi with her aria 'È Amore un ladroncello', but Fiordiligi decides to dress up in uniform and take herself off to the battlefield. Despina realises she has lost her mind. Fiordiligi has dressed in Ferrando's uniform, not Guglielmo's, because it fits her better (a symbolic point lost in most productions). As she – as it were – turns into Ferrando, he appears. In Mozart's greatest love scene, and the emotional climax of the opera, he turns her noble A major declamation (with throbbing undercurrents in the orchestra) towards C major – 'instantly raising the emotional pitch by his harmonic boldness', as Andrew Steptoe has noted, for C major in this opera reminds us of the men's initial realism and cynicism. But for the moment of seduction Ferrando falls back into the genuine emotion of A major with his phrase 'Volgi a me', marked 'tenerissamente'. (Steptoe aptly points to the comparison with Pamina's 'moment of truth', 'Tamino mein', though how different the the orchestration makes the two moments sound.) 'Turn your eyes to me with compassion, only in me will you find husband, lover and more.' He has conquered her, and it is left to the solo oboe to join their phrases achingly together as they then embrace and the duet ends with rejoicing. 'Only Mozart's music could make this psychological somersault credible, could transform the cynical game into real human feelings,' comments Alfred Beaujean. Now it is Guglielmo's turn to rage. But Alfonso must carry through the whole plan, and orders them to marry: in 'Tutti accusan le donne' he cites the motto of the opera: 'Così fan tutte'.

The finale starts as an effervescent wedding feast, but Mozart suddenly deepens the emotion with a slow, poised canon for the four lovers, each lost in their own world, three sublimely happy but Guglielmo still complaining bitterly. (This wholly exceptional but musically complex scene, which Mozart sketched out in advance, was later replaced, as Tyson has shown, with a far easier but inferior setting that survives in Mozart's hand.) Despina is now the notary, and just as they put quill to parchment the chorus announces the return of the soldiers. The Albanians rush out, and come back in their original garb to discover the wedding contract. Horror ensues, but then the deceit is revealed and forgiveness is handed out all round with remarkable rapidity considering the seriousness of the moment. (There is one oddity: in each recalling the music they just sang in disguise, Ferrando sings a little of an aria that must have disappeared from the score.) But do they end up with their original lovers? 'Join hands, you are betrothed,' says Don Alfonso, but to whom? We would naturally expect that Fiordiligi the high soprano and Ferrando the tenor would form a pair, particularly as their uniforms are the same size; while Dorabella the more mezzo of the two sopranos and Guglielmo the baritone are a natural match. That's one of the many conundrums that productions of this most sublime of love comedies have to address. The music presses on in celebratory C major, as if to cover up the turbulence and emotional depths that have been exposed.

The disapproval of *Così fan tutte* may conceivably have started at home. The early biography of Mozart by Franz Niemetschek set the tone by saying, 'everywhere, people wonder how that great mind could lower itself to waste its heavenly melodies on so feeble a concoction of a text. But it was not in his power to refuse the commissions and the libretto was expressly served on him.' Niemetschek often reflects Constanze's view of Mozart's life, and it was probably she

who expressed the general unease on the subject; she told the
Novellos she held a low opinion of the libretto. This view
took off in the nineteenth century and the opera was vilified
and rarely performed – when it was, the text was bowdlerised
– or the music was put to other uses: it became one of
Mozart's mass settings, for instance! But in the twentieth century it became recognised as one of Mozart's deepest and
most truthful creations, of a musical subtlety unequalled elsewhere, and it has received countless productions.

∩ Schwarzkopf, Ludwig, Steffek, Kraus, Taddei, Berry /
Philharmonia / Karl Böhm
EMI 5 67382–2 (3 CDs)
∩ Mattila, von Otter, Szmytka, Araiza, Allen, van Dam /
Academy of St Martin-in-the-Fields / Neville Marriner
Philips 422 381–2 (3 CDs)
∩ Roocroft, Mannion, Gilfry, Trost, James, Felle /
Monteverdi Choir / English Baroque Soloists /
John Eliot Gardiner
DG 437 829–2 (3 CDs)

La clemenza di Tito K621**

This was Mozart's last opera to be commissioned, in 1791,
but not the last to be finished or performed. It was written for
the celebrations in Prague of the coronation of Leopold II as
Emperor of Bohemia. Mozart had had little success when, the
previous year, he had travelled to Leopold's coronation in
Frankfurt and given concerts there. But this was different: in
Prague, where he was feted, he was asked by the impresario
Domenico Guardasconi to write an opera for the official celebrations. However, in strong contrast to his experience in
Vienna with Da Ponte, Mozart was given the commission
only when the subject and the libretto of the opera were set:
it was to be, in deference to the Emperor, Metastasio's *La
clemenza di Tito*, a tried and tested *opera seria* text. The commission was issued on 8 July and Mozart, in the middle of

writing *Zauberflöte*, had to turn his hand immediately to the very different text of *Tito*. The libretto had been set many times by composers such as Hasse, Jommelli and Traetta, but Mozart had firm ideas on the pacing and content and gave strict instruction to Caterino Mazzola, poet to the court of Saxony, on the changes he wanted. These Mazzola followed, and Mozart was able to describe the result in his thematic catalogue as 'an *opera seria*, turned into a true opera by Sigr. Mazzola'. This both acknowledges Mazzola's work and suggests that by this time in his life Mozart did not regard *opera seria* as the real thing, even though it was still alive and well in the world outside.

The contract with Guardasconi has survived and is a fascinating document which reveals the priorities of those who commissioned the opera: singers first, appropriate libretto second, spectacle third, and composer a poor fourth. Nevertheless, Mozart used the occasion to transform the conventions of *opera seria* into something that could have ensured its survival: there is a leaner, tauter structure with no over-extended ritornelli and da capo arias, and a reduction in the number of arias in favour of duets and ensembles. At this late point in his life, it is a profoundly forward-looking piece. Rumour had it that Mozart was ill while composing the piece, and this seems to have affected its reception. But it was also not quite the upbeat celebratory piece that everyone wanted. It may be apocryphal that Maria Luisa called it 'German piggery', but her actual opinion in her diary is not so different: 'In the evening to the theatre. The grand opera is not so grand, and the music very bad, so that almost all of us went to sleep. The coronation went marvellously.' Observing that it was not popular with the court, the populace of Prague, who had been so supportive towards Mozart in the past, stayed away too. And Guardasconi had to petition for money to make up his box-office losses.

La clemenza di Tito is launched with a fine, martial but expressive overture in C. Vitellia, daughter of the dethroned Emperor Vitellius, wants to marry the new Emperor Titus, but he intends to marry Berenice. Vitellia inveigles Sextus, who is in love with her, to conspire against Titus, 'Come ti piacce imponi'. But Vitellia becomes more hopeful when it emerges that Berenice has been sent back home: she pledges herself to Sextus in the G major aria 'Deh se piacermi vuoi'. Sextus and Annius (who wishes to marry Servilia) pledge their friendship in a lilting C major duet. The Roman people assemble to praise Titus. He distributes some help to the victims of the eruption of Vesuvius. He decides to marry Servilia instead of Berenice and sings of his own wisdom. Annius refuses to object and in a duet with Servilia renews their pledge of love. This gentle, perfectly blended duet in A major was regarded as a paragon of pure beauty by the early nineteenth century, and Grillparzer wrote a poem about it. Titus is about to denounce the conspirators against him when Servilia pleads that she loves Annius. Titus praises her honesty, but Vitellia is furious and incites Sextus to set the Capitol on fire and kill Titus at once. He reluctantly goes to do just that, with a magnificent concertante aria, 'Parto parto', with a solo clarinet part that Anton Stadler would have played. Now it is Vitellia who is chosen as empress, and she vainly tries to call Sextus back in the Terzetto with Annius and Publius, 'Vengo, aspettate'. Sextus is now trying to prevent the plot unfolding, and in a dramatic accompanied recitative, 'Oh Dei che smania è questa', he reveals his dilemma. But the Capitol is now seen on fire, and the rumour spreads that Titus is already dead. In the magnificent first-act finale sequence Vitellia tells Sextus to be quiet about the plot and the Roman people mourn their Emperor.

In Act II Sextus learns from Annius that Titus is unharmed. Annius encourages him to remain faithful to the Emperor in the aria 'Torno di Tito a lato', but he is arrested. Vitellia, Sextus and Publius express their feeling in a trio, 'Se al volto mai ti senti'. The chorus arrives to give thanks for Titus's survival in a gentle pastoral number. Publius admits that an honest man finds it harder to recognise disloyalty, but Sextus has confessed his guilt. Titus is riven by doubt as to whether he should be punished, and longs for the life of a simple farmer, in the recitative 'Che orror! Che traditmento!' Then in another brilliantly compressed Terzetto, Sextus, Titus and Publius confront each other. In a large-scale Rondo in A major echoing his first act duet, Sextus insists on death. Titus tears up his death warrant, and would rather give up the throne: 'Se all'impero, amici Dei'. Vitellia becomes more and more exercised, realising that Sextus did not betray her, and in a long recitative and set-piece aria 'Non più di fiori' (with an obbligato for basset horn that would also have been played by Stadler) she bids farewell to her ambitions for the throne. (It has long been a puzzle that this aria appears to date from before Mozart started to write the opera, and even predates the commissioning. Could it have been a separate concert aria, written perhaps with Stadler in mind, that then became useful?) The aria turns at its close into a march, and the chorus comes in to one of Mozart's very grandest entrances. As Titus is about to pardon Sextus, Vitellia confesses her guilt and begs his pardon. Once again Titus's clemency overcomes all his emotions, and in a final sextet with chorus he is praised by all as the Saviour of Rome.

The reputation of *La clemenza di Tito* is fascinating: in the decade after Mozart's death, it became the symbol of his noblest work and was frequently performed. Especially when we see the massive neo-classical sets in which the opera was performed, it's easy to understand that this was the work that most effortlessly made the transition to the massive classicism of the nineteenth century. It also became the central feature of Constanze Mozart's efforts to advance her husband's reputation; she arranged concert performances of the score. Niemetschek, who generally reflects her views, made the interesting comment that '*La clemenza di Tito* is considered, from the aesthetic point of view and as a beautiful work of art, Mozart's most perfect work.' Perhaps that implies that it is not his most perfect work from the purely theatrical point of view, which is certainly true. But its time did not last, and soon it was overtaken by bigger and bolder pieces of nineteenth-century opera. The critical tradition that led *Clemenza* to be ignored by most Mozart scholars is thoroughly explored by John Rice in his *Cambridge Opera Guide*, where he also chronicles its reawakening in contemporary productions. In the UK this was particularly associated with the Covent Garden production by Anthony Besch first seen in 1974; on the continent it was Jean-Pierre Ponnelle's series of productions from 1969 through to Zurich in 1986 which re-established the work in the canon. Recent successful productions have included David McVicar's for English National Opera in 2005.

⌒ Rolfe Johnson, von Otter, McNair, Varady, Robbin, Hauptmann / Monteverdi Choir / English Baroque Soloists / John Eliot Gardiner
DG Archiv 431 806–2 (2 CDs)
⌒ Baker, Minton, Borrows, von Stade, Popp, Lloyd / Royal Opera House Orchestra and Chorus / Colin Davis
Philips Complete Mozart Edition Vol. 44 422 544–2 (2 CDs)

Die Zauberflöte K620****

Mozart's two final operas were written in overlapping periods during his final year, 1791. *Die Zauberflöte* was begun first, but finished last, so to be consistent with the way Mozart's other output has been catalogued it should count as his last opera. Mozart had had his biggest success in opera with the German Singspiel *Die Entführung*, and he felt it was a form in which he wanted to write again. The composition of Italian operas during the second half of the 1780s was largely a reflection of the fact that the repertory of the Burgtheater had shifted back to Italian works. The succession of Leopold II, after the death of Joseph II in 1790, did not help Mozart; even though he claimed to like Italian opera, as did his wife, it was unlikely because of court intrigues that Mozart would receive a commission for Vienna (though he did receive one for *Clemenza* in Prague, after Salieri turned it down).

Mozart was still on the lookout for the opportunity to write a German piece with dialogue, and the chance presented itself through his contact with the remarkable polymath – impresario, singer, author, producer, arranger – Emanuel Schikaneder, whom he had met in Salzburg back in 1780, when Schikaneder's theatre company appeared there. He was by now running the Freyhaustheater, the Theater auf der Wieden, which opened in a Vienna suburb in 1789, and in early 1791 Mozart wrote a concert aria for the bass of the company and the virtuoso double-bass player of the orchestra (K612), as well as a set of keyboard variations K613. Schikaneder's theatre was part of a rambling complex in Vienna which included 225 apartments, courtyards, inns, gardens, and workshops as well as the theatre. In one of the gardens was the wooden pavilion which (much rebuilt) has now been transferred to the garden of the Mozarteum in Salzburg, and that is where myth has it that Mozart composed *Die Zauberflöte*.

Work on *Die Zauberflöte* began in the spring of 1791, though some planning may have preceded this. There is little evidence of the collaboration between Mozart and Schikaneder, and some doubt has been cast on the latter's solo authorship of the libretto, though he said that he thought it out in great detail with Mozart. It draws on a wide variety of literary sources, and the confusions and intricacies of the plot have absorbed much effort to disentangle them over the last two centuries. It is also based very clearly on some of the rituals of Freemasonry, albeit altered and disguised; they are greatly modified – in particular, by including women as part of the initiation ceremonies. The cast included Mozart's sister-in-law Josepha Hofer as the Queen of the Night, Benedict Schack as Tamino (who also played the flute) and Schikaneder himself as Papageno, singing the sort of good-natured ballads for which he was well known. The orchestra of the Freyhaustheater was comparatively large, about thirty-five players, and the scoring of *Zauberflöte* – one of its many surprises – is large-scale, with horns, trumpets and trombones, and timpani, but used with astonishing restraint and variety. Almost every number has a different scoring, and the orchestration has a transparency which is unequalled elsewhere in his music (though there are similar touches in the contemporary completion of the B flat Piano Concerto K595). Charles Rosen has written that *Zauberflöte* 'is Mozart's late style developed as far as he carried it: the purity and the bareness are almost exotic, so extreme have they become, and this almost wilful leanness is only emphasised by the exquisite orchestration'. And Joseph Kerman in *Opera as Drama* concurs: 'since the underlying conception is so pure, the almost crazy variety of musical styles which Mozart dared bring together can harmonise as beautifully as the solemn animals of the Peaceable Kingdom . . . There is a new serenity, a new sense of control over basic processes, a distillation of technique to the purest essentials of the art.'

The overture in the Masonic key of E flat starts with three calls-to-attention, which quickly give way to a brilliant fugal section, energetically propelling itself forward with the accent on the last beat of the bar. Three more groups of chords lead to the same fugal material, but this time chromatically developed in sonata form and exhilaratingly brought to a conclusion. This overture was entered (with the march that opens Act II) in Mozart's thematic catalogue for 28 September 1791, a long time after the main entry for the opera in July; only two more entries were to follow before Mozart's death, but there was certainly no falling-off in his powers at this point. The stage directions in the libretto of the opera give an unusually clear idea of the pictures intended. The curtain rises with Tamino – 'in a rocky landscape, overgrown with trees; there are hills on both sides and a rocky temple' – pursued by a serpent, in C minor. 'Zu Hilfe!' he cries, and three ladies come to his rescue, killing the serpent and taking more than a maternal interest in him. Papageno appears, singing his bird-catcher's G major song with panpipes, 'Der Vogelfänger bin ich ja', and claims to have disposed of the serpent himself. The three ladies return and padlock his mouth in punishment for this lie. They give Tamino a picture of Pamina, and he is overcome by her beauty: 'Dies Bildnis ist bezaubernd schön', in E flat with clarinets, bassoons and horns.

'The mountains part, and the theatre is transformed into a resplendent chamber.' The Queen of the Night appears: from a B flat introduction and a G minor slow section the aria bursts into B flat major, 'Du, Du, Du wirst sie zu befreien gehen', and we hear her coloratura in full flight, up to top D and then touching top F. She promises her daughter Pamina to Tamino if he can rescue her from Sarastro. Papageno returns, still padlocked, but he can hum and he launches a witty B flat Quintet in which the ladies first unlock his mouth and then give Tamino a magic flute and Papageno a set of magic bells for their journey. In an ethereally transparent Andante, set for clarinets and high bassoons over pizzicato violins, with no bass line, the ladies say that three young boys will accompany them on the journey. They bid farewell.

The scene shifts again to 'a magnificent Egyptian chamber' where the Moor Monostatos has prevented Pamina from escaping. He threatens her, but Papageno appears, and he and Monostatos frighten each other so much that after an irresistible, tiny comic ensemble both run off. Pamina and Papageno celebrate the joy of love in a perfect duet in E flat (which was, according to later myth, the subject of much trouble between Mozart and Schikaneder, the composer having to revise it endlessly before it met his Papageno's demands). Whoever took the credit was astute, for apart from a moment of elaboration for Pamina at the close, this is a completely simple construction. 'The theatre is transformed into a grove . . . at the back of the stage is a beautiful temple, from this temple colonnades lead to two other temples . . .' The extended C major finale begins with the appearance of the three boys, who lead Tamino towards the temples of Wisdom, Reason and Nature. He is driven back from two of the temples, but from the third the Speaker emerges and Tamino insists on seeing Sarastro. From the singing of the offstage chorus Tamino learns that Pamina is alive, and he plays his flute in C major in an aria that brings the birds and beasts onstage: 'Wie stark ist nicht dein Zauberton'. He hears Papageno's panpipes, and rushes off to find Pamina. Pamina and Papageno enter, but Monostatos stops them; Papageno remembers his bells and plays them. They magically turn Monostatos and his slaves into innocent dancers and they skip away. (This is the moment in the opera during which Mozart recounted causing confusion by playing the bells himself from the wings.) Pamina and Papageno again point the moral of true harmony, but no sooner has the music finished in G than C major fanfares and a march announce Sarastro's arrival. 'What shall we say?' asks Papageno. 'The truth,' declares Pamina in a ringing, C major cadence of complete confidence. She begs Sarastro for forgiveness, but Monostatos drags in Tamino in an agitated, busy F major. Pamina and Tamino recognise each other, Sarastro sends Monostatos to be whipped and separates the happy couple, so that they can undergo the trials. The chorus praise Sarastro – divinely wise, 'alike he rewards and punishes' – and in an oppressive C major the act ends.

Act II opens with a solemn march, *sotto voce* in F, which Mozart must have finished last, along with the overture, and entered into his catalogue on 28 September. (Alan Tyson points out that three further numbers from the second act are on the same late music paper, though possibly they were merely revised rather than composed late.) 'The theatre is a palm grove; all the trees are of silver, the leaves of gold.' Sarastro asks the priests to agree that Tamino should undergo the trials, and says he abducted Pamina only to save her for Tamino. They agree, and the Masonic chords from the middle of the overture are sounded again. Sarastro sings 'O Isis und Osiris', whose utterly distinctive sonority comes from the absence of violins and the use of violas with three trombones, two basset horns and bassoons. The Priests join in the solemn chorus. Two priests take Tamino and Papageno to embark on the trials and urge silence, 'Bewahret euch', but immediately three ladies arrive and a quintet in sparkling G major tests their resolve. The end of the quintet is masterly: the priests are suddenly heard behind stage, complaining that the threshold has been breached. The music slides into the minor, the ladies disappear, and Papageno collapses to a moan, along with the music.

'The theatre changes to a pleasant garden, with a horse-shoe pattern of trees.' Monostatos is still persecuting Pamina in an aria with yet another new sonority, using piccolo to double the flute. The Queen of the Night appears and in a tempestuous D minor aria, 'Der Hölle Rache', demands that Pamina take revenge on Sarastro by killing him. Monostatos threatens to denounce Pamina, but Sarastro enters and dismisses him. He promises not to take revenge on the Queen: 'In diesen heil'gen Hallen' – in these holy bounds, revenge is unknown. This E major aria uses pairs of flutes, oboes and horns, again with great simplicity. 'The scene is transformed into a hall . . . adorned with rose bushes and flowers, where later a door opens.' Papageno and Tamino are left alone; Papageno is visited by an old crone who comes with some water and says she has an admirer called Papageno. Worried, he decides to keep quiet.

The three boys return; this time in a trio in A major built on little wisps of ascending figures in the violins, answered by descending trills. Again one marvels at Mozart's piercingly direct musical language from which all decoration has been expunged. They encourage Tamino to remain silent, but Pamina is heartbroken by his lack of response. In her G minor aria, 'Ach ich fühl's', she laments her fate. This, the apotheosis of a long line of passionate Mozart G minor arias, achieves intensity through simplicity, with its lilting triple-time rhythm constant throughout, as the singer weaves chromaticism into her line, eventually echoed in the short orchestral postlude by the solo flute, oboe and bassoon.

Papageno prattles on. 'The scene changes to the vault of the pyramids.' The priests enter in a dignified D major chorus, singing that Tamino will soon be accepted into the brotherhood: 'soon he will be worthy to be one of us.' Pamina and Tamino are led in, and in a trio with Sarastro they contemplate their fate. This B flat Terzetto has a strong echo of Mozart's clarinet writing, with a phrase straight from the Clarinet Quintet, though the scoring uses the pairs of oboes and bassoons alongside the strings. Papageno is told that he will never be an initiate, which is fine by him, and he welcomes instead a good glass of wine which magically appears. 'Ein Mädchen oder Weibchen', he sings in F: he would be able to enjoy life if only he had a wife, and accompanies himself on his bells, becoming more virtuosic in each of the three verses. The old woman comes back, offers herself to Papageno, and he reluctantly accepts, whereupon she is transformed into a young girl and whisked away.

'The scene changes to a shallow garden.' In the home key of E flat, clarinets, horns and bassoons in Mozart's serenading manner bring back the three boys. They are just in time to prevent Pamina's suicide attempt, where the music shifts into a dark C minor as she persists in her despair in expressive chromatic lines. A plunging seventh and a rising line – the end seems near, but the boys interrupt her, bringing the music back to E flat. They reassure her that all will be well and that love will triumph. The music slips back into C minor as 'the scene changes to a prospect of two large mountains, in one of which a waterfall can be seen; the other is a volcano.' Two priests in armour lead Tamino in and sing a chorale, the Lutheran melody 'Ach Gott vom Himmel sieh darein', but set to Masonic sentiments: 'he who travels this path with burdens is purified by fire, water, air and earth.' Mozart here writes a complete chorale prelude over a walking bass, with chromatic counter-subjects, worked out with supreme skill, showing all his fascination with the music of the baroque. (Busoni so admired this passage that he made a remarkable piano transcription of it.)

Pamina calls from afar, and the priests say she can now accompany Tamino: from a cheerful A flat trio for the men, the music suddenly fades to F major, and Pamina enters.

There is a complete pause. The pair exchange phrases of utter beauty and radiant clarity: 'Tamino mein! O welch ein Glück'; 'Pamina mein! O welch ein Glück'. Everything stops again, except for a single horn note. As if not daring to go on, strings enter tentatively and Tamino and Pamina gather their strength for the trial ahead; Pamina says they will succeed because of the power of the magic flute that her father hewed from thousand-year-old oak. They will walk 'by the power of its music through death's dark night'. Pamina and Tamino pass into the trials. The libretto says, 'the crackling of the fire and the howling of the wind are heard, and sometimes also the sound of distant thunder and the rush of water. Tamino plays on his flute, accompanied by muffled drums.' This is a unique sonority: the single flute is balanced against isolated chords from horns, trumpets, trombones and timpani. They emerge from the first trial, and then enter the second. No sooner is the second trial over, than the chorus (now once more including female voices) sing of their triumph in blazing C major.

The scene reverts to the garden, where Papageno has had enough and resolves to commit suicide. In mock-earnest G minor he prepares to count down to death, but the three boys again burst in and remind him of his bells. He plays them and the young girl appears again, this time as his Papagena. They join in an exuberant, funny G major duet and look forward to many tiny Papagenos and Papagenas. The Queen of the Night is approaching with her ladies and Monostatos, but her C minor attempt to storm Sarastro's castle hardly gets off the ground before thunder and lightning sweep them all aside. 'The theatre is transformed into a great sun,' which emerges in glorious splendour in chains of suspensions, revealing Sarastro elevated, with Tamino and Pamina in priestly robes and the chorus. He praises the power of the sun's rays which 'drive away the night, and destroy the evil power of hypocrites'. The music lifts from B flat into a triumphant Masonic E flat: finally, and with the greatest splendour, all the instruments play together. The final chorus is a sparkling celebration of the conquest of virtue; it is a dancing sublimation of the popular style which Mozart has, throughout this opera, turned into the highest expression of human feeling.

Die Zauberflöte was a final, much needed success for Mozart. He clearly tapped into a vein of popular sentiment and humour that ensured that the audience was well pleased, and he carried out this task with unbelievable sophistication. There were twenty-four performances in October which were all sold out, and popular numbers were quickly published for piano, including the Pamina/Papageno duet and Sarastro's arias. Salieri and his mistress Caterina Cavalieri attended a performance at Mozart's invitation, and as Mozart reported: 'from the overture to the final chorus there was not a number that did not elicit a *bravo* or a *bello* from him.' Schikaneder said that by November 1792 there had been a hundred performances, and by October 1795 two hundred. Although the lack of enthusiasm on the part of the director of the Berlin National Theatre meant that the work was not seen there until 1794, it became extremely popular in Germany within a couple of years of Mozart's death. The huge and impressive designs for Berlin in 1816 by Karl Friedrich Schinkel symbolise the extravagance of the early nineteenth century's response to this opera. Great artists have been repeatedly drawn to the opera: Oscar Kokoschka, who designed it for Salzburg, Chagall for New York, and David Hockney for Glyndebourne. Ingmar Bergman made an unforgettable film set in a replica of the Drottningholm Court Theatre. Mozart's legacy has never been so universal as in this opera, expanding from the extremely specific circumstances of its performance in a suburban Vienna theatre during his last weeks to become a work which has sustained endlessly different interpretations and meanings across two centuries of our culture.

🎧 Oelze, Schade, Sieden, Finley, Peters, Backs / Monteverdi Choir / English Baroque Soloists / John Eliot Gardiner
DG Archiv 449 166–2 (2 CDs)

🎧 Ziesak, Jo, Heilmann, Kraus, Moll, Schmidt /
Vienna Philharmonic Orchestra / Georg Solti
Decca 433 210–2 (2 CDs)
🎧 Gedda, Janowitz, Berry, Popp, Frick, Crass, Schwarzkopf,
Ludwig, Hoffgen, Putz, Unger, Giebel, Reynolds, Veasey /
Philharmonia / Otto Klemperer
EMI CMS 567388–2 (2 CDs)

Arias and ensembles

Mozart wrote arias for concert performance, or for insertion
in other composers' operas, from a very early age; though
many of them are rarely performed, some of them are among
his finest and most original works. We know that the improvisation of such arias is something that he was trained in from
his earliest days. When the Mozarts were in London, one of
the musical skills he demonstrated for Daines Barrington was
the writing of an aria:

> Finding that he was in humour, and as it were inspired, I
> desired him to compose a Song of Rage, such as might be
> proper for the opera stage. The boy again looked back
> with much archness, and began five or six lines of a recita-
> tive proposed to precede a Song of Anger . . . in the mid-
> dle of it, he had worked himself up to such a pitch, that he
> beat his harpsichord like a person possessed, rising some-
> times in his chair. The word he settled upon for this sec-
> ond extemporary composition was 'perfido'.

This is supported by Leopold Mozart's account that he often
allowed people to offer Wolfgang at random any text of an
aria by Metastasio, and he would compose a setting 'with the
most amazing rapidity'.

In all these concert arias Mozart took considerable pride in
fashioning them for their intended singers with great care.
This is a summary of the important independent arias and
ensembles (arias that Mozart added to his own operas are

mentioned in the entry for that opera, and are generally omitted here). Except where mentioned, they are written for soprano.

'Va, dal furor portata' K21 (tenor)
'Conservati fedele' K23
'Per pieta, bell'idol mio' K78
'O temerario Arbace' K79
'Or che il dover' K36 (tenor)
'A Berenice . . . sol nascente' K70
'Cara se le mie pene' (not in K)

The earliest of Mozart's concert arias are set to texts by Metastasio: K21 was written in London in 1765 to a text of fury at treachery discovered; and K23 and K78–9 in The Hague on tour, setting arias from *Artaserse*. K79 contains an elaborate accompanied recitative and an increasingly virtuosic triple-time aria. Here the subject of a conflict between father and son, which was to be so important to Mozart in *Idomeneo*, first surfaces. K36 and 70, written after the return to Salzburg, were both extensive accompanied recitatives and arias known as a 'Licenza': a homage, performed at the end of an opera to convey greetings, in these cases for the anniversary of the consecration of the prince archbishop. The first was written for December 1766 and the second in 1769, with supine texts filled with praise. 'Cara se le mie pene', recently rediscovered, is an attractive C major da capo aria, perhaps the one mentioned by Leopold as having been written in Olmutz in 1767: 'If you wish to make me forget all my troubles, never separate me from your loving heart.'

'Fra cento affanni' K88
'Misero me . . . Misero pargoletto' K77
'Se ardire e speranza' K82
'Se tutti i mali miei' K83
?'Non curo l'affetto' K74b

'Si mostra la sorte' K209 (tenor)
'Con ossequio, con rispetto' K210 (tenor)
'Voi avete un cor fedele' K217*
'Ombra felice . . . Io ti lascio' K255 (alto)*
'Clarice cara mi sposa' K256 (tenor)

K88, yet another setting from Metastasio's *Artaserse*, was written in Milan in 1770; it has shooting scales and repeated top Cs: 'In hundreds upon hundreds of agonies I shake, tremble and feel my blood run cold.' Then there are five arias based on the same dramatist's *Demofoonte*, a text which had been set by Caldara, Gluck, Hasse and Jommelli. 'Misero me' K77 includes another impressive accompanied recitative before its fiery aria; it was performed in Milan, and its success probably contributed to the commissioning of *Mitridate*: 'Unhappy Thrace, here is your Oedipus, in me you will see the furies of Argos and Thebes renewed.'

K82, K83 and K74b also use this libretto, and Mozart found in it a fertile source of passion: K82 is an aria of despair, written for the castrato Giovanni Manzuoli, who had given Mozart lessons in London. K83 is similarly gloomy: 'in this bitter situation, even if you were a stone, you would shed tears.' K74b was written a little later for the theatre in Pavia, in the wake of the success of *Mitridate*, but no autograph survives. The remaining arias in this group were written after the Mozarts had returned to Salzburg, in connection with the visit of an Italian opera troupe to the city, where they performed an opera by Baldassare Galuppi in May 1775. The outstanding one is 'Voi avete un cor fedele', dated 26 October 1775, from a text by Goldoni for *Le nozze di Dorinda*. It marks a distinct advance in Mozart's *opera buffa* style. Gracefully slow and fiercely fast sections alternate, with a final outburst: 'You have a faithful heart like a passionate lover, but my bridegroom to be, what will you do? . . . for the moment I do not trust you.' Mozart's music sounds faintly ironic towards her loved one.

'Ombra felice' is the only example of a concert aria for alto, dated September 1776, for the castrato Francesco Fortini, with a recitative and an Aria en Rondeau: 'I leave you, and know not if this farewell will be the last . . . just gods, whoever endured more cruel torment.' Quite why Fortini came to Salzburg with the *opera buffa* troupe is not clear, but this is a serious piece. Unusually, after all the pyrotechnics, it ends quietly. K256 was probably an insertion into an opera by Piccinni for the tenor Antonio Palmini, and is a showy *buffa* aria – with interruptions from another character – in triplets (rather as Bartolo's in *Figaro* was to be). Marked with precision, 'In tempo comodo d'un gran ciarlone', it could be the ancestor of a Gilbertian patter song. The text is pretty well nonsense, but there is a nice section of musical parody: 'Se in questa musica / Non sian unisoni / Tritoni e dissoni / Vuo' fulminar' (if in this music there are no unisons, tritones and dissonances, then I will rage').

🎧 *K217 etc.*
Felicity Lott / London Mozart Players / Jane Glover
ASV CDDCA683

'Ah lo previdi . . . Ah t'invola' K272**
'Alcandro lo confesso . . . Non so d'onde viene' K294**
'Se al labbro mio non credi' K295 (tenor)
'Basta vincesti . . . Ah non lasciarmi, no' K295a*
'Popoli di Tessaglia . . . Io non chiedo, eterni Dei' K316**
'Ma che vi fece o stelle . . . Sperai vicino il lido' K368
'Misera dove son . . . Ah non son io che parlo' K369*

'Ah lo previdi' is the first of Mozart's really great concert arias, written for Josepha Duschek in August 1777. The text is from *Andromeda*, which had been set by Paisiello; the text is by Vittorio Cigna-Santi. This multi-section piece, full of powerful passion, concerns the crossing to Lethe's other shore by Perseus. It starts with a recitative, and the singer enters on a fierce dissonance – 'Ah I foresaw it' – and also begins the first aria on a dissonance: 'Ah, fly from my sight'. This section is fully developed, leading to another recitative and adagio, and then to a cavatina marked Andantino, with muted violins and violas, pizzicato second violins and cellos, and a prominent solo oboe: 'Ah, do not cross those waters, soul of my soul.' The mutes are lifted just for the brief final section, which is wonderfully restrained: 'I wish to come with you.'

'Alcandro lo confesso . . . Non so d'onde viene' is the first of a sequence of arias for a singer with whom Mozart was passionately in love, Aloysia Weber. It would have perfectly suited her silvery voice, rising to a top D and then touching E flat. This is a Metastasio text that J. C. Bach set, from *Olimpiade*: 'I know not whence comes this tender emotion, this feeling that rises in my breast, this chill that courses through my veins.' This is perhaps a first glimpse of Mozart's responsiveness to conflicting, uncertain emotions. This aria has a valuable set of autograph elaborations by Mozart to the vocal part, indicating what on other occasions he expected the singer to supply. 'Basta vincesti' K486a was for Dorothea Wendling, the first Ilia in *Idomeneo*, and is Dido's plea to Aeneas not to leave her, as written by Metastasio ('My life will end if I must say farewell'), an eloquent slow triple-time aria. Mozart reported that Wendling chose the text and that her and her daughter loved the setting.

'Popoli di Tessaglia . . . Io non chiedo' is again for Aloysia Weber, dated Munich 8 January 1779, boldly resetting a text which had already been successful, from Calzabigi's libretto for Gluck's *Alceste*. Mozart treated it with typical brilliance, rising right up to a G above top C. The first section of the aria is marked 'sotto voce, sostenuto e cantabile': 'Eternal gods, I do not ask for all my skies to be clear, but at least let some ray of pity console my grief.' Then follows a tumultuous Allegro assai: 'No one can understand my woes or the terror that fills my breast.' This aria has been criticised for its extravagance, and is certainly the music of someone for whom too much was not quite enough, but it reflects the passionate commitment Mozart then had for Aloysia.

The next aria of this group, 'Ma che vi fece' K368, is more restrained in compass, but no less vocally taxing; it might have been intended for Elisabeth Wendling, the first Electra in *Idomeneo* and the sister of Dorothea Wendling's husband. Finally, there is 'Misera, dove son!' from March 1781 in Munich, for a different singer, Countess Josepha von Paumgarten. She was an accomplished amateur, but Mozart's setting is admirably restrained in its vocal demands, despite the impassioned text: 'The cruel grief that rends my heart makes me rave'. The orchestration highlights the flutes in the texture, no doubt for Mannheim friends.

🎧 *K272 etc.* Kiri te Kanawa / Vienna Chamber Orchestra / Georg Fischer
Decca 455 241–2
🎧 *K272 etc.* Lena Lootens / La Petite Bande / Sigiswald Kuijken
Virgin Classics 561573

'A questo seno deh vieni . . . Or che il cielo' K374
'Nehmt meinen Dank' K383****
'Mia speranza adorata! Ah non sai qual pena sia' K416**
'Vorrei spiegarvi' K418****
'No, che non sei capace' K419***
'Per pieta, non ricercate' K420 (tenor)

These arias are dated between April 1781 and June 1783 and show Mozart working in Vienna at the very peak of his skills. 'A questo seno deh vieni', for the castrato Francesco Ceccarelli, is not especially interesting, doubtless because it was written for a visit of the Archbishop of Salzburg. By contrast, 'Nehmt meinen Dank', completed on 10 April 1782, is exquisite: a farewell piece for Aloysia probably written for her benefit concert in April 1782 ('Accept my thanks . . . never in my life shall I forget your gracious favour'). It is completely unlike other arias: a simple strophic setting, reminiscent of the finale of *Entführung* for its directness and simple emotion.

Mozart as ever works his special magic: here, the upward-drifting arpeggios from solo flute, oboe and bassoon that create a ravishing texture for the simple melody. Aloysia was back in Vienna for 'Mia speranza adorata', performed twice in 1783, one of the finest arias Mozart wrote. He generously takes her no further than high E flat in a text from Anfossi's *Zemira* (once again, he is tempting fate because this opera had already been performed in Vienna): 'Ah, you do not know what pain it is to have to leave you . . . for what cruel fate have you destined me, hostile gods.'

The next three arias were written by Mozart to be inserted in another Anfossi opera, *Il curioso indiscreto*. This opera had first been performed in Rome but Anfossi was not a member of the Vienna circle. The episode was full of intrigue which Mozart gleefully repeated: to allay the fears of those who thought he wanted to improve on Anfossi's opera (which must have exactly been his aim) he caused a disingenuous notice to be printed in the libretto, saying that he only wrote the arias 'because the originals did not suit Mme Lange's voice, so that the name of the most famous Neapolitan may not suffer in any way whatsoever'. Only the first two of the three arias were performed; Adamberger unwisely said he would not sing a substitute and thus was a failure. The second of Aloysia's arias brought the house down (according to Mozart it was 'a bravura . . . [and] had to be repeated'). But it is the first aria that is really outstanding and unique: an Adagio in A major for solo oboe and voice vying with each other in expressiveness, using Aloysia's unique range to rise gently to a top E and down again in vocally perilous circumstances. In the Allegro she has to jump more than two octaves from a bottom B to a top D. This is a superb picture of repressed emotion: 'I would like to tell you the reason for my anguish, but fate condemns me to weep in silence.' Surely here is all Mozart's grief at losing Aloysia herself. The companion bravura aria K419, in the mood of Constanze's 'Marter allen arten', is a flamboyant display piece. Adamberger was indeed foolish to refuse his insertion aria, an attractive number written in the style of Belmonte's part in *Entführung*.

🎧 *K383 etc.* Lucia Popp /
Salzburg Mozarteum Orchestra / Leopold Hager
Philips 464 880–2
🎧 *K383 etc.* Elisabeth Schwarzkopf /
London Symphony Orchestra / George Szell
EMI 574803–2

'Così dunque tradisci' K432 (bass)
'Misero! o sogno . . . Aura che intorno spiri' K431
  (tenor)
'Dite almeno in che mancai' K479 (soprano, tenor, two
  basses)**
'Mandina ambile' K480 (soprano, tenor and bass)
'Ch'io mi scordi di te' K505*** (soprano, piano)

The first two arias here, for bass and tenor, are of uncertain date, probably from Vienna in 1783. Mozart was now extremely busy with composing and teaching, and found little time for this kind of writing. But in November 1785 he was asked to provide two ensembles for Bianchi's opera *La villanella rapita*, which he did – a quartet and a trio, both very lively and benefiting from the experience of the ensembles he drafted for his own incomplete pieces *L'oca del Cairo* and *Lo sposo deluso*. The Terzetto is a relaxed triple-time movement in A major, which gains in intensity but ends quietly; the Quartet is a superb act-finale which points forward to the great ensembles of the Da Ponte operas with their conflicting views and ever-building excitement.

'Ch'io mi scordi di te' is one of Mozart's most famous and popular concert arias, for two reasons: the soprano part, written for Nancy Storace at her farewell concert in December 1786, makes no unreasonable demands in terms of range and agility, and the aria comes with a wonderful piano obbligato which Mozart wrote for himself and has recommended itself to generations of Mozart concerto pianists. The vocal range is indeed restrained, but the writing is very expressive and beautifully entwined with the piano. It is in the form of a Recitative with Rondo, and the text is adapted from one which was added to *Idomeneo* in 1786: 'Do not fear, my love, my heart shall be yours for ever, I can no longer bear such pain, my spirit fails me.'

🎧 *K505 etc.* Cecilia Bartoli, András Schiff /
Vienna Chamber Orchestra / Georg Fischer
Decca 430 513
🎧 *K505 etc.* Christine Schäfer, Maria João Pires /
Berlin Philharmonic Orchestra / Claudio Abbado
DG 457 582–2
🎧 *K505, K272, K528, opera arias* Soile Isokowski /
Tapiola Sinfonietta / Peter Schreier
Ondine 1043

'Alcandro lo confesso . . . Non so d'onde viene' K512
 (bass)
'Mentre ti lascio, oh figlia' K513 (bass)
'Bella mia fiamma, addio . . . Resta oh cara' K528***
'Ah se in ciel, benigne stele' K538**
'Ich mochte wohl der Kaiser sein' K539 (bass)
'Un bacio di mano' K541 (bass)

Two bass arias, 'Alcandro lo confesso' K512 (not to be confused with the earlier setting for soprano of the same text) and 'Mentre ti lascio' K513, one for Johann (Karl) Ludwig Fischer (the first Osmin) and one for Gottfried von Jacquin (a close friend), were both written in 1787. 'Bella mia fiamma' K528 is a superb scene written for Mozart's Prague friend Josepha Duschek. The style here is significantly more concentrated than in earlier arias – we are now in a post-*Figaro* musical world – but no less passionate. The text is a powerful suicide scene from an opera by Jommelli: 'It did not please heaven to make us happy . . . my death will absolve you from

the faith you pledged . . . My dearest, farewell for ever!' 'Ah
se in ciel' was specially revised for Aloysia, possibly as an
interval piece in the C. P. E. Bach oratorio that Mozart conducted in March 1788. It initially looks like a reversion to an
earlier style, but Tyson believes it was begun as early as 1778
and only completed in 1788. It is not stratospheric in range,
but demands great agility and poise. The jovial aria K539 is
an oddity, a strophic war aria for bass, set to doggerel verse:
'I'd like to be the Emperor.' It was written for a concert on 7
February 1788 for Friedrich Baumann.

Later that year, for another Anfossi opera, he wrote 'Un
bacio di mano', for bass, to be sung by his Vienna Don
Giovanni, Francesco Albertarelli; one of the aria's themes was
copied directly in the first movement of the 'Jupiter'
Symphony later that same year.

🎧 *K528 etc.* Barbara Frittoli /
Scottish Chamber Orchestra / Charles Mackerras
Erato 8573 86207–2

'Alma grande e nobil core' K578*
'Chi sa qual sia' K582*
'Vado ma dove? Oh Dei' K583**
'Per questa bella mano' K612 (bass with double bass)*

'Alma grande e nobil core' K578 was an insertion in a popular opera by Cimarosa, *I due baroni*, which was staged at the
Burgtheater in Vienna in September 1789. The singer was
Louise Villeneuve, the first Dorabella in *Così*, but this is a far
grander piece than anything he wrote for her in the opera.
She also sang in Martin y Soler's opera *Il burbero di buon core*
in November 1789, for which Mozart provided the bouncy
aria 'Chi sa qual sia', and the lyrical 'Vado ma dove?' The first
is an aria of puzzlement: 'what is it that torments my
beloved?' – in fact, it is the fact that he is hopelessly in debt, a
situation which might not have been unknown to Mozart at
this point. The second is an aria of departure: 'Love, guide

my steps, dispel my misgivings that cause me to doubt.'
Mozart's final concert aria is an unusual piece from 1791,
connected with Schikaneder's theatre, for which he was writing *Die Zauberflöte*: the piece was written for the theatre's
principal bass Franz Gerl (who was to sing Sarastro) and its
double-bass player Friedrich Pischelberger. Mozart manages
with amazing facility, in a skipping, gentle rhythm, to conjure
an unexpected lightness of texture from bass and double bass,
as the anonymous text tells that 'the breezes, the plants and
the winds tell you how constant is my fidelity.' (Finally, there
was one more contribution to another opera, Sarti's *Le gelosie
villane*, for which Mozart wrote a final chorus on 20 April
1791 and noted this in his thematic catalogue – but it has
disappeared.)

♫ *Concert arias complete* Te Kanawa, Gruberova, Berganza,
Laki, Hobarth, Winbergh / Vienna Chamber Orchestra /
Georg Fischer and London Symphony Orchestra / John
Pritchard
Decca 455 241–2
♫ *Fifty years of Mozart singing on record (operatic arias and
concert arias)*
EMI mono 7 63750–2 (4 CDs)

Songs

Mozart's songs were an entirely domestic side of his output, probably not intended at all for concert use. Some were deliberately intended for publication, but also for domestic use, a couple at a time, perhaps intended for a specific evening's private music-making. But they are all written with the same scrupulous care that he brought to all aspects of his work. Although he would have wished his operas and symphonies to have survived, he would probably have been astonished at the thought of these little miniatures still being performed and studied. Paul Nettl called them 'a by-product of his muse'.

'An die Freude' K53
'Wie unglücklich bin ich nit' K147
'An die Freundschaft' K148

These early songs are for voice and continuo, rather than fully written-out keyboard parts. The first has been linked to *Bastien und Bastienne*, from Vienna in 1768; the other two originated in Salzburg and the second, K148, is the earliest example in Mozart's work of a text inspired by Masonic ideals.

'Oiseaux si tous les ans' K307*
'Dans un bois solitaire' K308*

Two songs written in French for the daughter of Mozart's friends in Mannheim, the Wendlings, written for her to sing in late 1777 or early 1778. These have fully written-out piano parts of great charm.

'Die Zufriedenheit' K349

'Komm liebe Zither' K351
'Ich würd auf meinem Pfad' K390
'Sei du mein Trots' K391
'Verdankt sei es dem Glanz' K392
'Lied zur Gesellenreise' K468

K349 and K351 were written, anticipating Don Giovanni's serenade, to mandolin accompaniment. K390–2 are settings of Johann Timotheus Hermes, from his novel *Sophiens Reise*. It's difficult to say why Mozart set them, and each has a very specific marking: 'indifferent yet content', 'sadly yet calmly', 'moving with restraint'.

'Der Zauberer' K472*
'Die Zufriedenheit' K473
'Die betrogene Welt' K474
'Das Veilchen' K476**
'Lied der Freiheit' K506
'Die Alte' K517
'Die Verschweigung' K518
'Das Lied der Trennung' K519

K472–4 are three settings of the well-known poet C. F. Weisse, of which 'Der Zauberer' is the most dramatic and the others more conventionally pastoral. 'Das Veilchen' (The violet), Mozart's only setting of Goethe, is exceptionally free in its treatment and expressive in its result. The other pieces are more traditional in style.

☊ *K476 etc.* Dawn Upshaw, Richard Goode
Nonesuch 7559 79317–2

'Als Luise die Briefe' K520**
'Abendempfindung an Laura' K523**
'An Chloe' K524**
'Des kleinen Freidrich Geburtstag' K529
'Das Traumbild' K530

'Die kleine Spinnerin' K531

The first three are among Mozart's finest songs, all written in May or June 1787. The first was one of the pieces associated with the family circle of Gottfried von Jacquin and was indeed thought to have been composed by him, as was K530. The second two were published by Artaria in Vienna in 1789; 'Abendempfindung' weaves a long solo vocal line over undulating sixths in the piano part, perfectly suited to the sonority of the instrument, and sounds like a genuinely personal statement from the composer. The remaining two are relatively conventional strophic songs.

𝇇 *K523 etc.* Juliane Banse, András Schiff
ECM 461 899–2

'Sehnsucht nach dem Frühling' K596*
'Im Frühlingsanfang' K597
'Das Kinderspiel' K598

'Longing for spring' has become one of Mozart's best-known melodies because a version of it also appears as the last movement of the B flat Piano Concerto K595. All these three songs were written at the start of Mozart's last year, and were published as part of a collection of songs for children. The texts are by Overbeck and Sturm. Their carefree mood gives the lie to Mozart's being oppressed by thoughts of death at this time.

𝇇 *Songs* Anne Sophie von Otter, Melvyn Tan
DG 447 106–2
𝇇 *Complete Lieder* Elly Ameling, Dalton Baldwin
Philips Complete Mozart Edition Vol. 24 422 524–2

'Liebes Mandel, wo is's Bandel' K441
?Notturni K436–9, K346
Canzonetta K549

One of Mozart's best family friends was Gottfried von
Jacquin, whose sister was one of Mozart's piano pupils (for
whom he wrote the misnamed 'Kegelstatt' trio) and whose
brother Josef Franz is the subject of a touching entry in
Mozart's autograph album in broken English (see K228
below). The Bandel Trio, with its parts marked for
Constanze, Mozart and Jacquin, dramatises a little domestic
incident, the loss of a ribbon, and works it up into a little
drama. Alan Tyson suggests the date 1786/7 for this piece,
rather than the usual 1783, which would fit better with those
that follow.

The Notturni were also written for Jacquin, and maybe are
partly by him; they are simple settings for a trio of singers and
basset horns or clarinets, perhaps showing that the Stadler
brothers were also part of this domestic circle. They were
probably written in Vienna sometime in 1787, but the
Canzonetta is more exactly dated 16 July 1788, though the
accompaniment may have been conceived by the singer
Michael Kelly. Neal Zaslaw suggests that in these pieces
Mozart played the role of the editing, collaborating, encouraging hand to Jacquin and Kelly, much as his father had for
him.

♫ *Complete Notturni etc.*
Philips Complete Mozart Edition Vol. 24 422 524–2 (2 CDs)

Canons

Finally, a bit of fun! There are many of these informal works,
some written as counterpoint exercises, some written to sing
as part of social gatherings, others inscribed in the albums of
friends: these canons were to Mozart and his circle, as they
had been to J. S. Bach, a natural but ingenious way of communicating. But where Bach aspired to the spiritual in the

meanings of his canons, Mozart reflected the down-to-earth
bawdiness that is contained in some of his letters. Such pieces
appear to have been a traditional part of Salzburg life, where
Michael Haydn also wrote many such examples, and some
may be by Mozart's colleagues rather than by him. They also
remind us how the whole compositional technique of the day
was grounded in the study of traditional counterpoint and the
reinvention of the style of Palestrina preserved through the
agency of Fux; so it is no surprise that the earliest examples
come from the time of Mozart's study with Padre Martini in
Bologna. Much more fun, however, are the later examples
with amusing texts. You are not likely to hear many of them
these days, especially as many were published only with their
texts bowdlerised.

?'Leck mich im Arsch' K231 ('Lasst froh uns sein')
Canon in D K347
'V'amo di core' K348*

'Leck mich im Arsch' is an example of a canon preserved
under its real title, but with its text emasculated: publishers
replaced it with the innocent lines 'Lasst froh uns sein'. It is
sung thus even in the rigorous Philips Complete Mozart
Edition, but a fully underlayed version of the original text
turned up just in time for the Mozart celebrations of 1991.
Whether Mozart originated the music is less certain: K231 is
based on an old-style tag reminiscent of the 'Jupiter' finale
theme, and gains its energy from the much quicker counter-
subjects. (Its companions in the *Neue Mozart Ausgabe*, K233
and K234, are now attributed to a composer called Trnka.)
The D major Canon K347 has been given a drinking text,
'Wo, der perlende Wein'. 'V'amo di core' is an ingenious
twelve-voice quadruple canon for four choirs: it probably
originated with Mozart's study of Padre Martini's canons, but
Stadler may have realised or completed it.

Canon in F K507
Two canons K508 and K508a
Canon in F K228
'Lieber Freistadler, liebe Gaulimauli' K232

These canons were all written between 3 June and August 1786; some were given words. Some come from the teaching notebook of Thomas Attwood, Mozart's English pupil. The second of the four-voice canons was copied into the notebook of his friend Josef Franz von Jacquin on 24 April 1787 with the touching line in English: 'Don't never [*sic*] forget your true and faithfull [*sic*] friend Wolfgang Amadé Mozart.' Possibly he was learning some English from Attwood, and discussing with his friends a possible visit to London. The canon was later given a text. Then there is a joke canon designed to make fun of Franz Josef Freistadler, one of Mozart's students in Vienna, rather foursquare compared to the others.

Alleluia K553*
Ave Maria K554*
'Lacrimoso son'io' K555*
'Nascoso e mio sol' K557
'Gretchtelt's enk' K556
'Gehn wir im Prater' K558
'Difficile lectu mihi mars' K559
'O du eselhafter Peierl/Martin' K560
'Bona nox! Bist a rechta Ox' K561
'Caro bell'idol mio' K562

These ten canons, all with texts by Mozart, were precisely entered in his catalogue for 2 September 1788. K553 and K554 are on sacred texts, one of them with what sounds like a plainsong theme, the Alleluias using beautiful suspensions across the bar-line, and the 'Ave Maria' using subtly varied phrase-lengths to create a haze of imitative entries. The Italian canons are more elaborate and demonstrative: they must have been challenging (especially the chromatics of K557) but enjoyable to sing. K556 and K558 are both in Viennese dialect, arguing about whether to go to sample the new attractions of the Prater Park. The nonsense Latin of K559 and the joke at the expense of tenor Johann Peyerl (also reworked as an insult to someone called Martin instead of Peyerl) are good fun, particularly when the Latin is sung with the right accent to turn it into dubious German. The names can be changed at will: as one Mozart scholar put it, who knows when you may unexpectedly need to insult someone and require a ready-made canon for the purpose.

K561 wishes us good night in five languages, commending us (as Mozart did even to his mother) to stick our arse in our mouth as we sleep, creating what has been described as 'a scatological extravaganza'. K562 is altogether more serious, a lyrical canon in A major which looks forward to the heart-stopping canon in the finale of *Così fan tutte*. It is yet one more example of Mozart's genius that 'Caro bell'idol mio' can co-exist with the cheerful vulgarity of 'Bona nox!' and be, convincingly, part of the same composer's creative spirit.

🎧 *Wolfgang Amadeus Mozart: Soirée chez les Jacquin. Notturni, Canons K439, K580b, K346, K484b, K410, K411, K549, K428, K437, K441, K561, K498* Piau, Gabail, Caton, Thome, Moreno / Ensemble 415
Zig Zag Records 990701
🎧 *Canons* Chorus Viennensis etc.
Philips *Complete Mozart Edition* Vol. 23 422 523–2

Further reading

There are many hundreds of books on Mozart, and thousands of significant articles; I have chosen those which contain significant recent research, are as jargon-free as possible, and have provided information for this book. All the recommendations below are of books in English, but readers with German may wish to turn to the comprehensive introductions and critical commentaries to the volumes of the *Neue Mozart Ausgabe* (*NMA*); the authoritative edition of the Mozart family letters by Wilhelm Bauer, Otto Erich Deutsch, and Joseph Eibl (*Mozart: Briefe und Aufzeichnungen: Gesamtausgabe*, 7 vols., 1962–75); and Rudolph Angermüller's survey of Mozart's singers, *Vom Kaiser zum Sklaven, Personen in Mozarts Opern* (Salzburg, 1989). The New Köchel catalogue of Mozart's work, edited by Neal Zaslaw, is due for publication soon, while a new 'Little Edition' of Köchel is due from Cliff Eisen and Ulrich Konrad in 2006.

GUIDES

The Mozart Compendium, ed. H. C. Robbins Landon
(Thames and Hudson, 1990)
The best single-volume guide to the whole of Mozart's output and cultural background; no narrative biography, but a vast amount of information from different writers on many relevant topics.

The New Grove Mozart, Stanley Sadie and Cliff Eisen
(second edition, Macmillan, 2001)
The most up-to-date and detailed list of works, with a scholarly overview of both the biography and the music, well-judged and reliable analysis and description. The second edition should be used.

Mozart: A Documentary Biography, Otto Erich Deutsch, trans. Eric Blom, Peter Branscombe, Jeremy Noble (A. & C. Black, 1965)

The indispensable collection of all extant documents about Mozart known in the 1960s; an astonishing achievement which has helped to form all subsequent writing about the composer. In a vitriolic but amusing review, W. H. Auden described this collection of uninterpreted facts as 'an unbook unwritten by an anal madman'.

New Mozart Documents, Cliff Eisen (Macmillan, 1991)
Recent additions and discoveries since the 1960s to add to Deutsch's work, many minor but all fascinating.

The Compleat Mozart: A Guide to the Musical Works of Wolfgang Amadeus Mozart, ed. Neal Zaslaw with William Cowdery (Norton, 1990)
Reliable programme notes from very mixed sources on the whole of Mozart's output, but no biography or context; designed to support the Mozart Festival of 1991 at Lincoln Center, New York, when all his works were performed.

The Cambridge Companion to Mozart, ed. Simon Keefe (Cambridge, 2003)
The most recent important publication: a stimulating guide to the newest scholarship and context: includes fine essays by Cliff Eisen on Salzburg and Dorothea Link on Vienna, and significant discussions of the works, reception and performance. The bibliography provocatively lists all biographies under 'Reception'.

LETTERS
The Letters of Mozart and his Family, ed. Emily Anderson (third edition, Macmillan, 1985)
The pioneering English translation, still the most comprehensive available, and now well annotated, but increasingly criticised for its lack of accurate reflection of Mozart's unique writing style, missing musical and cultural detail, and for its tacit censorship of some scatological and sexy passages (though these went far beyond what had previously been available). The first edition of 1938 also included Constanze's later letters to the publisher André.

Mozart's Letters, Mozart's Life, Robert Spaethling
(Norton/Faber, 2000)
A more racy, idiomatic translation than Anderson, but
includes far fewer letters.

Mozart Speaks: Views of Music, Musicians and the World,
Robert Marshall (Schirmer, 1991)
A compilation of Mozart's opinions, especially about other
composers.

BIOGRAPHY

Mozart, Wolfgang Hildesheimer (Dent, 1983)
A stimulating reinterpretation of the composer's life, based
on a properly sceptical attitude, especially to Mozart's own
letters, which created a huge stir, especially in Germany.

Mozart in Vienna 1781–1791, Volkmar Braunbehrens
(Grove /André Deutsch, 1990)
A compelling picture of the composer's Viennese years,
based on extensive knowledge of the cultural life of the city.

Mozart: A Life, Maynard Solomon (HarperCollins, 1995)
A biography by the most stimulating thinker about Mozart
in recent years.

Mozart's Death: A Corrective Survey of the Legends, William
Stafford (Macmillan, 1991)
A rigorous look at the myths surrounding Mozart's death.

Mozart in Person: His Character and Health, Peter J. Davies
(Greenwood, 1989)
Gruesomely fascinating but only partly convincing detail on
Mozart's illnesses and personality.

The Mozart Family: Four Lives in a Social Context, Ruth
Halliwell (Oxford University Press, 1998)
Exhaustingly thorough and scrupulously fair consideration
of the Mozart family in the light of the most recent
research.

Mozart and his Circle: A Biographical Dictionary, Peter Clive
(Dent, 1993)

Reliable and fascinating entries on many of Mozart's contemporaries, singers, friends, and patrons, and some biographers; lacks the composers by whom Mozart was influenced.

SCHOLARLY STUDIES

Mozart: Studies of the Autograph Scores, Alan Tyson
(Harvard University Press, 1987)
A seminal collection of essays, bringing together a selection of Tyson's articles which changed our whole understanding of Mozart's composing process.

Mozart Studies, ed. Cliff Eisen (Oxford University Press, 1991)
Includes Maynard Solomon's important article on the Rochlitz Anecdotes and Christoph Wolff on the Requiem, as well as a crucial list of re-datings by Alan Tyson and other scholarly analyses.

Conceptions of Mozart in German Criticism and Biography 1791–1828, William Robinson (Yale University, thesis, 1974)
A fascinating thesis, unfortunately never published in book form, discussing many interesting views of Mozart in the years after his death.

Mozart and Posterity, Gernot Gruber (Quartet, 1991)
A subject of major importance, but disappointingly superficial, and not well translated.

Performing Mozart's Music: A Conference at Lincoln Center, ed. Neal Zaslaw, in *Early Music* (OUP) Mozart issues, November 1991, February 1992, and May 1992
Papers given at the Mozart bicentennial conference in New York, gathered in three volumes of the leading early-music journal.

Wolfgang Amadé Mozart: Essays on His Life and His Music, ed. Stanley Sadie (Oxford University Press, 1996)
Proceedings of a major Mozart bicentenary conference in London, published five years later.

On Mozart, ed. James M. Morris (Woodrow Wilson Center and Cambridge University Press, 1994)
Important symposium containing Neal Zaslaw on 'Mozart as a working stiff' and Christoph Wolff on 'The challenge of blank paper'.

MUSIC

Haydn, Mozart and the Viennese School 1740–1780, Daniel Heartz (Norton, 1995)
The best survey of all Mozart's music up to 1780, and the context within which he worked.

The Classical Style: Haydn, Mozart, Beethoven, Charles Rosen (second edition, Norton/Faber, 1997)
The most original and thought-provoking study of Mozart's music published in our lifetime, this book offers insights into many musical aspects of his output.

1791: Mozart's Last Year, H. C. Robbins Landon (Thames and Hudson, 1988)
A classic of gripping, popular scholarship, hugely successful, and using original sources; Landon's profound sympathy for his subject shines through the sometimes patchwork structure. No scholar has done more to make scholarship accessible to the music-lover.

Mozart's Symphonies: Context, Performance Practice, Reception, Neal Zaslaw (Oxford University Press, 1989)
The authoritative work on the symphonies, closely linked to the complete recordings of the cycle on Decca Oiseau-Lyre, and an indispensable source for performing information of all kinds.

OPERA

Mozart's Operas, Daniel Heartz, ed. Thomas Baumann (California University Press, 1990)
The most important collection of essays published in recent times on Mozart's operas, with valuable chapters by Heartz's co-editor Thomas Baumann. Defines our current, ever-

expanding understanding of the circumstances and cultural context within which Mozart wrote his masterpieces, high-lighting his innovations.

Cambridge Opera Handbooks (all published by Cambridge University Press):
Die Entführung aus dem Serail, Thomas Baumann (1987)
Le nozze di Figaro, Tim Carter (1987)
Don Giovanni, Julian Rushton (1981)
Così fan tutte, Bruce Alan Brown (1995)
Die Zauberflöte, Peter Branscombe (1991)
La clemenza di Tito, John A Rice (1991)
The most up-to-date accounts of the Mozart operas, each of which includes analysis, context, and a significant final section on the reception history of each opera and its productions.

AND YOU MUST READ . . .
Amadeus, Peter Shaffer (Penguin Plays, with new postscript, 1993)
The text of the New York version of the play, with a note on the film. Whatever you think about its view of Mozart, it is unarguably a superb piece of stagecraft, which has formed the approach of our generation to the problems of Mozart's genius.

ON THE WEB
Increasingly, the Internet provides a wealth of relevant material. It cannot be guaranteed that links remain constant, and sites change regularly, but among the most useful sources of Mozartian material at the time of publication are:
www.nma.at
www.mozart.at
www.mozartproject.org
www.mozartforum.com
www.mozart2006.at

Index of Mozart's works

The main entry for each work is in **bold** type

All works are listed under their first letter, even if they begin with the definite or indefinite article (e.g. under E for *Eine kleine nachtmusik* or under L for *Le Nozze di Figaro*)